The Northern Sanctions Playbook

The Northern Sanctions Playbook

How Trade Blocks Will Be Enforced in Ice Waters

By

Rayan Veldaskar

Vij Books

New Delhi (India)

Published by

Vij Books
(Publishers, Distributors & Importers)
4836/24, 3rd Floor, Ansari Road
Delhi – 110 002
Phone: 91-11-43596460
Mobile: 98110 94883
e-mail: contact@vijpublishing.com
www.vijbooks.in

ISBN: 978-93-7794-029-4 (PB)

This book was developed using advanced writing tools to support the drafting and ideation process. All content has been thoughtfully curated, refined, and reviewed to ensure quality and relevance.

Contents

Introduction

On 2 November 2023, the United States Treasury moved against Arctic LNG 2, a flagship Russian liquefied natural gas project on the Gydan Peninsula. The designation was an administrative act, dry on the page and cold in its prose, yet its force travelled outward through places far from Washington: through shipbrokers' inboxes, through insurers' underwriting screens, through ports where diesel hangs in the air and steel gangways ring under heavy boots. That is how modern maritime coercion works. A sanction does not begin on the water. It begins in documents, in payments, in permissions, and only then does it reach the hull.

The sea was never lawless.

It only looked that way from shore. Commercial shipping has always depended on a dense architecture of recognition: a flag accepted as genuine, a certificate treated as current, a cargo description believed, a payment cleared, a master admitted to berth, a club prepared to insure the liabilities that make trade tolerable. What appears, at a distance, as movement across open water is in fact movement through institutional gates. In northern waters, those gates become fewer, narrower, and more consequential. Ice does not merely harden the sea. It hardens choices.

This is the paradox at the heart of maritime sanctions in cold regions. Remoteness can strengthen control because alternatives are scarce. The same remoteness can weaken control because evidence is harder to gather, services are more concentrated, and ambiguity can linger longer before anyone with authority is compelled to settle it. A vessel in temperate, densely monitored trade lanes leaves a thick trail: pilots, terminals, chandlers, customs agents, repair yards, traffic services, financiers. A vessel moving at the edge of seasonal access may leave a thinner, more brittle record. The hinge is often small. A registry update filed in one jurisdiction, a fuel supplier's hesitation in another, a classification question raised after midnight, a discrepancy between a bill of lading and a payment instruction—each can alter the fate of a voyage more decisively than any dramatic interception.

That helps explain why maritime sanctions are so often misunderstood. Public debate likes the image of decisive interdiction: a vessel stopped, a cargo seized, a state visibly enforcing its will. The working reality is more administrative and, for that reason, more revealing. Enforcement is usually exercised by institutions that were not built as instruments of geopolitical theatre at all. A port authority asks for one more certificate. A bank declines to process a transaction whose ownership chain does not withstand scrutiny. An insurer delays cover pending clarification of a cargo's origin. A classification society's decision becomes commercially fatal without ever looking like a political act. These are not side details. They are the machinery. The sea may appear borderless; the voyage is anything but.

Northern trade gives this machinery unusual clarity. The physical environment strips away comforting assumptions about endless substitution. In the high latitudes, there are fewer harbours capable of handling specialised cargoes, fewer yards equipped for difficult repairs, fewer bunkering options, fewer pools of ice-qualified expertise, and narrower weather and seasonal windows within which a commercial promise can still be kept. A delayed clearance in Rotterdam is costly. A delayed clearance near the edge of ice season can rewrite the economics of an entire operation. Here, "risk" ceases to be an abstract noun favoured by committees and becomes a visible sequence of decisions: whether a charterer accepts a vessel whose ownership has recently shifted; whether a port operator tolerates documentary inconsistencies; whether a manager takes on a ship that has lost mainstream insurance; whether a bank will finance cargo that may arrive after the profitable window has closed.

For that reason, sanctions in ice waters are best understood not as isolated prohibitions but as systems of dependency. Law matters, certainly. So do diplomacy and intelligence. Yet the durable question is operational: which dependencies can a state or coalition influence, and which dependencies can an evasion network reroute, mimic, or temporarily replace? To ask that question is to move away from slogans and towards sequence. One does not need to moralise a voyage to understand it. One needs to reconstruct it. Who flagged the vessel, who managed it, who insured it, who classed it, who paid for the fuel, who vouched for the cargo, who accepted the paper trail as good enough, and at which point did doubt become expensive enough to stop the movement of steel?

A second, older case shows the point from another angle. In July 2014, after the downing of Malaysia Airlines Flight 17 and Russia's actions in Ukraine, the United States and the European Union widened sectoral sanctions against Russian entities, including measures affecting energy and finance. Much commentary at the time focused on headline restrictions. Less visible, but more instructive, was the slower tightening of private behaviour around Arctic and offshore activity: financing became harder to arrange, partnerships grew more cautious, and specialised service relationships acquired geopolitical weight they had not previously carried in public discussion. Nothing about that shift was theatrical. It was cumulative. A project in a remote region does not fail only when the state says no. It can fail when enough surrounding institutions decide that uncertainty itself has become too costly to carry.

There is a temptation to think of such developments as the triumph of central command, as though modern sanctions were a seamless expression of state power flowing outward through obedient commercial actors. They are not. The closer one looks, the more jagged the picture becomes. Shipping has long used layered corporate structures for ordinary reasons: tax planning, financing, liability management, joint ventures, and the compartmentalisation of risk across assets. A special-purpose company does not prove concealment. A reflagging is not, by itself, an admission of wrongdoing. A ship-to-ship transfer can be routine commerce rather than covert manipulation. The discipline required in this field is precisely the discipline that public argument often resists: to separate indicators from proof, suspicion from substantiation, pattern from prejudice.

Still, patterns matter.

They matter because the operational world runs on thresholds of trust rather than on omniscience. A port does not need metaphysical certainty before delaying a berth. A bank does not require a courtroom standard before declining to move funds. An insurer does not wait for a criminal conviction before reassessing whether a voyage remains within appetite. This is where maritime sanctions derive much of their real force. Not from perfect knowledge, which nobody possesses, but from the ability to raise questions that others cannot afford to ignore. The practical contest is therefore less about dramatic intent than about evidentiary burden. Who must explain what, to whom, and under what time pressure?

That burden sharpens in the Arctic and the sub-Arctic because the informational environment is thinner and the consequences of hesitation are heavier. Automatic Identification System signals may be patchy or interrupted by geography, weather, equipment practices, or human choice.

Port records in remote locations may be less standardised or less rapidly shared across institutions. Surveillance can be expensive, episodic, and technically constrained. Even when data exist, interpretation is not simple. A vessel that loiters in a congested southern anchorage may invite one inference; a vessel that changes speed or route in northern waters may reflect ice, safety, convoying arrangements, or operational caution. Harsh environments generate ambiguity, honestly. That is why they are attractive to evasion networks and frustrating to enforcers at the same time.

The third instructive scene lies not at a grand project site but at the ordinary threshold of port state control. A vessel arrives with papers that are nearly, but not quite, right. The deficiency may appear trivial to an outsider: a stale insurance confirmation, a mismatch in ownership details, a certificate whose amendment has not propagated across every database, a crew list altered too recently to sit comfortably with the rest of the file. Yet this is the point at which abstract governance becomes tactile. Someone must decide whether to treat the inconsistency as harmless administrative lag or as the exposed edge of a deeper deception. Here the playbook of northern enforcement becomes visible. Formal sanctions law may sit in the background, but the decisive action is often a demand for clarification, a temporary detention, a refusal to accept a document at face value, a call placed from one institution to another to test whether the story remains coherent when told twice.

The instinct to search for a single master lever is therefore misguided. Flags matter because they package reputations and administrative standards into market signals, and because changing them can be faster than changing the conduct behind them. Beneficial ownership matters because control can hide behind corporate layers even while payments, crewing, and technical management reveal continuity to anyone patient enough to compare them. Insurance and classification matter because modern shipping depends on third parties willing to attach their names to a vessel's legitimacy. Port access matters because every long voyage ends in a place where documents meet local authority. Financial compliance matters because cargo is not only moved through water; it is moved through systems of credit, settlement, and verification. None of these nodes is sufficient on its own. Together they form the operational map on which both enforcement and evasion are plotted.

And yet a sober account must admit the limitation: pressure applied at one node can thicken demand at another. Restrict mainstream insurance and high-risk alternatives emerge. Close one transhipment corridor and activity shifts towards remoter anchorages or more fragmented parcel sizes. Tighten screening standards and disposable companies proliferate, each designed to absorb suspicion briefly before being abandoned. The effect of sanctions is not linear. Success in one sense may generate adaptation in another. The result is neither futility nor triumph, but a moving contest in which every improvement in detection alters the incentives for concealment. A useful analysis must be frank about this. To pretend otherwise is to confuse the existence of friction with the achievement of control.

That frankness also matters for legitimacy. Coercive measures imposed in harsh maritime environments do not act upon an empty sea. They reshape costs for allies, neutral carriers, insurers, ship managers, terminal operators, and port officials whose first obligation may be safe and lawful commerce rather than geopolitical signalling. A voyage delayed for scrutiny may be a justified intervention or an avoidable distortion; sometimes it is both, depending on where one stands in the chain. Humanitarian cargoes, safety-related deviations, emergency repairs, seasonal windows, and the simple fact of sparse northern infrastructure complicate any easy celebration of denial as virtue. If sanctions are to retain political and commercial support, they must not only target effectively. They must also preserve a reputation for proportion, clarity, and correction when mistakes occur.

That is why evidence occupies the centre of this subject. Not evidence in the grand rhetorical sense, but evidence as institutions actually use it: registry extracts, beneficial ownership filings, charter records, bills of lading, port call histories, AIS traces, claims documents, invoices, sanctions-screening alerts, emails sent at awkward hours, names that recur across companies supposedly unrelated, dates that do not line up, signatures that appear too often. The hinge returns here. An enforcement system lives or dies on small hinges of proof. Push too little, and concealment flourishes in the spaces between agencies and markets. Push too crudely, and legitimate trade begins to bear costs that erode the coalition required to sustain pressure at all.

From that vantage point, the northern maritime world becomes less a frontier than a diagnostic instrument. It reveals what is usually hidden in denser trade lanes: how much shipping depends on quiet acts of verification; how frequently private actors serve as unwilling constitutional organs of economic statecraft; how quickly a vessel's apparent identity can diverge from its commercial continuity; how strongly safety regulation and sanctions enforcement can overlap without becoming identical; how often the practical question is not whether a state possesses legal authority, but whether enough institutions can recognise the same risk in time to act on it. These are not merely technical problems. They are problems of governance under strain.

The wider stakes lie there. Climate change, infrastructure investment, route politics, and the uneven opening of northern waters will not make these issues disappear. They will make them more ordinary. As access shifts and commercial interest deepens, the fragile balance between openness and control will come under greater pressure. More routes may create more options for lawful trade, but they can also create more opportunities for rerouting, relabelling, and jurisdictional arbitrage. More private rulemaking by insurers, standards bodies, and classification societies may strengthen discipline, yet it may also displace public accountability into domains where commercial caution operates faster than legal review. The likely future is not a simple expansion of state authority across a melting map. It is a denser struggle over who gets to decide when a voyage is credible enough to proceed.

The question, then, is neither romantic nor abstract. When a ship heads north under commercial urgency, through waters where delay is expensive and evidence incomplete, what should count as enough certainty to move, enough doubt to stop, and enough coordination to make that decision legitimate rather than merely forceful? That question hangs over every registry filing, every port inspection, every insurance renewal, every transfer of ownership that preserves the network while changing the paper. It is a question of threshold, of proof, of how institutions behave when steel, ice, and money meet. The northern sanctions playbook is written there, on the cold hinge between what can be alleged and what can be made to hold.

Chapter 1

Sanctions as Maritime Systems

How can a ship be free to sail and yet unable to move? The answer sits in the ordinary transactions that surround any voyage. A vessel may float, fuel may be aboard, cargo may be ready, and the weather may hold, yet the journey can still fail before the mooring lines are cast off. A payment does not clear. A declaration does not satisfy. A service provider hesitates. A certificate invites a second look. What appears, from a distance, to be a matter of open water turns out to be a matter of gates.

That contradiction matters because sanctions are often imagined in the wrong shape. They are pictured as bans that fall like a wall across trade, decisive and visible, with the state standing plainly at the centre. Maritime commerce works differently. It depends on a chain of recognition in which many actors, public and private, decide whether a voyage remains acceptable. The ship is only the most visible object in that chain. Less visible are the approvals, confirmations, bookings, attestations, and transfers of responsibility that make the voyage legible to everyone who must touch it.

The invoice matters.

So does the booking email sent at an awkward hour, the change of manager recorded without much notice, the cargo description that grows vaguer as it passes through intermediaries, the insurer's question that cannot be answered cleanly. Sanctions gain force through these small points of contact because shipping does not move on physical capacity alone. It moves on confidence. A charterer must trust the paper enough to commit tonnage. A port must trust the documentation enough to admit the vessel. A bank must trust the transaction enough to process the payment. Once that confidence weakens, movement slows long before any patrol boat appears on the horizon.

The central tension lies here: sanctions need complexity in order to bite, yet that same complexity gives evasion room to manoeuvre. Every commercial voyage relies on sequence. Ownership must be intelligible enough to satisfy screening. Insurance must be credible enough to support access. Routing must align with regulation, contract, and practical seamanship. Cargo identity must survive translation from one document to the next without losing legal meaning. This sequence creates multiple chances to test a voyage, but it also creates multiple chances to disguise one. The same system that permits auditing permits manipulation, because both depend on how information travels from desk to desk.

That is why maritime sanctions are better understood as systems rather than commands. A rule written in legal language does not enforce itself. It enters the world through operations. Someone reads the restriction and adjusts a charter party. Someone rethinks a route because a planned call may trigger scrutiny. Someone amends cargo declarations to preserve market access or to obscure what should not survive scrutiny. Someone refuses a booking because too many details remain unstable. The distance between law and action is not a gap to be crossed once. It is the terrain on which the real contest takes place.

Pressure gathers at recurring nodes because trade cannot avoid them for long. Ports matter because geography eventually becomes administration. Insurers matter because risk without recognised cover is often commercially useless. Classification matters because technical legitimacy is rarely judged from scratch by every counterparty. Finance matters because cargo cannot live by steel alone; it must also live on paper, timing, and settlement. Communications matter because the plausibility of a voyage rests not only on what is filed formally but on what is asked, answered, delayed, or left oddly vague. None of these points is absolute. Each can be worked around for a time. Yet every workaround leaves traces of its own.

A change of flag may look like routine commerce until it coincides with a change of manager, a new trading pattern, and a fresh reluctance from established service providers. An intermediary may look like a harmless commercial layer until no one can explain why it adds cost without adding function. A blended cargo may look like ordinary logistics until the supporting documents begin to describe origin in terms so elastic that they explain everything and certify nothing. The significance of such patterns lies not in any single detail taken alone, but in the way they accumulate into a test of coherence. Honest trade can usually survive coherent questioning. Concealment often cannot.

And yet caution has its own dangers. Shipping is messy even when no one is cheating. Corporate structures can be convoluted for legal reasons. Documents can conflict because clerks, systems, and jurisdictions do not update at the same speed. A vessel may alter course for weather, safety, or congestion rather than for concealment. A prudent compliance culture recognises this untidy reality. It distinguishes between a risk indicator and proof, between a troubling pattern and an admissible case, between suspicion that justifies more questions and evidence strong enough to support denial. Without that discipline, sanctions lose credibility precisely where they most need it: among the institutions expected to carry them into practice.

The deeper stakes are therefore institutional as much as political. If sanctions are treated as slogans, they invite theatre, overreach, and easy disappointment. If they are treated as systems, harder questions come into view. Which dependencies are truly decisive, and which merely look impressive from a distance? Where does delay serve legitimate scrutiny, and where does it become a substitute for judgement? How much ambiguity can commerce bear before private actors withdraw more broadly than the law requires? These questions do not belong only to lawyers or ministers. They belong to insurers, brokers, port officials, ship managers, analysts, and bankers whose daily decisions give sanctions their practical shape.

What follows proceeds along the route a voyage itself must take. Legal text hardens into operational choice; pressure concentrates at specific choke points and provokes its own evasive replies; the argument returns, at last, to the stubborn problem of proof. The movement matters. A sanctions regime is rarely strongest where it speaks most loudly. It is strongest where doubt can be measured, compared, and acted upon before the ship has gone too far for the paper trail to matter. The question hanging over every departure is therefore not whether a rule exists, but whether the voyage can still hold together once every document, service, and claim is asked to bear weight.

From legal text to voyage plan

On 25 September 2019, the United States Treasury designated COSCO Shipping Tanker (Dalian) Co. and related entities under its Iran programme. The legal act took only a few lines on a sanctions list in Washington. Its commercial force appeared elsewhere: in chartering rooms in London and Singapore, in hurried calls between brokers and compliance staff, in terminals asking whether a nominated ship was still acceptable, in traders recalculating whether a voyage could proceed without breaching internal controls. Steel did not change overnight. Paper did. A vessel that remained seaworthy could become commercially unusable because a name on a fixture recap, an invoice, or a beneficial ownership screen no longer passed the checklist.

That is the point worth holding. Sanctions do not travel from law into practice as a single command that everyone hears at once. They move by contact. A regulation reaches a voyage when it touches the people and institutions that must commit to that voyage in sequence: the charterer who books tonnage, the owner or manager who accepts the employment, the insurer who confirms cover, the bank that processes payment, the terminal that expects a clean cargo declaration, the port authority that tests the papers against its own procedures. A prohibition may look singular when published. A voyage never is.

This translation from legal text to operational decision is where maritime sanctions gain their real shape. The law names restricted persons, cargoes, services, places, or forms of dealing. Commerce then asks a harder question: what must be true, and provable, for this specific movement of ship, cargo, money, and documents to go ahead? Show the problem in ordinary form and its importance becomes plain. A charter party is circulated. The vessel appears technically suitable. Freight is commercially tolerable. Laycan dates line up. Then the compliance queries arrive. Has the vessel changed manager recently? Does the cargo description match previous movements? Do the payment instructions point to a bank or intermediary that raises concern? Is the insurer recognised by the ports on the intended route? Each question seems narrow. Taken together, they decide whether the voyage exists in practice.

That is why enforcement is shaped less by a dramatic ban than by the order in which shipping depends on outside recognition. Chartering comes early because no cargo moves until someone commits a ship to service. Here sanctions bite through due diligence rather than spectacle. A broker may circulate a candidate vessel whose ownership chain requires extra checking. A charterer may reject a ship not because guilt has been proved, but because the time needed to resolve uncertainty exceeds the commercial value of the fixture. Trust, in this setting, is not a mood. It is a visible willingness to sign a recap, issue voyage instructions, and expose capital to delay. Once trust thins, the law has already entered the voyage plan.

Routing translates sanctions in a different register. A route is not simply a line on a chart. It is an argument about what services will be needed, which ports may be called, what straits or canals may be used, what contingencies can be tolerated, and how much scrutiny the operator is prepared to invite. After the United States and the European Union expanded sectoral measures against Russia in 2014, Arctic and offshore energy projects did not only face legal restrictions in the abstract; they faced altered routing and service calculations in the concrete. Counterparties had to ask whether a particular voyage required support, equipment, financing, or technical assistance now treated as restricted or reputationally dangerous. The route ceased to be merely geographic. It became legal architecture. A course through remote waters may reduce public visibility, yet it can also narrow the field of acceptable ports, repair options, insurers, and emergency support. Every nautical choice drags a contractual one behind it.

Cargo declarations are another hinge. They look clerical until pressure rises. A bill of lading, a certificate of origin, a customs description, a terminal manifest: each presents the cargo in slightly different language, to slightly different audiences, for slightly different purposes. Honest trade can survive that variation. Evasive trade often relies on it. The legal text may prohibit dealings in a particular commodity of particular origin. The voyage plan then turns on whether origin is described consistently enough to satisfy the port, the buyer, the bank, the insurer, and any regulator who later reconstructs the transaction. This is why maritime sanctions are rarely enforced by staring at the cargo alone. They are enforced by comparing the paper trail against itself. A declaration that becomes vaguer as the voyage progresses does not prove deception, but it changes the burden of explanation. The checklist lengthens.

The same logic governs service bookings, which are often treated as secondary details rather than decisive points of control. Yet a ship cannot trade on law alone. It needs bunkers, agency services, towage if required, pilots where mandated, terminal windows, waste disposal, repairs, spare parts, crew changes, and routine administrative support. Each booking is a moment when someone outside the immediate commercial bargain asks whether the voyage still looks legitimate enough to touch. A fuel supplier that asks for fuller counterparty details is not making a geopolitical speech. It is protecting credit and regulatory exposure. A port agent that delays confirmation pending document review is not merely being cautious. It is deciding whether to bind its own local reputation to the movement. These are quiet acts, but they are the acts that give sanctions operational density.

The Northern setting sharpens this because dependency is harder to hide. In crowded trade lanes, a doubtful voyage may still find substitute providers, alternative bunkering ports, or enough transactional noise to blur its profile. In colder and more remote waters, options thin. A vessel needing ice-class support, specialist handling, or a narrow seasonal window cannot improvise endlessly. That scarcity turns legal language into a more exacting commercial filter. If a mainstream insurer hesitates, the replacement market may be smaller, dearer, or less acceptable to ports. If a port declines a call, the next feasible harbour may sit far enough away to disrupt the economics of the entire movement. If a payment query remains unresolved for a few days too long, the weather and the calendar may settle the matter more harshly than any regulator. Distance magnifies administration.

A named example from the Russian Arctic makes the mechanism plain. In November 2023, the United States imposed sanctions on Arctic LNG 2. The designation did not physically immobilise platforms or tankers at the stroke of midnight. It changed the viability of surrounding decisions. Ship operators, insurers, financiers, and potential buyers had to judge whether association with the project remained lawful, insurable, financeable, and tolerable within their own risk frameworks. The decisive question was not simply whether gas could be produced. It was whether the chain of chartering, carriage, insurance, payment, and port acceptance could still be assembled without one link refusing the load. Sanctions rarely defeat a voyage by sinking it. They more often defeat it by making the assembly fail.

A credible limitation must be admitted here. Not every sanction travels cleanly through commercial sequence, and not every delay proves that law is working as intended. Shipping remains full of lawful complexity. Companies use layered structures for tax, finance, and liability reasons that predate any sanctions regime. Cargo descriptions can vary for mundane reasons across customs systems and contractual forms. A route may change for weather, safety, congestion, or mechanical caution. Even a last-minute service cancellation may reflect ordinary credit concerns rather than sanctions exposure. This matters because over-reading ambiguity imposes its own cost. If every irregularity is treated as concealment, legitimate trade pays for the weakness of the evidence, and private actors begin refusing business more broadly than the law demands. That may still choke targeted flows for a time, but it can also erode the credibility that makes coordinated enforcement sustainable.

The answer is not to imagine a perfect evidentiary world. Maritime practice has never offered one. The answer is to see sanctions as a system of dependencies that can be audited, stressed, and, just as surely, manipulated. An evasion network studies sequence as carefully as an enforcement agency does. It knows that changing the registered owner shortly before fixing a voyage may create enough formal distance to survive an initial screen. It knows that a new manager, a fresh flag, an intermediary trader, and a revised cargo description can each absorb suspicion if no single institution compares the whole chain. It knows that service providers often see only their slice of the movement. What defeats such manoeuvres is not rhetorical toughness but patient comparison: name against name, date against date, cargo paper against payment paper, declared route against commercially sensible route, technical need against booked service. Systems fail at the joins. They are also repaired there.

This is why the voyage plan matters more than the headline prohibition. A sanction may sound comprehensive when written in legal prose, yet its practical effect depends on whether enough institutions can recognise the same problem soon enough, with enough confidence, to refuse participation. That recognition is sequential, not simultaneous. It unfolds through fixtures, bookings, declarations, confirmations, amendments, and the awkward silences between them. The law starts the process. Commerce tests it. The ship then carries the outcome into water, where uncertainty grows more expensive with every mile. The unresolved question is never merely whether a rule exists. It is whether the next signature on the checklist can still be given without exposing the signer to a risk no document can satisfactorily explain.

Choke points and workarounds

In May 2020, the United States Treasury issued guidance warning about deceptive shipping practices linked to sanctions evasion, drawing unusual attention to a truth long familiar to maritime operators: a cargo does not need to disappear to become difficult to govern. It only needs to pass through enough hands, papers, and service relationships that responsibility blurs. The warning mattered not because it revealed a hidden ocean, but because it named the ordinary mechanics through which trade can be made less legible. A ship approaching a terminal still needs a berth, cover, class, banking, and credible communications. The route remains visible at each hinge, even when the cargo story grows murky.

That is where pressure gathers. Not everywhere at once, and not mainly in the dramatic places. Sanctions work by narrowing the set of institutions willing to say yes. A port can delay. An insurer can exclude. A classification society can withhold confidence. A bank can refuse to clear. An agent can stop replying. None of these decisions looks decisive in isolation. Together they create the corridor through which lawful trade must pass. The corridor is the quiet motif here: narrow it enough, and even a physically capable vessel begins to lose commercial room to move.

Ports sit closest to the visible end of this corridor because they convert legal uncertainty into operational friction. A vessel may be technically able to berth, yet a port authority, terminal operator, harbour master, or local agent can still ask for documents that expose deeper problems. Show the scene plainly. A ship arrives with a cargo declaration that appears serviceable until compared with previous port calls. The insurer's details require checking. The identity of the beneficial owner does not align neatly across databases. The port does not need to stage a geopolitical drama. It can ask for clarification, prolong review, or insist on updated attestations before services begin. This is the leverage of gatekeeping. The port becomes a site where law, commercial caution, and local procedure meet, and that meeting matters because delay itself has force. Time can become a sanction before any formal refusal is issued.

The practical importance of ports is often misunderstood because the word suggests a single authority acting from a single motive. Real ports are coalitions of actors with different exposures. Terminal operators worry about cargo integrity and contractual performance. Harbour authorities worry about navigation, safety, and public order. Agents worry about local liability and reputation. Towage firms, pilots, waste contractors, and bunkering providers worry about being drawn into a transaction they do not fully control. Trust, here, is not a principle floating above the scene. It is visible in a berth confirmation, a services order, a pilot booking, a willingness to take payment after the ship has sailed. Once any of those actors begins to doubt the coherence of the voyage, pressure concentrates quickly.

Insurers form another choke point because they convert suspicion into price, exclusion, or silence. Marine insurance does not merely cushion loss after the fact; it signals to ports, charterers, financiers, and counterparties that a voyage has passed through a recognised process of scrutiny. Show what happens when that signal weakens. A charterer reviewing a vessel for a time-sensitive cargo checks not only the ship's suitability but the standing of the cover behind it. If the insurer is obscure, newly substituted, or subject to its own reputational questions, the vessel may remain technically employable and yet commercially unattractive. Insurance becomes a permission structure without ever announcing itself as one. The concept is dependency. Shipping relies on third parties to absorb portions of uncertainty. When those third parties retreat, the voyage does not simply become riskier in theory; it becomes harder to fixture, harder to finance, harder to admit to port.

Classification works differently, but its influence can be just as sharp. A classification society does not declare a cargo politically acceptable. It assesses technical compliance and seaworthiness against recognised standards. Yet markets often treat class as shorthand for seriousness. A vessel that loses class, changes to a less trusted society, or struggles to maintain consistent survey records may find that counterparties no longer separate technical doubt from commercial doubt. The distinction matters in law and may matter morally, but commercial actors often decide under time pressure. They do not hold seminars on theory. They compare documents, note who stands behind them, and decide whether to proceed. Classification thus becomes a form of technical legitimacy that sanctions pressure can indirectly affect. Not by turning surveyors into diplomats, but by making every surrounding actor more sensitive to the credibility of technical paper.

Finance closes the corridor from another direction. Cargo may travel by sea, but it travels commercially through letters of credit, documentary collections, correspondent banking, freight settlements, agency fees, and insurance premiums. If banks decide that a transaction cannot be understood cleanly enough to process, the steel may still float while the trade ceases to function. Show the mechanism. Payment instructions arrive with an intermediary company that appears only briefly in the paperwork. Freight rates look oddly structured. The declared seller and the receiving account do not sit comfortably together. A compliance team escalates. Settlement slows. The vessel waits. This is not theatrical. It is administrative suffocation. Banks do not need to prove the entire scheme. They need only to conclude that they cannot explain it well enough to carry it.

Communications deserve a place among choke points because maritime trade remains astonishingly dependent on small acts of correspondence. Emails, port calls, fixture notes, cargo updates, last-minute amendments, confirmations from agents, notices of readiness, insurance confirmations, survey reports, and instructions from managers create the practical narrative of a voyage. Evasion often depends on fragmenting that narrative. One party sees only the charter. Another sees only the bunkering request. Another sees only a certificate forwarded without context. The workaround lies in the gaps between inboxes. When communications are inconsistent, overly routed through intermediaries, or curiously reluctant to answer simple identity questions, the problem is not merely tone. It is auditability. A system that depends on distributed trust becomes vulnerable where no one actor can see the whole message chain.

The most familiar workaround is reflagging, in part because it is both visible and legally ordinary. Ships change flag for many legitimate reasons: cost, service quality, financing structures, labour arrangements, or commercial strategy. That lawful background makes reflagging attractive to evasion networks. A flag change can create fresh administrative distance, reset assumptions about scrutiny, and complicate pattern recognition across databases that update at different speeds. Show why the move matters without exaggerating it. A vessel with a recent flag change approaches a new market after losing access to mainstream business elsewhere. The flag itself does not prove misconduct. The implication emerges when reflagging coincides with altered management, opaque ownership, insurance substitution, and a trading pattern that depends on less demanding service environments. Reflagging is powerful not because it erases identity, but because it briefly interrupts continuity for anyone not comparing the whole record.

Intermediaries perform a similar function in the commercial chain. A trader, broker, ship manager, nominee director, freight forwarder, or shell company may each have legitimate uses in shipping's divided labour. Yet intermediaries also absorb scrutiny by distributing responsibility thinly enough that no single participant feels fully responsible for the entire voyage. This is the workaround of dilution. One company charters. Another markets the cargo. A third appears in the invoice trail. A fourth receives payment. A fifth manages the vessel. The arrangement need not be illicit to be confusing. That is precisely why it can be exploited. Each layer gives the next layer a reason to say that someone else verified the difficult part. Enforcement pressure therefore concentrates on continuity rather than labels: who keeps recurring, who gives instructions, who benefits from the freight, who remains when paper owners come and go.

Cargo mixing presents a different difficulty because it exploits the fact that commodities often travel in forms that are commercially blendable before they are politically legible. Oil can be co-mingled in storage or during transfer. Refined products may be aggregated through terminals and trading chains that smooth differences for market efficiency. Blending has legitimate commercial functions. It can also be used to soften origin and complicate attribution. The workaround here is not disappearance but dilution. Once cargo leaves its original administrative frame and joins a larger stream, the question becomes whether subsequent documents preserve a meaningful account of origin or merely inherit the credibility of a respectable hub. The visible behaviour to watch is not a mystical change in the cargo's nature. It is the way descriptions, certificates, and trading narratives become less precise as commercial distance increases.

A named example helps. In April 2018, the United States sanctioned COSCO Shipping Tanker (Dalian) Seaman and Ship Management Co., and in September 2019 it designated COSCO Shipping Tanker (Dalian) Co. and related entities under its Iran programme, prompting immediate disruption in tanker markets and forcing counterparties to recalculate vessel acceptability. The case is instructive less for market drama than for sequencing. Charterers did not merely ask whether a ship could sail. They asked whether the ownership and management connections behind particular ships, and the services attached to them, remained compatible with their own compliance duties. The pressure concentrated on fixture decisions, insurance assumptions, and contractual appetite. Even where legal exposure remained contested or technically narrow, commercial caution widened the effect. A choke point need not be formal to be decisive.

A second example lies in the repeated scrutiny of ship-to-ship transfers connected to Iranian and Venezuelan oil movements in waters near Fujairah, the eastern Mediterranean, and parts of East and Southeast Asia during the late 2010s and early 2020s. Public reporting, regulatory notices, and enforcement actions repeatedly pointed to a pattern: cargoes moved through transfer zones, documentation grew less stable, and intermediary traders or shell entities appeared at moments when origin or destination required reframing. What mattered operationally was the clustering of workaround techniques. AIS transmission anomalies alone were not enough. A ship-to-ship transfer alone was not enough. A new commercial counterparty alone was not enough. Pressure built when multiple deviations converged around the same movement and the corridor narrowed at once - port scrutiny, insurance doubt, banking hesitation, documentary inconsistency.

A credible limitation should be faced squarely. Not every choke point holds. Some ports value throughput and local revenue more than strict alignment with distant enforcement priorities. Some insurers outside mainstream clubs may continue to write business that established markets refuse. Some banks and intermediaries operate in jurisdictions less responsive to allied pressure. Some classification arrangements persist where reputation costs bite less sharply. This matters because sanctions analysis becomes lazy when it assumes universal obedience. Trade does not stop merely because a coalition intends it to stop. It reroutes through institutions with different incentives, lower visibility, or higher tolerance for ambiguity. The corridor narrows, but it rarely closes completely.

That limitation does not empty the concept of choke points; it clarifies it. A choke point is not a magical switch. It is a place where costs rise, options contract, and inconsistency becomes harder to carry. The effectiveness of pressure depends on how many such places act in rough alignment, and how quickly evasion networks can replace one corridor with another. This is why communications matter so much. Every workaround requires coordination, and coordination leaves traces - delayed confirmations, altered instructions, cautious language, substitution of counterparties, recurring names where clean separation should exist. Even a fragmented network must still tell a story coherent enough for enough institutions to keep saying yes.

The map that emerges is less geographical than functional. Ports test whether a voyage can physically enter commerce. Insurers test whether uncertainty can be priced and borne. Classification tests whether technical legitimacy remains persuasive. Finance tests whether the paper can survive scrutiny. Communications test whether the whole sequence holds together when asked twice. Workarounds do not abolish these tests. They try to spread them thinly across enough jurisdictions, companies, and documents that no one actor sees the corridor as a whole. That is the unresolved pressure running beneath every sanction's regime at sea: whether enforcement can compare the right fragments fast enough to make the next refusal stick, or whether the voyage will keep moving because each gate sees only a plausible slice of a larger design.

Evidence, not slogans

On 4 July 2019, Royal Marines and Gibraltar law enforcement boarded the tanker *Grace 1* off Gibraltar and detained it on suspicion that it was carrying Iranian crude oil to the Banyas refinery in Syria, contrary to European Union sanctions. The boarding was dramatic enough to dominate headlines, yet the real dispute turned on quieter material: destination, ownership, documentary intent, and what could actually be established from the ship's movements and papers. The vessel was not detained because outrage had been expressed loudly enough. It was detained because officials believed they could connect cargo, route, and end-use to a prohibited transaction. When that connection became contested, politics remained noisy, but the case itself narrowed to proof.

That narrowing matters. Maritime sanctions are often discussed as though moral certainty and operational certainty were the same thing. They are not. A ship may look suspicious, a trading pattern may invite inference, a cluster of intermediaries may smell of concealment, and still the decisive question remains stubbornly practical: what can be shown, by whom, from which records, quickly enough to justify action that can survive scrutiny later? Evidence lives in sequence. The signal must hold.

The distinction between suspicion, risk indicators, and admissible evidence is not a lawyer's nicety imported into commercial life. It shapes decisions every day. Suspicion is an intuition with reasons, often thin ones: a recent change of flag, an awkward ownership history, a cargo description that grows less specific as the voyage progresses. Risk indicators are more structured. They include recognisable warning patterns such as AIS irregularities, repeated ship-to-ship transfer behaviour in unusual locations, poorly explained management changes, insurer substitutions, or payment routes that do not fit the declared trade. Admissible evidence stands somewhere harder and narrower. It is material an institution can rely upon when it delays a berth, blocks a payment, declines cover, makes a designation, or defends a decision against challenge. The movement from one category to the next is where maritime enforcement succeeds or falters.

Show how this works in ordinary form. A compliance officer receives a file on a tanker nominated for charter. The vessel has traded in a region associated with sanctions evasion. AIS history shows gaps. The registered owner has changed. Payment instructions involve an intermediary the officer has not seen before. None of these facts alone proves a breach. Together they may justify enhanced due diligence, internal escalation, or refusal to proceed until explanations arrive. That is not yet an evidentiary case in the strong sense. It is a threshold judgement: the file no longer clears on routine assumptions. The implication is decisive. Commercial enforcement often begins before proof is complete because institutions act on the cost of unanswered questions, not only on the existence of finished cases.

This is why slogans are so unhelpful. "Dark activity", "shadow fleets", "front companies", "illicit cargoes" - such terms may orient attention, but they do not resolve decisions. A port authority cannot defend delay by citing atmosphere. A bank cannot explain a blocked transaction by invoking a mood. An insurer cannot comfortably decline a claim on rhetoric alone. Each needs some chain of material that links identity, conduct, and exposure. The chain may be indirect, but it must still be made. Compare names across registries. Match IMO numbers despite vessel renamings. Read charter dates against port calls. Compare bills of lading with payment records. Test whether certificates remain consistent when copied into different systems. Evidence is built by comparison, not by incantation.

The practical difficulty is that maritime information is rarely born clean. Data are produced by different institutions for different reasons and at different speeds. Registry records may lag. Port logs may vary in detail. Corporate filings may be incomplete or filed in jurisdictions with uneven disclosure standards. AIS data can mislead through human error, equipment failure, or deliberate manipulation. Satellite imagery can sharpen suspicion without settling ownership or intent. Even basic documentary items may contain transliteration problems, stale addresses, typographical mistakes, or legitimate discrepancies between legal owner, beneficial owner, manager, and operator. The challenge is not simply access. It is provenance. Before a fact can persuade, someone must know where it came from, how current it is, what exactly it records, and what it leaves unsaid.

A second named example shows the problem from the enforcement side rather than the port side. In May 2020, the United States Departments of State, Treasury, and Coast Guard issued a sanctions advisory on deceptive shipping practices. The document drew attention to conduct such as AIS manipulation, physically altering vessel identifiers, falsifying cargo and vessel documents, and using complex ownership or management structures to disguise sanctioned interests. Its value lay not in announcing that deceptive behaviour exists - the industry knew that already - but in clarifying that these features are indicators requiring further examination rather than automatic proof in themselves. An AIS gap can arise for more than one reason. A reflagging can be commercial. A complex ownership structure can be lawful. The advisory's institutional logic was clear: assemble indicators, then compare them against documents, counterparties, cargo claims, and service patterns until a coherent account either emerges or breaks apart.

That distinction between indicators and proof matters even more under time pressure. Ships do not wait kindly while institutions think. Laycans expire. Berths are reassigned. Weather turns. Charterers demand answers. A payment held for review can unsettle an entire chain of performance. Under those conditions, the temptation to collapse categories becomes severe. If the signal looks bad, why not act as though the case were proved? Because overreach creates its own operational damage. Wrongful delays impose costs on innocent cargo owners, vessel operators, and ports. Reputational overstatement can chill legitimate trade. Weak cases make poor precedents. Most importantly, institutions that repeatedly act on thin grounds may lose credibility with the very private actors whose cooperation gives sanctions force. Evidence is not only about catching evasion. It is also about preserving confidence that enforcement distinguishes between justified friction and arbitrary obstruction.

A credible limitation deserves candour. Sometimes regulators and firms must act without complete information because waiting would empty the enforcement of practical meaning. That is not hypocrisy. It is the condition of trade under uncertainty. A bank screening a transaction does not enjoy the luxury of a multi-year investigation. A port deciding whether to grant entry may need to weigh incomplete records against safety, schedule, and external pressure. Intelligence held by states may not be fully shareable with commercial actors, who are asked to bear the consequences. These constraints mean that sanctions enforcement will never operate at the serene evidentiary standard imagined by textbooks. The relevant question is narrower and harder: whether the basis for action is proportionate to the action taken, and whether it can be revisited if better material emerges.

That is where contestation becomes part of the evidence process rather than an embarrassment to it. A designation may be challenged. A detention may be lifted. A refusal to insure or finance may later appear overcautious. None of this proves the system broken. It shows that sanctions operate in an institutional environment where claims are made, resisted, corrected, and sometimes reversed. The important measure is not perfect foresight. It is whether institutions record enough of their reasoning that they can explain why a given file crossed a threshold on a given day. Who checked the ownership chain? Which documents conflicted? What route pattern raised concern? What explanation was offered, and did it answer the specific inconsistency or merely generate a better story? Procedure matters because memory fails quickly once a voyage has moved on.

The investigative method that follows from this is more modest than the language often used around sanctions, and more demanding. It does not begin by asking whether an actor is wicked. It asks how information was produced. A bill of lading did not descend from the sky; someone drafted it for a purpose, at a moment, using data from somewhere. A registry extract reflects a filing system with its own update cycle and disclosure rules. AIS traces are not raw reality but machine-generated records shaped by transmission conditions, equipment behaviour, and interpretation. Corporate records tell the truth about certain legal relations while often obscuring others. When several such records line up independently, confidence grows. When they diverge, the divergence itself becomes evidence - not evidence of guilt, necessarily, but evidence that the story needs further testing.

This is why the strongest sanctions cases often look almost boring when laid out carefully. No single fact dazzles. The power lies in accumulation. A vessel's IMO number stays constant through renaming. A management company recurs after paper ownership changes. Payment instructions connect to entities already known from other files. Port calls contradict declared destination patterns. Insurance arrangements shift at precisely the point mainstream scrutiny intensifies. A cargo description loses specificity after a transfer. Each element alone may support only suspicion. Together they can produce something institutions are willing to treat as reliable enough to act upon. The signal holds because different records, generated for different reasons, point in the same direction.

And yet the reverse also happens. A case that appears compelling in public can weaken under disciplined examination. A vessel may loiter because of congestion or weather. AIS anomalies may prove operational rather than deceptive. A purported ownership link may collapse once common names, bad transliteration, or stale registry data are corrected. A cargo trail may look damning until one sees the underlying contractual structure. This is not a nuisance at the edges of enforcement. It is central to integrity. If the standard becomes "sounds plausible", then the difference between sanctions administration and maritime rumour starts to erode. For states that want allies, insurers, banks, ports, and registries to absorb enforcement burdens voluntarily, that erosion is costly.

The deeper truth is almost austere. Maritime sanctions are information contests conducted under commercial time. They reward actors who can compare fragments faster and more carefully than their counterparts. They punish institutions that mistake volume of data for quality of proof.

They expose the weakness of public language that confuses a red flag with a finished case. In northern waters, where distance, weather, and sparse infrastructure can already thin the record, these pressures grow sharper. The file arriving on a desk may be incomplete. The route may be plausible. The names may half-match. The cargo may carry just enough documentation to proceed if no one asks a second question. The signal must still hold. The unresolved test is simple to state and hard to meet: at what point does a pattern become solid enough to justify action that can withstand not only immediate urgency, but the slower, colder scrutiny that comes afterwards?

Chapter 2

Ice-Water Trade Routes and Constraints

How can a route become both easier and harder to control at the same time? That is the central paradox of northern trade. Cold-water passages strip shipping down to its essentials. They remove the illusion of endless substitution. A voyage cannot casually change course when harbours are sparse, repair options thin, and the next safe haven lies far enough away to turn hesitation into danger. Scarcity sharpens authority. It also sharpens concealment, because where fewer eyes watch and fewer records are generated, uncertainty lasts longer and denial can sound more plausible.

The map looks severe for a reason. Ice waters do not simply add risk to an ordinary voyage; they reorder the whole logic of movement. A temperate sea lane often allows for delay, diversion, and redundancy. A northern passage asks harsher questions. Which port can actually receive the vessel? Which yard can fix what fails? Which crew can operate safely in the conditions encountered? Which supporting services can be reached before weather, ice, or darkness narrows the margin again? These are not background matters. They decide whether a ship can keep moving without slipping from commercial calculation into emergency planning.

A cold route punishes fantasy.

That severity gives geography unusual political weight. Enforcement at sea is often discussed as though it begins with law and only later meets the world of weather, steel, and distance. In practice, the physical route can decide what the law is able to achieve. Where options are scarce, pressure applied at one service node can travel much further than it would in a dense maritime network. A port denial means more when there is no easy alternative. A compliance query matters more when the next acceptable provider is days away. Geography becomes enforcement architecture not because states suddenly acquire magical reach, but because the environment reduces the number of exits available to a doubtful voyage.

Yet the same features that strengthen pressure also weaken certainty. Sparse infrastructure rarely produces rich documentation. Remote movements do not always leave the same layered trail found in crowded commercial zones. Monitoring becomes episodic. Records arrive late, or in forms that do not align neatly across institutions. A vessel can remain perfectly visible in one sense and still be evidentially elusive in another. This is the deeper tension of northern sanctions practice: scarcity makes dependency easier to exploit, while remoteness makes proof harder to assemble. The corridor narrows, but the view through it may not improve.

That tension matters because maritime enforcement never acts upon geography alone. It acts upon timing. Northern routes are governed by windows rather than by continuous availability, and windows change behaviour. When access is short, scheduling hardens into pressure. Cargoes must move before conditions shift. Service bookings carry more weight because missing one slot can disturb an entire chain of performance. Administrative imperfections that might be tolerable elsewhere begin to look consequential. A hurried declaration, a late amendment, an unexplained change in routing, a service request that arrives with too little supporting detail: each may reflect innocent compression of time, or something less innocent using that compression as cover. Seasonal constraint therefore does more than shape navigation. It shapes the quality of compliance itself.

Safety deepens the dependency further. Harsh waters demand more from vessels, from crews, and from the institutions that stand behind them. Technical fitness is not a decorative matter in such conditions. Nor is competence. The need for specialised standards, recognised classification, trained personnel, reliable emergency planning, and trusted support services gives private actors unusual influence over what can trade and what cannot. A ship may satisfy a commercial desire to move, yet still depend on a narrow circle of providers willing to confirm that it can move safely enough to be tolerated. Those providers are not neutral scenery. They form part of the governing structure, whether or not they wish to play that role.

A useful understanding of northern enforcement therefore resists two easy mistakes. One is to romanticise remoteness, as though distance naturally dissolves oversight and turns the high latitudes into a permissive frontier. The other is to imagine that harsh conditions automatically strengthen control because everything important passes through a small number of gates. Both ideas contain a fragment of truth and fail as complete explanations. Remote waters can frustrate scrutiny and still intensify dependency. Tight service concentration can aid enforcement and still leave investigators with patchy evidence. The governing question is not whether geography helps or hinders in the abstract. It is which forms of control survive contact with operational reality, and which collapse once the route itself starts making decisions.

The path ahead follows that reality rather than stepping around it. The argument begins with geography as an institutional fact, then moves into the pressures created by seasonal timing, the disciplined dependencies imposed by safety and specialised service provision, and the stubborn incompleteness of remote observation. Taken together, these problems force a more exact way of thinking about control. They ask not only where a ship can go, but when it must commit, whom it must trust, and how much of that sequence can be known while the voyage is still under way.

The result is a colder account of maritime power than public rhetoric usually allows. Control in ice waters rarely appears as dramatic interruption. More often it appears as narrowed choice, delayed confirmation, brittle scheduling, and thin records that must bear more interpretive weight than they can comfortably carry. The map remains severe. So does the question hanging over every northern voyage: when a route offers fewer alternatives but also fewer certainties, where exactly should an institution place its confidence - in the scarcity of options, or in the quality of the evidence those options leave behind?

Geography as enforcement architecture

In March 2014, when sanctions pressure on Russia began to widen after the annexation of Crimea, much of the public discussion centred on finance, diplomacy, and headline restrictions. Less visible was a harsher fact of northern trade: geography itself was already doing part of the sorting. In the Russian Arctic, as in other cold-water regions, a voyage could not simply be rerouted with the shrug familiar to temperate commerce. Harbours were fewer. Repair capacity was unevenly distributed. Distances between safe havens lengthened the consequence of every misjudgement. The map had teeth.

That matters because enforcement at sea is often imagined as something laid *onto* geography by law, patrols, or policy. In cold waters, geography does not wait politely in the background. It shapes the field before a regulator, port authority, or insurer says a word. A doubtful voyage approaching a crowded southern corridor may still find another port, another yard, another supplier willing to absorb uncertainty for a price. A doubtful voyage in northern waters faces a colder arithmetic. Fewer alternatives mean that refusal travels further. So does delay.

The chart narrows options fast.

That narrowing is what makes geography an architecture of enforcement rather than a mere setting. Show the problem in operational terms. A vessel planning to move cargo through icy or sub-Arctic waters must line up admissible ports, acceptable insurance, capable crews, weather margins, and contingency plans that would look excessive on gentler routes. If one element fails, the others do not remain untouched. A missed service slot can disturb the route. A problem with class can affect port acceptance. A port denial can create not just inconvenience but exposure, because the next viable harbour may be far enough away to alter fuel planning, safety posture, and contractual performance. Geography turns each administrative decision into something heavier because the sea offers fewer forgiving exits.

The first claim, then, is straightforward: scarcity magnifies choke points. Consider ports. In a dense maritime region, port access is important but often substitutable. In cold-water trade, substitutability shrinks. A port with suitable depth, handling capability, ice support, and administrative willingness may have no near-equivalent along the practical route. Name the concept properly and its force becomes clearer. This is not simply remoteness. It is infrastructural concentration. Where usable harbours are sparse, the ordinary acts of gatekeeping - asking for additional certificates, delaying confirmation, requiring proof of insurance from a recognised market, querying ownership, deferring berthing until documents align - gain outsized influence. The implication is not theatrical state power. It is more precise. Geography makes modest decisions bite harder.

The same logic applies to repair and maintenance capacity. A ship in cold waters does not merely need a place to berth; it may need access to yards and service providers capable of dealing with specialised wear, ice-related stresses, or systems that cannot safely be improvised at sea. That creates another layer of concentration. Show the practical sequence. A vessel with a technical deficiency that might be manageable in a dense commercial basin now faces a route where specialist yards are scarce and distances long. Owners, managers, insurers, and charterers must weigh whether the defect remains tolerable given how few credible repair options lie ahead. The concept here is operational dependency. Geography creates it. Enforcement can then ride on it indirectly, because any service restriction in such an environment carries more force than the same restriction would elsewhere. A ship does not need to be formally blacklisted to become commercially stranded.

A named example from the Russian Arctic illustrates the mechanism. After the United States imposed sanctions on Arctic LNG 2 in November 2023, the question was never only whether gas could be produced on the Gydan Peninsula. The sharper question was whether cargoes connected to the project could move through a northern logistics chain that depended on specialised vessels, ice-capable support, acceptable insurers, willing buyers, and ports prepared to receive the trade. The northern setting mattered because it concentrated dependency. A project in an ordinary maritime environment may test market appetite. A project in Arctic conditions tests market appetite *and* the capacity of a narrow service corridor to remain intact under pressure. The outcome turns not just on legality in the abstract, but on how many scarce nodes continue to say yes.

This is where a second claim becomes important: geography does not merely strengthen sanctions pressure; it also produces blind spots. Remoteness can sharpen dependency and weaken observation at the same time. Show the contradiction in plain form. A ship travelling through sparsely serviced waters leaves fewer of the routine traces that accumulate almost automatically in busy zones: fewer pilotage interactions, fewer terminal hand-offs, fewer casual port calls, fewer layers of commercial paperwork generated by dense logistical choreography. Monitoring still exists, of course, but it becomes costlier, more intermittent, and often more interpretive. An AIS signal may tell part of the story. Satellite imagery may supply another fragment. Port records may arrive later or in forms less easily matched across systems. The concept is evidentiary thinness. Geography does not create lawlessness; it creates a thinner documentary skin.

That thinness matters because sanctions enforcement lives on comparison. Investigators and compliance teams test one record against another until a coherent pattern emerges or breaks apart. In cold-water routes, there are simply fewer records to compare, and the gaps between them are harder to bridge. A vessel may behave oddly for innocent reasons: ice conditions, weather avoidance, convoying constraints, or operational caution in difficult waters. Those same conditions can also provide cover for concealment. The implication is unsettling but necessary. Northern geography makes some interventions easier because alternatives are scarce; it makes proof harder because the record is sparse and ambiguity can be honest. Enforcement becomes stronger and less certain at once.

A second named example sits further west. The Northwest Passage has long occupied political imagination far beyond the volume of actual commercial use, and that imbalance itself is instructive. When the tanker *Manhattan* transited the passage in 1969 as part of a proof-of-concept effort tied to Alaskan oil transport debates, the episode exposed more than navigational difficulty. It demonstrated that Arctic routing is governed by infrastructure and political control at least as much as by raw physical possibility. The ship could move; the route could not be treated as ordinary commerce. That older moment still helps here. Cold-water trade is never only about whether a hull can pass through ice. It is about whether the surrounding network of authority, rescue capability, support services, and administrative recognition can sustain the movement as a credible commercial act. Geography does not merely challenge ships. It disciplines institutions.

Still, any argument that treats cold-water routes as naturally governable by scarcity alone would be too neat. A credible counter-example comes from the very remoteness just described. Sparse infrastructure can reduce alternatives for sanctioned trade, but it can also reduce the density of scrutiny that gives sanctions practical force. If a vessel can avoid major service nodes for longer, if cargoes can be shifted through less observed locations, if communications travel through a thinner chain of providers, then geography can shelter evasive conduct rather than suppress it. A route with few ports may create fewer chances for a port authority to intervene. A sea with fewer commercial witnesses may produce less incidental intelligence. Scarcity, in other words, does not automatically favour enforcers. Sometimes it favours the party better prepared to exploit silence.

The apparent contradiction dissolves once geography is treated not as a single variable but as a patterned distribution of dependence and visibility. Some forms of scarcity intensify control. Others diminish it. A narrow set of harbours can strengthen port leverage. A narrow set of observation points can weaken the evidentiary chain. Long distances between safe havens can make insurers and managers more cautious. The same distances can delay detection of suspicious deviations because fewer institutional eyes observe the voyage in real time. The map does not deliver one verdict. It arranges pressures unevenly. Good analysis therefore asks where geography concentrates authority and where it thins information, rather than assuming the two always coincide.

That distinction has consequences for how one thinks about risk. In ordinary policy language, risk often floats as an abstraction. Here it becomes visible. It appears in a charterer's decision not to nominate a vessel because the route leaves too little room for service failure. It appears in an insurer's hesitation when a project depends on scarce northern infrastructure and uncertain contingency planning. It appears in a port's insistence on cleaner documentation because diversion options are limited. It appears in a manager's reluctance to accept commercial employment that could leave the ship too far from trustworthy repair capacity if difficulties arise. Geography presses risk out of theory and into sequence. People must sign, commit, and move under conditions that punish optimism.

The quiet motif running through all of this is the harbour. Not the harbour as a romantic image, but the harbour as a test. Every northern voyage is planned against the fact that there are only so many places where paper, services, weather, and safety can be reconciled after something goes wrong. That fact sharpens compliance behaviour long before the ship reaches the water. It sharpens enforcement, too, because a harbour with no close substitute gains influence over actors well beyond the quay. Yet the same sparse chain of harbours leaves long stretches where observation is partial and interpretation uncertain. The harbour is both answer and absence: a point of control because it exists, a source of ambiguity because there are too few of them.

For sanctions analysis, the deeper lesson is institutional. Geography does not act alone; it acts through the organisations that must translate spatial constraint into decisions. A state can only exploit distance if its regulators, ports, insurers, financiers, and service providers understand where the route genuinely pinches. A commercial actor can only navigate pressure if it recognises which constraints are hard and which are merely inconvenient. An evasion network can only survive if it maps not just the coastline but the pattern of tolerances embedded in ports, yards, and support services. The contest is therefore less about abstract control of space than about knowing which places matter enough that refusal will cascade through the voyage plan.

That leaves a harder question hanging over every cold-water route. When the sea offers fewer alternatives, should enforcement trust the scarcity of physical options to do part of its work, or should it distrust that same scarcity because long distances and patchy observation leave too much room for stories that cannot be checked until the voyage is almost over? Geography gives sanctions unusual force. It also makes errors more expensive. The decisive issue is not whether the map is harsh. It plainly is. The issue is whether institutions can tell, in time, which part of that harshness is tightening the corridor and which part is merely hiding what moved through it.

Seasonal windows and routing incentives

In September 2018, Maersk announced that the *Venta Maersk* had completed a trial voyage along the Northern Sea Route from Vladivostok to St Petersburg. The passage drew attention because it was not merely a navigational experiment. It was a commercial argument made against a calendar. A northern route can look attractive on a map, yet the map says less than the season. Ice conditions, convoy support, port readiness, crew planning, insurance assumptions, and cargo timing all have to align within a narrow period in which the route is not only passable, but commercially tolerable. A ship can be able to sail and still miss its moment.

The calendar hardens into steel.

That is the first fact to grasp about seasonal access in cold waters. Time is not an external condition laid gently over trade. It is part of the trade itself. A charterer fixing a voyage in temperate waters may think in terms of freight, distance, berth availability, and ordinary operational risk. A charterer looking north must think in terms of closing corridors, degrading margins, and the cost of losing even a few days to document queries, service delays, or route changes. Seasonal pressure does not merely make transport more difficult. It changes what counts as an acceptable delay, what counts as a tolerable ambiguity, and what kinds of compliance behaviour are more likely to fray at the edges.

Show the sequence plainly. A vessel is nominated for a voyage that depends on a short navigable period. The cargo has a buyer expecting delivery within a contractual slot. Bunkering, ice advice, pilotage if required, local agency work, and port services have all been booked around a route that only makes sense if the ship moves more or less as planned. Then a discrepancy appears. A certificate has not updated across all systems. A cargo declaration requires clarification. An intermediary in the payment chain raises questions. A port authority or insurer asks for one more document. In ordinary trade, that might produce irritation. In cold-water trade under seasonal compression, it can unravel the economics of the entire movement. The concept is temporal dependency. The implication is blunt: sanctions and compliance measures gain force when time itself becomes scarce.

This helps explain why routing decisions in northern waters are never purely geographical. They are bets on timing. A route is chosen not only because it is shorter on paper or politically attractive to a sponsor, but because it offers the best chance of keeping the whole commercial sequence intact before conditions deteriorate. Seasonal access, therefore, shapes where enforcement can be applied with maximum effect. A documentation query raised before departure may stop a voyage cleanly. The same query raised too late may create pressure to let the ship proceed because reversal has become more costly, more dangerous, or simply harder to administer. Timing changes institutional behaviour. Ports, insurers, charterers, and banks do not respond only to legal text; they respond to how much room the calendar leaves them to verify, refuse, or defer.

A named example from the Canadian Arctic makes the point from the other side of the ledger. In September 2013, the bulk carrier *Nordic Orion* completed a transit of the Northwest Passage carrying coal from Vancouver to Pori, Finland. The voyage was widely discussed for its routing implications, but its real lesson lies in planning discipline. Such a passage depends on careful seasonal judgement. Draft, ice conditions, local support, timing of arrival, and downstream commercial commitments must line up with much greater precision than on more forgiving routes. The point is not that northern voyages are inherently suspicious or inherently fragile. It is that their success depends on a narrower tolerance for disruption. Once that is understood, compliance behaviour starts to look less like a legal afterthought and more like part of the voyage design itself.

That design can encourage unhealthy shortcuts. Not always, and not only in illicit trade, but often enough to matter. When the window is short, the temptation grows to treat paperwork as something to be regularised en route rather than settled before sailing. Cargo descriptions may be drafted in language broad enough to get a booking confirmed, with details to be sharpened later. Service requests may be pushed through before every supporting document is cleanly aligned. Counterparty checks may be handled at speed by people under commercial pressure to preserve a fixture. None of this proves evasion. Much of it can arise from ordinary haste. Yet the distinction between haste and concealment becomes harder to police when the same compressed timeline serves both innocent urgency and strategic ambiguity. The relevant behaviour is visible: late amendments, inconsistent attachments, rushed declarations, unexplained substitutions of managers or agents close to departure, and a general tendency for the paper trail to catch up with the ship rather than precede it.

Short seasonal windows also affect transhipment incentives. A cargo that cannot move directly to its final buyer within the favourable period may be broken into stages, shifted through intermediate storage, or transferred between vessels in order to keep commercial options alive while the season still permits movement. Some of these arrangements are legitimate. They belong to the ordinary repertoire of maritime logistics. But time pressure can make them harder to interpret because speed favours simplification. A terminal wants the cargo processed. A charterer wants the ship turned around. A buyer wants delivery risk contained. The documents describing origin, title, destination, and handling can become less precise as more parties touch the transaction in quick succession. The concept is documentary compression. The implication is not that every hurried transhipment masks wrongdoing, but that seasonal pressure increases the number of situations in which enforcement agencies and private compliance teams must judge incomplete files under narrowing time.

This is where routing incentives and sanctions pressure meet most clearly. A vessel or cargo exposed to regulatory or reputational scrutiny may seek a route that reduces the number of high-friction service points it must pass through before the commercial objective is secured. In a northern context, that can mean preferring a voyage plan with fewer port calls, fewer mainstream intermediaries, or a sequence that pushes scrutiny to the latest possible stage. Again, the route is doing legal work. It is not simply moving cargo across water. It is organising when the trade will encounter institutions able to demand clarification. A route that minimises those encounters during the short accessible season may look commercially elegant. It may also look like an effort to outrun the paper trail. The same plan can plausibly be read both ways. That ambiguity is the enforcement problem.

Risk, in this setting, stops being a broad managerial word and becomes measurable in decisions. It appears when an insurer decides that a late change in voyage details, benign in summer trade elsewhere, is intolerable on a northern route nearing the edge of navigability. It appears when a bank or charterer refuses to rely on a promised document because the cost of waiting for a correction now exceeds the value of the fixture. It appears when a port demands earlier confirmation of insurance, class, cargo origin, or agency authority because seasonal congestion and limited alternatives make corrective improvisation more dangerous. Efficiency also changes meaning. It no longer means only moving quickly. It means moving with enough evidentiary discipline that speed does not hollow out the record needed to justify the voyage later.

A credible limitation must be faced. Seasonal compression does not always weaken compliance. In some trades it does the opposite. Operators that know a route offers little room for error may prepare more carefully, not less. They may front-load document review, commit earlier to service providers, build in larger safety margins, and reject commercially tempting cargoes that cannot be documented cleanly enough in time. The narrow window can foster discipline precisely because failure is so costly. Northern operators with experience often understand this well. The strongest files are sometimes assembled where the consequences of sloppiness are most obvious. That is an important corrective to any theory that equates time pressure with inevitable corner-cutting.

Yet the limitation does not overturn the larger argument. It refines it. Seasonal windows do not produce one uniform behavioural effect; they intensify whatever governance culture already exists around the voyage. In disciplined organisations, the calendar prompts earlier checking and cleaner sequencing. In marginal or evasive networks, the same calendar becomes an excuse for vagueness, delay, and strategic incompleteness. That is why the calendar matters so much as a diagnostic tool. It does not merely constrain navigation. It reveals which actors can still maintain documentary coherence when time is no longer generous. The pressure exposes institutional quality.

The same pattern appears in service markets surrounding northern routes. Ice-capable vessels, experienced crews, suitable insurers, and specialised local support do not sit endlessly available, waiting to be summoned without notice. Their availability is itself shaped by season. That scarcity sharpens incentives to commit early, but it also creates temptation to conceal marginal details that might cause a provider to say no. A ship manager may delay disclosing a complication until a booking is secure. A charterer may present the voyage in simplified terms to keep optionality alive. An intermediary may promise that paperwork will follow once operational momentum has been established. These are not exotic manoeuvres. They are recognisable forms of commercial behaviour under pressure. What cold-water trade does is raise the cost of discovering them late.

The quiet motif here is the calendar, because the calendar does not merely record the season; it governs the credibility of the trade. Every date entered into a fixture recap, service booking, insurance confirmation, or cargo schedule carries more weight when the route's tolerable period is short. Delay changes meaning. A document received a week late in an ordinary corridor may be an irritation. A document received a week late near the shoulder of an Arctic season may be the difference between a controlled voyage and a costly, exposed, or impossible one. Enforcement should be understood against that backdrop. Institutions do not intervene in a vacuum. They intervene in relation to time remaining.

This is why seasonal windows should not be treated as a colourful feature of northern navigation, but as part of the sanctions environment itself. They determine where scrutiny is most potent, where actors are most tempted to compress or postpone inconvenient checks, and where an apparently minor administrative question can acquire the force of a commercial veto. They also complicate judgement, because the same haste that signals possible concealment may also reflect the ordinary desperation of legal trade trying to keep a narrow route viable. The forward test is therefore uncomfortable and practical. When a voyage approaches the edge of its season, and the file is not quite clean, should an institution trust the urgency as evidence of normal trade under pressure, or distrust it as the very condition under which evasive conduct becomes easiest to hide?

Safety regulation and operational dependency

On 1 January 2017, the International Maritime Organization's Polar Code entered into force, giving formal shape to a principle northern operators had long understood in practice: a ship in ice waters is not judged by cargo and route alone, but by whether the vessel, the crew, and the surrounding support system can carry the voyage safely enough to be tolerated. The Code did not invent operational dependency. It named and organised it. A northern voyage now had to speak more clearly through certificates, manuals, assessments, and training records. Safety moved closer to the centre of commercial legibility.

Paper can keep ships moving.

That phrase sounds bureaucratic until one remembers what northern conditions do to error. In warmer, denser trade lanes, commercial shipping can often survive small failures of planning because alternatives remain within reach. In cold waters, the margin contracts. A vessel may require an ice-class appropriate to the voyage, crew competence that can withstand fatigue and unfamiliar conditions, and emergency arrangements credible enough to persuade ports, insurers, managers, charterers, and coastal authorities that the voyage will not become someone else's problem. Safety regulation, in such an environment, does more than reduce accidents. It decides who gets access to the scarce network of trust on which the voyage depends.

This is where operational dependency becomes a sanctions issue without ceasing to be a safety issue. Show the sequence in ordinary form. A ship is commercially available. The cargo is lawful on its face. The route is technically open. Yet the vessel still needs recognised class, acceptable insurance, up-to-date certification, competent crewing arrangements, suitable operational manuals, and support services prepared to stand behind the movement. If any one of those elements weakens, the voyage becomes harder to defend. The concept is concentrated enablement. Northern trade rests on a narrow band of specialised institutions willing to certify, insure, service, and support difficult movements. The implication follows quickly: where enabling services are concentrated, pressure on supply can do the work that direct interdiction often cannot.

Ice-class requirements show the mechanism sharply. They are usually discussed as technical matters, and in one sense they are. Hull strengthening, machinery suitability, and operational limitations belong to the world of marine engineering and classification. Yet the institutional meaning is broader. Ice class is a passport into a particular kind of trade, but only because third parties agree to treat it as one. A charterer reads class notation as evidence of suitability. An insurer reads it as part of underwriting logic. A port or coastal authority reads it as part of a wider safety judgement. A manager reads it as a constraint on employment choices. Once those readings align, class becomes more than a technical label. It becomes a gate through which cold-water commerce must pass. The ship does not self-certify. Others decide whether to trust the paper and the institutions behind it.

That trust is operational, not sentimental. It appears in concrete decisions. A charterer nominates a vessel for a northern cargo because the class records and operational profile withstand scrutiny. An insurer confirms cover because the voyage falls within an acceptable safety framework. A coastal administration accepts a passage plan because emergency arrangements and vessel capability seem coherent. A port agent agrees to represent the call because the documentation does not force them into needless exposure. When any of these actors hesitates, the practical effect can be larger than a formal prohibition. Safety regulation turns private caution into a visible narrowing of options.

Crew competence works in the same way, though with a more human texture. Harsh routes do not merely demand paperwork; they demand people able to interpret the route, the vessel, and the margin of safety under stress. Competence is not an abstract virtue here. It appears in manning plans, endorsements, training records, bridge procedures, familiarisation, fatigue management, and the plain commercial fact that experienced personnel are not infinitely available. A ship manager trying to crew a northern voyage may discover that suitable officers or specialist support cannot be assembled without attracting closer scrutiny of ownership, routing, or counterparties. That is operational dependency in its most immediate form. The voyage relies on a labour market and training structure that can quietly refuse by not providing credible people for the job.

A named example helps to ground the argument. The *Yamal LNG* project at Sabetta depended not merely on a terminal and willing buyers, but on a tightly organised chain of Arc7 ice-class LNG carriers, specialist design approval, insurance acceptance, crewing competence, and northern operational support. The commercial success of such a project has often been discussed in terms of energy strategy and Arctic infrastructure. Less often acknowledged is the institutional lesson: trade of that kind rests on a dense cluster of specialised service relationships. Pressure on those relationships - class support, insurance comfort, maintenance pathways, crewing arrangements, spares logistics, technical management - can alter viability without any dramatic act at sea. The cargo may exist. The route may exist. The enabling structure can still fray.

A second example lies in the tightening web around Russian Arctic energy after sanctions linked to the 2022 invasion of Ukraine and, more specifically, the 2023 designation of Arctic LNG 2 by the United States. What mattered for present purposes was not only the legal status of the project, but the practical question of whether specialised shipping and support arrangements could be sustained. Ice-capable vessels require credible maintenance, insurable operation, recognised class standing, and crews competent for demanding northern service. If mainstream insurers, managers, technical partners, or service providers step back, the burden does not vanish. It shifts to a smaller set of actors with weaker reputational standing, reduced global acceptance, or thinner operating margins. The concept here is supply-side fragility. Sanctions may appear to target trade directly, but in northern conditions they often bite hardest by thinning the pool of institutions able to make the trade operationally respectable.

Emergency planning adds another layer to the same architecture. A northern voyage is judged not only by how it intends to proceed, but by what it will do when something fails. Search and rescue capacity, towing options, communications resilience, pollution response arrangements, medical contingencies, port refuge possibilities, and the chain of command for difficult decisions all matter because the environment punishes improvisation. Again, the technical detail matters less here than the institutional structure. Emergency planning ties a vessel to maps of dependence beyond the ship itself. It forces operators to identify who will answer, who will assist, who will admit, who will coordinate, and under what assumptions. Where those services are concentrated, they become indirect tools of enforcement. No dramatic refusal need be issued. A provider can simply decline to support a movement that sits outside acceptable legal or reputational bounds, and the voyage's safety case may collapse with it.

The logic can be seen in smaller, quieter moments too. A spare part for a northern-capable vessel cannot always be sourced casually from the next port. A specialist survey cannot always be deferred without consequence. A technical superintendent cannot always be replaced with a generalist when the route and vessel demand more. Each small dependency gives shape to the wider corridor. That is why supply-side restrictions in cold-water trade can have disproportionate effect. Restrict access to generic finance or shipping services, and markets may adapt. Restrict access to highly specialised enabling services, and the room for adaptation narrows because substitution is neither quick nor widely accepted. The route becomes politically constrained through the very institutions meant, in ordinary times, to keep it safe.

A credible limitation should be stated plainly. Safety regulation is not a sanctions instrument by design, and it should not be romanticised into one. A poorly governed or over-politicised use of safety arguments can damage the legitimacy of both safety oversight and sanctions enforcement. If every technical query is treated as a proxy sanction, operators may begin to see genuine safety concerns as politically contaminated. If authorities or private service providers stretch safety rationales too far, they risk chilling legitimate trade and encouraging substitution into weaker, less transparent service markets. That would not strengthen northern governance. It could degrade it. The boundary between prudent caution and opportunistic obstruction matters.

There is another limitation. Concentrated services do not always remain concentrated. Pressure creates markets. When mainstream insurers, managers, classification relationships, or crewing networks withdraw, alternative providers sometimes emerge. They may offer thinner assurance, narrower geographic acceptance, weaker claims-paying reputation, or less persuasive technical standing, yet they can still keep some trade alive. This is especially true where state backing, political urgency, or strategic commodity value encourages the construction of parallel support systems. The existence of such alternatives complicates any easy claim that safety-linked dependency guarantees enforcement success. It does not. It raises costs, narrows options, and often degrades quality. Those effects matter, but they are not the same as closure.

That complication does not weaken the main argument. It sharpens it. The real issue is not whether safety regulation can stop every targeted voyage. It is whether concentrated enabling services can shape the terms on which trade proceeds, forcing operators to choose between widely recognised support and more marginal substitutes. In northern waters, that choice is unusually consequential because the safety margin is already thin. A vessel operating with weaker cover, weaker technical backing, less trusted emergency support, or thinner crewing depth does not merely carry reputational baggage. It carries operational fragility. The market reads that fragility. So do ports, charterers, and counterparties. Safety and sanctions do not merge, but they begin to press on the same fault line.

The quiet motif running through this problem is the permit. Not a single government paper, but the wider idea of permission embodied in certificates, endorsements, service bookings, acceptance letters, operating manuals, and emergency plans. A northern voyage proceeds because enough institutions, each holding a small portion of the permit, agree that the movement remains safe enough and lawful enough to touch. Withdraw too many of those permissions, and the trade may remain theoretically possible while becoming commercially or operationally implausible. That is how indirect enforcement works in harsh environments. It does not need to dramatise itself. It lets dependency do the work.

For sanctions analysis, the deeper lesson is that northern trade cannot be understood by looking only at the ship and the cargo. One must look at the support lattice: classification, insurance, crewing markets, technical management, emergency planning, specialist maintenance, and the organisations that lend their names to difficult voyages. Those names matter because they are how institutions distribute responsibility in places where failure travels quickly from one actor to another. A ship in ice waters rarely stands alone. It arrives wrapped in borrowed confidence.

That leaves an uncomfortable question at the edge of every northern voyage subject to political pressure. When a ship is technically capable but increasingly dependent on thinner, less trusted, or more politically exposed support, at what point does the withdrawal of specialist services cease to look like ordinary commercial caution and begin to function as the decisive form of enforcement? In cold waters, that threshold comes sooner than many legal texts admit, and later than many public slogans assume.

Remote monitoring limits

On 13 June 2019, two oil tankers, the *Front Altair* and the *Kokuka Courageous*, were struck in the Gulf of Oman. The incident did not occur in the Arctic, yet it exposed a truth that matters even more in remote northern waters: a ship may be seen by many systems and still remain only partially known. AIS records, commercial tracking feeds, port data, satellite imagery, state intelligence, crew testimony, and corporate filings can all exist at once without producing a settled account. Observation does not equal certainty. The file can stay thin.

That distinction grows sharper as trade moves north. In dense maritime corridors, ships generate records almost accidentally. They pass through traffic schemes, call at major ports, interact with pilots, agents, terminals, customs systems, bunkering providers, and repair services, leaving behind an administrative wake that thickens the story of the voyage. Remote routes behave differently. Fewer ports mean fewer routine checks. Longer intervals between service points mean fewer commercial encounters that generate paperwork. Weather, distance, communications limits, and sparse infrastructure make surveillance more selective and interpretation more fragile. The sea does not fall silent, but it speaks in shorter fragments.

Five minutes can matter.

That is not because remote monitoring fails absolutely. It fails unevenly. Show the pattern in ordinary form. A vessel transits a northern route with AIS transmitting for most of the voyage. The track appears broadly plausible. Then the signal weakens, drops, or behaves oddly in a zone where weather, satellite coverage, equipment condition, geography, or human intervention could all play some part. Later, a port record confirms arrival, but the interval between departure and arrival contains less detail than an analyst would like. The concept is probabilistic visibility. Monitoring provides clues whose reliability varies by place, technology, and context.

The implication is important for sanctions enforcement: a suspicious gap may justify further questions, but it does not answer them by itself.

AIS illustrates the problem because it occupies an awkward place between routine navigation aid and evidentiary object. The system was not designed as a perfect sanctions tool. It was designed to support safety, awareness, and traffic management. Compliance analysts and investigators use it because it is often the best available public or commercially accessible record of where ships say they are and how they move. Yet AIS can mislead in several ways without any elaborate conspiracy. Signals may be interrupted by equipment faults, power issues, atmospheric conditions, reception limits, or harsh operating environments. Data aggregators may display incomplete or delayed coverage. Manual entries may be wrong. Human beings mistype. Equipment ages. Remote routes do not forgive such fragility; they expose it. When analysts treat AIS as a clean mirror of the voyage, they import certainty the system never promised to provide.

A named example clarifies the point. Public scrutiny of ship-to-ship transfers associated with sanctioned oil movements in the eastern Mediterranean and parts of Asian waters during the late 2010s and early 2020s often relied heavily on AIS anomalies: periods of silence, odd loitering, or suspicious proximity between vessels. Sometimes those indicators pointed to conduct later supported by broader evidence. Sometimes they remained just that - indicators. The lesson matters in northern waters because harsh conditions can create superficially similar signatures for less sinister reasons. A vessel may reduce speed, alter course, or behave irregularly because of ice, convoying constraints, weather avoidance, or safety decisions taken on the bridge. The data point looks dramatic. The context can make it ordinary. Good enforcement practice, therefore, compares AIS against other records rather than treating it as a verdict generator.

Port records are often imagined as the cleaner alternative, but they too deserve caution. A port call appears official, and in one sense it is. Yet port documentation is produced by different institutions for different purposes, with different update cycles and levels of detail. Some records are rich and timely. Others are sparse, delayed, or poorly harmonised across agencies and jurisdictions. In remote regions, that unevenness can deepen. Show the sequence. A vessel departs from a northern loading point with documents generated under local administrative conditions, then arrives days later at a port that logs its entry according to a different set of practices. The records may both be accurate in their own terms while still leaving wide interpretive gaps between them. The concept is administrative discontinuity. The implication is that enforcement rarely receives a single continuous record; it receives islands of information and must decide whether the water between them hides anything important.

Remote surveillance from aircraft, patrols, or satellites complicates rather than solves the problem. Each tool sees something real, but none sees everything that matters. Imagery may confirm presence, proximity, movement, or physical characteristics, yet remain silent on ownership, instructions, cargo title, or the legal meaning of a transfer. Patrol assets can observe behaviour but not necessarily reconstruct the paperwork that made the behaviour possible. State intelligence may fill some gaps but often cannot be shared in full with commercial actors or foreign partners expected to act upon it. Monitoring is therefore layered but not seamless. The record resembles a patchwork quilt: useful, sometimes persuasive, rarely complete. That is why remote detection can be delayed even when observation exists. The hard part is often not looking. It is connecting.

The Arctic setting adds its own distortions. Darkness, weather, ice conditions, communications constraints, sparse coastal infrastructure, and long distances do not merely reduce the amount of data collected; they alter the balance between what is seen and what can be confidently inferred. A vessel may be visible in broad outline but evidentially indistinct in detail. A route deviation may look suspicious from afar but prove prudent when read against local conditions. A long interval without fresh records may reflect remoteness rather than concealment. This matters because plausible deniability does not always require deception. Sometimes it grows naturally where the environment makes full verification expensive and slow. A party under scrutiny does not need to invent an entirely false story if the gaps in the record already permit several partially credible ones.

A second named example sits close to the northern theme. The 2018 transit of the *Venta Maersk* along the Northern Sea Route drew attention partly because commercial observers tracked it as a proof-of-concept movement under closely watched conditions. The voyage was unusually visible because it was unusual, public, and commercially symbolic. That visibility itself is instructive. High-profile passages often produce abundant records because many actors are watching them. Ordinary or politically sensitive movements in remote regions may not enjoy the same density of observation. The contrast shows why selective visibility can mislead analysis. We know more about some voyages not because the route is inherently transparent, but because publicity, commercial interest, or state attention temporarily thickens the record. The monitoring environment is therefore not merely technical. It is social and political.

This has consequences for how sanctions evidence is built. A compliance team or regulator working on a remote-route case rarely starts with a complete narrative. It begins with fragments: AIS traces, registry entries, port call data, insurance records, satellite images, charter information, perhaps customs documents or cargo certificates, perhaps reporting from reputable media or specialist intelligence providers. Each fragment arrives with its own reliability profile. Some are machine-generated. Some are self-reported. Some are lagging. Some are curated by commercial vendors. The task is not to celebrate data abundance, but to compare fragments until either a coherent account holds or the contradictions become impossible to ignore. Risk, in this setting, is visible in decisions: whether to permit a port call, process a payment, confirm cover, accept a cargo description, or escalate a file for deeper review.

A credible limitation must be admitted. Remote monitoring is often better than critics suggest. Satellite capability, commercial vessel tracking platforms, improved data integration, and more sophisticated open-source methods have narrowed the informational advantage once conferred by distance alone. Some evasive conduct that might once have passed unnoticed now leaves a trail visible to analysts willing to work patiently across systems. That matters, and it should not be understated. The old romantic claim that remote seas naturally swallow evidence has become less persuasive in an age of persistent observation and rapid cross-border information exchange.

Yet this improvement does not erase the central problem. Better monitoring produces more data, not automatically better judgement. Incomplete coverage remains incomplete, however refined the interface displaying it. A richer stream of AIS records still requires interpretation. Higher-resolution imagery still leaves legal and commercial questions unresolved. Data integration can reduce some blind spots while encouraging overconfidence in others, particularly when users forget that different records were generated for different purposes and with different thresholds of reliability. A false sense of omniscience may be more dangerous than admitted uncertainty, because it tempts institutions to treat pattern recognition as proof and absence of evidence as evidence of absence.

That tension explains why plausible deniability persists. It is not simply a trick used by bad actors; it is an effect produced by the structure of remote monitoring itself. Where records are intermittent, parties can anchor their explanations in the same ambiguities analysts must confront. A signal gap becomes a technical fault. A routing anomaly becomes a weather decision. A slow reporting interval becomes ordinary administrative lag. Sometimes those explanations are true. Sometimes they are merely available. The enforcement challenge lies in distinguishing between the two without pretending that every unresolved gap contains guilt. Delayed detection follows naturally from this structure. If the record only becomes legible once port data, payments, imagery, and corporate records are assembled after the event, then the relevant decision may already have passed from prevention to reconstruction.

The quiet motif here is the signal, because a signal is never the same as the thing it reports. A clean track on a screen can conceal uncertainty about who instructed the voyage, who benefited from it, or what changed hands between sparse reporting points. A lost signal can indicate malfunction, conditions, or manipulation. A late signal may still be useful, but only if the institution reading it understands delay as part of the evidence rather than an embarrassing flaw to be wished away. Northern monitoring requires that discipline. One must read signals for what they are: partial transmissions from a system built for practical use, then repurposed for scrutiny under conditions it handles unevenly.

For maritime sanctions, the wider lesson is austere. Remote monitoring should be treated as a probability machine with known failure modes, not as a theatre of omniscient watching. It narrows uncertainty. It does not abolish it. That is why the most careful institutions combine surveillance with slower forms of verification - comparing documents, testing ownership continuity, checking port records against payment patterns, and resisting the urge to let a compelling visual trace do all the argumentative work. Remote regions punish both naivety and overconfidence. The first assumes nothing can be known. The second assumes that enough has already been seen.

The unresolved question comes down to threshold. When a vessel moving through remote waters leaves a track that is plausible but incomplete, and the surrounding records do not fully agree, should enforcement act on the probability that the gaps matter, or hold back until the missing pieces arrive and risk learning too late that the voyage was structured to exploit precisely that delay?

Chapter 3

Jurisdiction, Port State, and Control

On 10 December 1982, in Montego Bay, Jamaica, states signed the United Nations Convention on the Law of the Sea. That moment is often remembered as a grand settlement of maritime order, a legal architecture spread across oceans that seem, from a chart room or a shoreline, too fluid to govern neatly. Yet the enduring lesson is less majestic and more practical. The sea was not placed under one hand. It was divided into relationships: flag, coast, port, transit, service, approach, entry, inspection. Authority was distributed rather than solved.

That distribution still governs the life of a voyage. A ship may sail under one flag, pass near another state's coast, seek refuge or trade in a third state's port, insure through a fourth jurisdiction, bank through a fifth, and answer, in commercial reality, to private firms operating across several more. The law does not vanish in that movement. It multiplies. Each stage attaches a different kind of claim, a different burden of proof, a different appetite for delay, a different fear of getting the judgement wrong. The passport changes hands.

How can control become stronger as direct power becomes harder to use? That is the paradox. High-profile interdiction on the open sea draws public attention because it looks like real force. Much of maritime enforcement, however, grows more effective as it becomes quieter, more administrative, and more dispersed. A vessel may be difficult to stop lawfully in one place and quite easy to slow in another. The same trade that resists overt confrontation at sea may become vulnerable when it asks for bunkers, seeks insurance confirmation, files entry papers, requests classification support, or tries to settle payment through institutions that would rather not carry the exposure. Control shifts from the horizon to the desk.

That shift matters because jurisdiction is rarely a simple map question. It is a sequencing question. Who can act depends not only on where the ship is, but on what the ship is trying to do. Passing is different from calling.

Trading is different from transiting. Seeking services is different from asserting freedom of navigation. A flag state claims continuing authority through registration and legal identity. A coastal state asserts powers linked to waters, resources, security, and navigation in its vicinity. A port state exercises authority at the point where the voyage asks to become administratively legible. The practical significance lies in the hand-off. Once a ship seeks entry, support, or recognition, the legal and commercial room around it narrows quickly.

That narrowing creates one of the most consequential features of modern sanctions enforcement: port state control and related documentary scrutiny can carry more weight than coercive action at sea while appearing, on the surface, much more ordinary. Inspection regimes were not invented as sanctions theatres. They were built around safety, seaworthiness, certification, manning, and operational compliance. Yet the very habits that make them routine also make them useful. A vessel already under suspicion does not need a dramatic sanctions deficiency to be delayed. An insurance inconsistency, a crewing problem, a certificate issue, or a mismatch in management records may be enough to hold the file open. Safety and compliance do not merge, but they begin to press against one another in ways no serious operator can ignore.

The stakes reach well beyond port officials and coast guards. States increasingly influence maritime behaviour by making private actors internalise public risk. Banks screen transactions not because they aspire to naval power, but because penalties, reputational harm, and regulatory exposure alter their tolerance for ambiguity. Insurers ask harder questions because claims, cover, and sanctions liability can no longer be separated cleanly. Ship managers, agents, and classification bodies become reluctant carriers of state pressure because their own commercial survival depends on reading political signals correctly. This matters now and later because firms will carry only so much uncertainty on behalf of governments. Where legal boundaries blur or guidance remains thin, private caution may exceed public intent for a while, then harden into fatigue, inconsistency, or withdrawal.

That is why the language of escalation needs care. Maritime enforcement is too often imagined as a choice between weakness and confrontation, between doing nothing and seizing ships under cameras. Real practice offers a broader and more disciplined vocabulary. Documentation can be demanded without a spectacle. Services can be denied without a blockade. Investigations can be sequenced so that a weak point in one part of the voyage becomes decisive pressure in another. These are not evasions of power. They are forms of calibrated pressure designed to work below the threshold at which legal ambiguity, diplomatic friction, or military risk begin to swallow the original purpose. Quiet measures often travel furthest.

The argument ahead moves through these layers in the order the voyage itself encounters them. Authority begins with the vessel's legal attachment to flag, coast, and port, then tightens through inspection and administrative control, spreads outward through the commercial institutions that absorb extraterritorial pressure, and settles into the less visible arts of enforcement that seek effect without dramatic collision. The sequence matters because each layer alters the next. A dispute over legal reach becomes a delay in port. A delay in port becomes a problem for insurers and banks. A problem for insurers and banks becomes a quieter form of coercion than interdiction, and often a more sustainable one.

The deeper friction is not hard to state, only hard to resolve. States want maritime sanctions to bite without provoking broader conflict. Firms want clarity strong enough to justify refusal without making every doubtful file a permanent hazard. Ships continue to move through spaces where multiple authorities claim something, but none claims everything. The passport changes hands again. The decisive question is therefore not who owns the sea in the abstract, but who can require enough proof, at the right moment, to make a doubtful voyage pause without turning that pause into something much larger.

Flag state, coastal state, port state

On 4 July 2019, authorities in Gibraltar detained the tanker *Grace 1* off the southern tip of the Iberian Peninsula on suspicion that it was carrying Iranian crude oil to Syria in breach of European Union sanctions. The episode quickly became a diplomatic quarrel involving the United Kingdom, Gibraltar, Iran, and arguments about destination, ownership, and legal basis. Yet the most instructive feature was jurisdictional, not theatrical. The ship sailed under the flag of Panama at the time, moved near a coast claimed by one set of authorities, and became vulnerable at the point where territorial access and administrative control could be asserted with greater confidence than on the open sea. The sea looked continuous. Authority did not.

That discontinuity is the practical starting point for any serious account of maritime sanctions. A vessel does not move through one seamless legal field. It moves through layers of attachment that change with its location, status, and purpose. Its flag links it to one state in matters of registration and legal identity. Its proximity to a coast brings another state's powers into view, shaped by the law of the sea and by local enforcement choices. Its arrival at port places it within an administrative space where entry, inspection, and services can be conditioned in ways that are often more decisive than dramatic action offshore. The ship remains the same object. The governing relationship around it changes.

The passport keeps changing hands.

That is why maritime disputes so often arise from a category mistake. Public argument tends to ask who "has jurisdiction" as though a single winner must emerge. The more precise question is who has which authority, at which stage, for which purpose, and with what practical means to turn that authority into effect. Flag state authority is enduring but often distant. Coastal state authority is spatially immediate but carefully bounded. Port state authority is conditional, administrative, and frequently powerful precisely because the ship has asked to enter a controlled space rather than simply pass through one. Once these forms are separated, much of modern sanctions practice becomes easier to understand. Enforcement shifts towards ports and services not because legal principle has failed, but because legal principle itself distributes authority in ways that make open-sea coercion more difficult and administrative control more useful.

Flag state jurisdiction sits at the formal centre of maritime order. A vessel's registration is not decorative. It anchors nationality, documentation, certain safety obligations, crewing standards, and the legal identity through which a ship enters commerce. Show the ordinary sequence. A ship seeks insurance, classification, finance, charter employment, and port access through papers that all presume some recognised flag connection. The flag tells other actors which registry stands behind the vessel, which rules apply to aspects of its operation, and which state bears primary responsibility in the legal imagination of the law of the sea. The concept is continuing attachment. The implication is that flags matter even when the flag state is physically absent, because registration remains the first language in which the vessel presents itself to the world.

Yet flag authority is not the same as operational control. A flag state may possess formal competence and still lack the political will, regulatory capacity, or practical reach to monitor every questionable voyage conducted under its register. That does not make the flag irrelevant; it makes it incomplete. Sanctions enforcement often begins with questions about the flag because registration packages information into a usable form, but it rarely ends there. A vessel can be duly registered and still become problematic when it approaches another state's coast, seeks entry to port, or depends upon insurers, bankers, and service providers who read the flag as only one part of a wider risk picture. The law recognises the flag's significance. The market tests its credibility.

Coastal state authority enters when the vessel moves through waters or maritime zones where another state may lawfully regulate certain forms of conduct. This is where jurisdiction becomes most politically charged, because geography tempts states to claim more than the law cleanly grants, while security concerns tempt observers to treat proximity as permission. A coastal state can do much within its territorial sea. It can do far less simply because a ship is visible offshore. The difference matters. Freedom of navigation is not an empty slogan, but neither is coastal jurisdiction a mere courtesy. The practical problem is that sanctions cases often sit near the line where commercial movement, strategic suspicion, and legal restraint meet. A state that cannot readily stop a vessel on the high seas may still watch it, record it, prepare a file, or wait until the vessel seeks a form of access that activates a stronger set of controls.

This is one reason high-seas interdiction is less central to sanctions practice than public imagination suggests. It is legally riskier, politically louder, and often evidentially harder. A vessel moving beyond territorial waters has not yet asked for much. It may be observed, tracked, or questioned, but coercive interference raises immediate issues of legal basis, escalation, and international reaction. Show the contrast. A ship at sea presents suspicion. A ship at port presents paperwork, services, certificates, and jurisdictional hooks. The concept here is threshold. Offshore, the threshold for force is high and the permissible grounds narrower. In port, the threshold for administrative action can be lower because the ship has entered a domain where entry conditions, inspections, and service approvals already structure ordinary practice. The implication follows: port state power often carries more practical weight than offshore drama because it operates where maritime commerce becomes institutionally dependent.

Port state authority is therefore the quiet centre of many sanctions systems. It does not depend on romantic ideas of national power projected over empty water. It depends on the simple fact that ships trade by entering places where someone can ask questions and require answers before the movement continues. A port can inspect, delay, deny clearance, query insurance, test certificates, compare ownership records, and refuse services if the file will not hold together. None of this requires a sensational confrontation. It requires procedure. This is why a suspect voyage may escape direct challenge at sea only to become vulnerable the moment it seeks bunkers, a berth, agency representation, pilotage, cargo handling, or departure formalities. Ports turn jurisdiction into paperwork. Paperwork then turns doubt into leverage.

A second named example makes the distribution of authority clearer. In July 2022, the cargo vessel *Zhibek Zholy*, carrying Ukrainian grain under a Russian flag according to widely reported accounts, became the subject of dispute when it approached the Turkish port of Karasu. Ukraine requested action, claiming the grain had been stolen. Turkey, as port state, confronted a difficult file: allegations with political weight, a vessel present within its jurisdictional reach, and legal questions about evidence, ownership, and the basis for detention. The episode did not resolve into a simple morality play. It exposed the operational truth that port states are often asked to convert contested facts into enforceable decisions under intense time pressure. A ship may be visible, even notorious, and yet still require a defensible administrative basis before the port acts with confidence.

Disputes arise because these forms of authority overlap without merging. Flag states may insist upon the primacy of registration. Coastal states may stress security, resource protection, or the integrity of nearby waters. Port states may emphasise their right to police entry and services. Private actors - insurers, managers, banks, terminal operators - then add another layer by treating uncertain jurisdiction as commercial risk. Trust, in this setting, is not a mood. It is visible in choices: whether a port agent accepts the appointment, whether an insurer confirms cover, whether a bank clears the freight payment, whether a terminal allots a window, whether a classification society feels comfortable remaining attached to the vessel's record. Jurisdiction therefore does not live only in statutes or treaties. It lives in the behaviour of institutions deciding how much doubt they are willing to carry.

A credible limitation must be faced. Port state power, for all its practical strength, is not unlimited. States vary in administrative capacity, political appetite, legal culture, and economic dependence on maritime trade. Some ports apply scrutiny rigorously. Others hesitate, delay, or look for reasons not to inherit a disputed case. A vessel may also avoid the ports most likely to ask difficult questions, shifting trade towards more permissive jurisdictions or relying on intermediate transfers that reduce the need for direct entry into closely watched facilities. This matters because sanctions analysis becomes lazy when it assumes that jurisdiction, once located on a map, automatically produces action. It does not. Authority must be exercised, and exercise always depends on institutions, incentives, and the quality of the evidence they are asked to trust.

That limitation does not weaken the larger claim. It explains why enforcement tends to migrate from the open sea towards the thicker administrative world of ports and services. The more uncertain or contested a sanctions case becomes, the more attractive low-visibility forms of control tend to be. A direct interdiction may provoke diplomatic crisis. A port document check may delay the same voyage with less spectacle and often with stronger legal footing. A coastal state may have reasons to avoid confrontation offshore while quietly sharing information that later shapes port scrutiny elsewhere. A flag state may remain formally central while commercial actors treat its assurances as insufficient without confirmation from insurers, financiers, or port officials. Jurisdiction, in practice, works by relay rather than by monologue.

This relay helps explain why responsibility disputes can look so persistent and so unsatisfying. Each actor can point to another. The flag state can insist that enforcement beyond clear legal limits would be improper. The coastal state can say the vessel has not crossed the threshold that justifies stronger action. The port state can ask for better evidence before bearing the political cost of detention or denial. Private firms can claim they need clearer guidance before carrying public burdens. None of these positions is always cynical. Many are legally or commercially rational. Yet taken together they create the spaces in which doubtful voyages try to survive: between responsibility and reach, between formal competence and practical appetite, between visibility and action.

The quiet motif here is the passport, because maritime jurisdiction resembles a document checked repeatedly by different officials for different reasons. The vessel is the same. The questions change. One authority asks who the ship legally belongs to. Another asks where it is and what it is doing nearby. Another asks whether it may enter, unload, refuel, repair, or depart. Each check reveals something, and each leaves something unresolved. The mistake is to expect any single check to settle the matter completely. Maritime sanctions depend on accumulation. One jurisdictional touchpoint rarely decides the voyage; several in sequence often do.

The deeper lesson is austere. The sea does not abolish law, but it scatters law across institutions that act at different moments and under different constraints. Serious enforcement therefore relies less on fantasies of total control than on understanding where authority becomes operationally useful. A doubtful ship on the high seas may remain mostly a legal and diplomatic problem. The same ship approaching port, seeking services, or presenting documents to commercial actors becomes an administrative problem, and administrative problems are often easier to act upon without tearing larger holes in the legal order. The unresolved question is the one that keeps returning as voyages move north and scrutiny thickens: when a vessel's status, route, and paperwork trigger concern, which authority in the chain will decide that the file is finally strong enough to stop passing the passport on?

Port state control as a practical lever

On 4 July 2019, authorities in Gibraltar detained the tanker *Grace 1* on suspicion that it was carrying Iranian crude oil to Syria in breach of European Union sanctions. The headlines favoured the spectacle: boarding parties, diplomatic protest, retaliatory pressure, arguments about destination and legal basis. Yet the more durable lesson lay elsewhere. The ship became vulnerable not in some romantic contest for command of the sea, but at the point where a port-related authority could ask for documents, test explanations, and convert doubt into administrative action. The lever was procedural before it was dramatic.

That is why port state control matters so much in sanctions practice. It does not begin as a tool of geopolitical theatre. It begins as a practical regime for checking whether ships entering port comply with safety, certification, manning, and operational standards recognised across maritime commerce. The genius of the system, if that is not too generous a word, lies in its ordinariness. A port need not prove an entire sanctions case in order to slow a doubtful voyage. It can inspect. It can compare certificates. It can record deficiencies. It can delay departure until explanations arrive. Paper does the work.

Port state control sits at the intersection of routine oversight and strategic consequence. Show the scene in ordinary form. A vessel arrives with a history that has already raised quiet concern among insurers, banks, or cargo interests. Nothing in the arrival itself compels a sanctions detention. The ship nevertheless enters a space in which officials may lawfully inspect certificates, review manning documents, examine safety systems, test the consistency of class records, and decide whether the vessel should be detained for deficiencies unrelated to sanctions as such. The concept is jurisdictional conversion. Suspicion that could not easily justify action on the high seas becomes a practical reason to examine the ship with unusual care once it requests entry into port. The implication follows quickly: ports transform uncertainty into a sequence of reviewable decisions.

That sequence matters because inspections are not merely technical rituals. They allocate time, cost, and credibility. A deficiency noted by a port state control officer can disturb charter performance, unsettle insurance assumptions, trigger further scrutiny by classification societies, and make cargo interests or financiers ask whether the vessel remains worth the trouble. Trust, here, is not a general feeling about the shipping market. It is visible in decisions: whether the port lets the ship continue, whether the insurer maintains cover without further questions, whether the charterer accepts delay, whether the terminal still wants the cargo on its berth schedule, whether the next port is prepared to receive the same vessel with the same file. A detention is not merely a legal event. It is a redistribution of commercial patience.

That practical force explains why safety and compliance rationales often overlap without ever becoming identical. Port state control was built to keep substandard ships from moving risk from one jurisdiction to another. Sanctions enforcement, by contrast, is concerned with targeted trade, restricted parties, prohibited services, and the circumvention of economic pressure. The two regimes are conceptually different. A ship may be sanctions-compliant and still unsafe. It may be well maintained and still part of a prohibited transaction. Yet the operational world does not keep these categories in separate drawers. A vessel already viewed with suspicion is more likely to attract patient scrutiny. A file already weakened by sanctions concerns is less likely to survive ordinary safety irregularities without consequence. The overlap occurs in behaviour, not in theory.

A brief example makes the point. A vessel with a recent change of manager, an unusual trading pattern, or questions surrounding ownership may enter port with minor certification issues that, under less charged conditions, might have been corrected with limited fuss. Under closer inspection, those same issues can justify detention or delay. The deficiency need not be a hidden sanctions violation. An expired certificate, a crewing irregularity, a problem in safety management documentation, or a technical defect requiring rectification may be enough. The official reason remains a safety deficiency. The wider effect is to interrupt a voyage already viewed as commercially or politically doubtful. This is not a legal fiction so much as an institutional reality. Port state control does not need to become sanctions law in order to shape sanctions outcomes.

The power of such interventions lies in timing. A ship stopped offshore can provoke immediate legal and diplomatic argument. A ship detained in port for documentary or technical shortcomings enters a slower, denser process. Evidence can be gathered. Other agencies can be consulted. Service providers can reconsider their exposure. Cargo interests can decide whether continued involvement is worth the delay. Banks can reassess payment timing. Investigators can compare the ship's documentation with external records while the vessel remains physically fixed within reach. The port becomes a holding point for information as much as for steel. In sanctions terms, that is often more useful than a burst of overt coercion at sea.

A second named example comes from a different register. In August 2020, the *Wakashio* grounded off Mauritius and later broke apart, causing a major oil spill. The case was not a sanctions incident, and it would be wrong to force it into one. Its value here lies elsewhere. It reminded governments, insurers, and maritime professionals that administrative judgments about vessel condition, route risk, competence, and oversight are not abstract housekeeping matters. They are decisions with material consequences for coasts, cargoes, and public authority. Port state control draws strength from that memory. When a port inspects aggressively, it does so under the shadow of what happens when weak documentation, poor maintenance, or operational complacency is allowed to travel onward. The implication for sanctions practice is indirect but real: a port can justify close scrutiny of suspect shipping through safety logic without pretending that safety and sanctions are the same issue.

This indirectness is precisely why port state control can serve as such a powerful lever. It works through accepted institutional habits rather than exceptional force. Inspectors already know how to compare certificates, question manning arrangements, review records of drills and maintenance, and assess whether deficiencies warrant detention. Ports already understand the administrative consequences of holding a ship. Shipowners already know the commercial cost of appearing on the wrong side of inspection records. That accumulated routine means the port does not need to improvise a sanctions response from scratch. It can work with familiar tools, then allow the resulting delay or detention to trigger consequences across insurance, finance, chartering, and reputation.

The mechanism becomes especially potent when combined with the uneven quality of maritime records discussed earlier. A vessel may arrive with documentation that is not plainly false, yet not cleanly persuasive either. Names may have changed. Ownership chains may look complicated but not unlawful. Service histories may show gaps. Certificates may be current but recently amended. In such cases, port state control provides a disciplined method for asking whether the ship's technical and administrative condition supports the confidence its commercial backers are asking the port to extend. The question is not "Is this vessel sanctioned?" in the abstract. It is narrower and often more actionable: "Does this file hold together well enough for the port to allow the ship to proceed without exposing itself to avoidable risk?" Ports live by that question.

A credible limitation must be admitted. Port state control is not infinitely elastic, and it should not be treated as a convenient disguise for sanctions action whenever direct authority is weak. If ports begin using safety inspections as a pretext untethered from actual deficiencies, they risk damaging the legitimacy of inspection regimes that depend on broad professional respect. Shipowners, flag states, and courts can challenge overreach. Repeated misuse would also burden ports themselves, whose resources are finite and whose commercial role depends on preserving a reputation for procedural seriousness rather than political improvisation. A lever works best when it remains recognisable as a lever, not when it is mistaken for a crowbar.

There is another limitation. Administrative detention does not always yield strategic effect. Some vessels trade precisely because their operators have already accepted delay, weaker reputational standing, and the possibility of diversion to more permissive ports. A ship detained in one jurisdiction may reappear later under altered management, amended paperwork, or a different flag. Ports vary in appetite, resources, and political backing. A rigorous inspection regime in one harbour does not guarantee similar action elsewhere. Sanctions analysts sometimes overstate the coherence of port practice, as though one detention automatically radiated control across the whole system. Maritime trade remains too fragmented for that. A port can slow the voyage. It cannot, by itself, settle the entire map.

Still, the limitations do not diminish the central point. They clarify where port state control is strongest. It is strongest when it operates within its own logic, documenting real deficiencies, preserving procedural credibility, and allowing other institutions to absorb the consequences. A vessel delayed for safety reasons may lose a charter slot. A ship with documentary inconsistencies may find insurers, banks, and terminals less willing to indulge ambiguity. A detention can prompt deeper review of ownership, cargo origin, or service history without requiring the port to carry the entire sanctions case alone. The most effective port actions often look modest on paper and substantial in their consequences.

The practical culture of port state control also matters. Inspectors do not work like headline writers. They are trained to look for patterns of deficiency, maintenance quality, record-keeping discipline, and the relationship between paper compliance and the condition of the ship before them. That professional habit has real value in sanctions-adjacent cases because evasion networks often rely on fragmentation. One institution sees the ownership issue. Another sees the payment anomaly. Another sees the route oddity. The port sees the ship itself, its documents, and the immediate quality of its operational discipline. A vessel tied into opaque commercial arrangements may also reveal slippage in crewing, certification, maintenance, or safety management. Not always. But often enough that ports become natural places where broader doubt begins to harden into operational consequence.

The quiet motif here is the clipboard. Not because maritime enforcement is trivial, but because the clipboard represents something underestimated: the power of methodical inspection to hold a voyage still. A clipboard can check what a public argument cannot settle quickly. It can compare dates, signatures, endorsements, and deficiencies. It can ask why one document was reissued, why another remains stale, why a crew record does not align with the rest of the file, why a maintenance history suggests more neglect than the owner admits. The clipboard is not glamorous. It is often more effective than glamour.

Port state control therefore occupies a peculiar but decisive place in sanctions systems. It neither replaces direct legal authority nor serves as a mere bureaucratic accessory. It functions as the operational space in which suspicion can be tested without immediate escalation, and where deficiencies unrelated to sanctions may still change the fate of a suspect voyage. That is not institutional hypocrisy. It is the reality of a maritime order in which ships do not move solely by legal entitlement, but by satisfying a chain of gatekeepers that each measures a different kind of risk.

The unresolved question is not whether ports *can* delay doubtful voyages. Plainly they can. The harder question is when ordinary inspection remains ordinary and when it begins, quietly, to carry the political weight of sanctions enforcement itself. Once a vessel is held on grounds that are formally technical but strategically consequential, how much of the burden should the port bear, and how much should be passed outward to the states, insurers, banks, and managers whose doubts made that clipboard suddenly matter so much?

Extraterritorial pressure and private compliance

In September 2019, the United States designation of COSCO Shipping Tanker (Dalian) Co. and related entities under its Iran programme sent a jolt through shipping markets far beyond Washington. The legal act named particular companies. The commercial effect spread through chartering desks in London, trading houses in Singapore, banks handling letters of credit, insurers reviewing cover, and ship managers deciding which instructions they were still prepared to follow. A rule issued by one state had travelled across contracts and service relationships that did not belong to that state in any simple territorial sense. The ocean had not changed. The inbox had.

That is the essential fact behind extraterritorial pressure in maritime sanctions. States do not need to police every mile of sea directly if they can make enough service providers conclude that touching a doubtful voyage now carries too much regulatory, financial, or reputational cost. The force does not lie only in formal prohibition. It lies in anticipated exposure. A bank asks whether processing a payment may trigger sanctions liability or supervisory trouble. An insurer asks whether a claim linked to the voyage would be defensible. A ship manager asks whether providing crew, accounts, technical oversight, or operational instructions could place the firm inside a prohibited relationship or damage its standing with other clients and regulators. Each actor begins with its own survival. The burden travels from state power into private caution.

The email does the travelling.

This is what extraterritorial pressure looks like in practice: a web of commercial actors revising behaviour because the consequences of a wrong decision reach beyond the immediate transaction. Show the sequence plainly. A cargo movement may appear lawful under the local law of the port where it loads. Yet the freight is to be paid in a currency cleared through a bank with exposure to another jurisdiction. The vessel's insurance depends on a market that fears penalties or exclusion. The ship manager operates offices, staff, or corporate structures within states that expect compliance with sanctions rules framed far away from the voyage itself. The concept is risk internalisation. The implication is direct. Enforcement expands not because law becomes magically global, but because firms with cross-border exposure shrink the set of transactions they are willing to support.

Banks sit at the heart of this system because maritime trade remains inseparable from payment discipline. A ship can load without a bank physically present on the quay, but freight, insurance premiums, agency fees, bunker purchases, and cargo settlement all eventually require accounts, messaging systems, and institutions willing to move money in a form counterparties accept. Show the behaviour that matters. A bank receives payment instructions linked to a cargo whose ownership chain appears unusually layered. The vessel's recent trading pattern has already attracted internal concern. The named counterparties are not designated, yet the deal structure, documents, or intermediary accounts raise questions about true control or destination. The bank does not need a completed prosecutorial brief. It may simply freeze the process, request clarification, escalate to compliance, or decline the transaction. The legal state has not boarded a ship. It has still altered the voyage materially.

That power is often misunderstood as mere private over-caution. Sometimes it is that. More often it is an institutional adaptation to asymmetry. A bank usually knows less about the underlying cargo movement than the trader or shipowner does, but it bears a concentrated share of the regulatory consequences if the transaction proves problematic. This asymmetry encourages what the industry calls de-risking, though the phrase is thinner than the reality it describes. The visible behaviour is easier to trust than the label. Files are escalated. Payment timelines lengthen. Seemingly lawful trades are declined because ownership cannot be explained well enough, document chains do not align, or a route touches a sanctions-sensitive environment where later questions may be impossible to answer cleanly. Extraterritorial pressure works because uncertainty itself becomes expensive.

Insurers perform a related function, though their decisions speak through different instruments. Marine insurance is often described as financial cushioning after the fact, but for shipping it also operates as a passport to normal commerce. Ports, charterers, lenders, terminals, and counterparties want to know who stands behind the liabilities a vessel may generate. When sanctions pressure causes insurers to narrow cover, add exclusions, request deeper disclosure, or refuse renewal, the effect extends beyond the policy wording. Show the sequence. A ship can still float without mainstream cover. It may not, however, secure a berth, transit a canal smoothly, or satisfy a charterer's internal controls with an insurer nobody recognises or trusts. The concept is delegated gatekeeping. The insurer is not a sovereign authority, yet its willingness to attach its name to a voyage determines whether many others will do the same.

A named example makes the logic unmistakable. After the United States announced secondary sanctions pressure linked to Iran and later designated COSCO Shipping Tanker (Dalian) entities in 2019, shipping counterparties did not wait for a theatrical enforcement campaign at sea. Charterers reconsidered vessel nominations. Insurers and financiers examined their exposure to related shipping structures. Market participants tried to map which ships, contracts, and service relationships remained acceptable. The decisive point was not simply that law had changed. It was that private firms were forced to translate legal uncertainty into immediate commercial choices. The risk did not stay with the state that issued the measure. It moved into the firms that would process, insure, manage, or finance the voyage.

Ship managers are especially important here because they stand close to the daily mechanics of a voyage while often remaining outside public discussion. Management firms arrange crews, technical maintenance, regulatory paperwork, safety systems, accounts, procurement, and a range of operational support without which a vessel quickly becomes a steel shell rather than a trading asset. That position gives them unusual exposure. A manager may not own the cargo or even own the ship, yet it may still provide the human and administrative infrastructure that keeps the commercial movement credible. When sanctions pressure rises, managers become enforcement actors because continuing to serve a suspect vessel may endanger banking relationships, insurance arrangements, office operations, reputational standing, or access to other clients. The ship's technical life and the firm's corporate life begin to collide.

This is where extraterritorial pressure proves more subtle than popular arguments suggest. It is not merely that one state tells foreign firms what to do. It is that foreign firms operate within a commercial order dense with dependencies on jurisdictions, currencies, insurers, regulators, and service markets they cannot afford to lose. A ship manager based in one country may employ crew through another, pay suppliers through banks in a third, rely on insurance clubs centred in a fourth, and market its services to clients who care deeply about fifth-country regulatory expectations. The voyage becomes a convergence point for exposures accumulated elsewhere.

A state that can influence those exposures can shape behaviour far beyond its coastline.

A second named example lies in the broader response to Russian trade after February 2022. Measures adopted by the United States, the European Union, the United Kingdom, and partners did not affect maritime behaviour solely through formal prohibitions on named entities or cargoes. They also reshaped private decisions across insurance, trade finance, ship management, broking, and service provision. Firms reviewed whether ongoing involvement with certain voyages or counterparties remained worth the scrutiny and potential consequences. Some relationships ended not because a black-letter ban clearly required immediate termination in every instance, but because the surrounding compliance environment had changed enough that continuing became hard to justify to boards, auditors, insurers, or correspondent banks. Extraterritorial pressure, in other words, often works by raising the administrative cost of saying yes.

That pressure can be highly effective because it acts before a ship reaches the obvious choke points. A vessel denied port entry has already travelled far. A transaction refused by a bank or cover withheld by an insurer may fail before departure. So may a management instruction never issued, a crew contract never signed, a bunker order never confirmed, or a trade finance document returned for lack of comfort on ownership or origin. The state benefits from private screening capacity it neither fully controls nor fully funds. That arrangement is one reason sanctions often seem broader in practice than their legal wording alone would suggest. Private firms read not only the rule itself but the enforcement climate around it, and they tend to protect themselves first.

Still, this system has limits, and the limits matter. Firms will not carry state burdens indefinitely without clarity. A bank can block a file for a time, but if sanctions rules remain ambiguous, guidance contradictory, and exposure hard to bound, the institution may retreat from wider classes of business rather than continue making fine-grained judgements. An insurer can ask for more information, but it cannot underwrite permanent uncertainty without distorting its own business model. A ship manager can sever doubtful clients, yet if too much normal trade begins to look politically risky, the firm may either over-withdraw or seek markets less responsive to allied pressure. The visible behaviour here is fatigue: blanket refusals, fragmented internal policies, delays detached from actual risk quality, or quiet movement of business into less transparent channels.

A credible counter-example sharpens the point. Extraterritorial pressure does not always compel compliance; sometimes it stimulates substitution. If mainstream banks close payment rails, alternative financial arrangements emerge. If established insurers step back, higher-risk or state-backed cover may appear. If major management firms withdraw, other operators - perhaps smaller, less transparent, or more politically sheltered - may step in. The trade does not disappear. It changes shape. This matters because sanctions analysis turns sloppy when it assumes that private withdrawal automatically equals effective control. It may instead mean fragmentation, opacity, and a shift towards actors with weaker documentation cultures and higher tolerance for reputational damage.

That limitation does not make private compliance irrelevant. It defines its real value. The goal is often not total suppression, which may be unattainable, but the raising of costs, the narrowing of respectable options, and the forcing of trade into arrangements that are slower, thinner, less trusted, or easier to scrutinise later. A vessel backed by marginal insurance, obscure payment channels, and unstable management may still move. It does not move with the same commercial ease. Ports hesitate more. Buyers demand more discounts or assurances. Service providers ask harder questions. Claims become harder to settle. The voyage survives, perhaps, but under degraded conditions. Extraterritorial pressure works best when it imposes this cumulative friction without pretending it has erased the trade entirely.

That is why clarity matters so much. Private firms can absorb risk; they cannot govern by prophecy. They need enough precision to know which counterparties, cargoes, services, and structures remain defensible, and enough confidence that careful compliance will be recognised rather than punished retroactively. Without that, the state begins to outsource judgement while withholding the tools needed to make it. Firms respond rationally: some become over-cautious, others opportunistic, others inconsistent across offices and markets. The enforcement system then grows noisy. Similar transactions receive dissimilar treatment. Compliance departments become miniature foreign ministries without the legitimacy or information base that state institutions possess. The result is not disciplined pressure but institutional drift.

The quiet motif here is the signature. Maritime commerce advances by signatures of many kinds: a bank's willingness to process, an insurer's confirmation of cover, a manager's instruction to proceed, a broker's fixture recap, a supplier's acceptance of an order. Extraterritorial pressure works by making those signatures harder to give. The state does not need to supervise every movement physically if enough firms decide that signing has become too dangerous. But signatures withdrawn too broadly can also distort lawful trade, encourage weaker substitutes, and exhaust the private institutions being asked to carry public strategy in their balance sheets and inboxes.

The deepest issue is therefore one of burden, not merely reach. States may be tempted to celebrate the way banks, insurers, and managers amplify sanctions beyond territorial borders. They should be more sober. Private compliance is powerful because firms fear exposure and value continued access to the mainstream commercial order. It is fragile because those same firms will eventually ask how much ambiguity, cost, and reputational peril they are expected to bear without clearer lines, quicker guidance, or stronger public ownership of the policy choices being made. The unresolved test arrives when a doubtful voyage sits just inside the zone of discomfort rather than plainly inside the zone of prohibition: will the next signature be withheld because the law clearly requires it, or because the private actor no longer trusts the state to tell the difference?

Enforcement without escalation

In July 2019, after Gibraltar detained the tanker *Grace 1*, the episode quickly widened into a diplomatic crisis involving Iran, the United Kingdom, and wider arguments about sanctions, maritime law, and retaliatory risk. The spectacle was revealing precisely because it showed what many states would prefer to avoid. A ship can be stopped with cameras watching, statements issued, and prestige engaged. It can also be slowed, documented, denied services, and quietly rendered commercially immobile without inviting the same immediate spiral of confrontation. The difference is not cosmetic. It is strategic.

That distinction matters because maritime sanctions are often judged by the wrong image. Public discussion gravitates towards overt coercion: boarding, seizure, interdiction, dramatic rerouting under armed supervision. Such acts are visible, legible, and politically satisfying to those who want proof that enforcement means more than paperwork. Yet they carry obvious dangers. They raise legal thresholds. They invite reciprocal action. They harden nationalist narratives. They can transform a questionable commercial movement into a state-to-state test of will. A file can do more.

The central problem, then, is how to apply pressure without converting every contested voyage into a larger conflict. The answer is not passivity. It is calibration. Show the practical sequence. A vessel or cargo movement triggers concern because ownership looks opaque, destination unclear, payment channels awkward, or service providers increasingly uneasy. A state could attempt direct coercion at sea, but that may rest on uncertain legal footing or carry disproportionate political cost. Instead, institutions ask for fuller documentation, delay a service approval, compare certificates across registries, notify insurers and banks of elevated concern, and allow the movement to encounter friction at points where the law is clearer and the consequences quieter. The concept is graduated interference. The implication is decisive: the most effective pressure often works by slowing commercial certainty rather than dramatising sovereign force.

Documentation demands are the first instrument in this quieter vocabulary because they look ordinary even when they are doing serious work. A request for beneficial ownership detail, proof of cargo origin, confirmation of insurance validity, updated class status, or clarification of ship management may appear procedural. In practice it can reorder the voyage. A charterer may decline to proceed while the answer is pending. A port may defer berth allocation. A bank may hold payment instructions. A terminal may refuse to schedule discharge. None of these actors needs to proclaim a sanctions enforcement action. Each simply insists that the paper carry the weight the voyage now requires. This is not theatrical weakness. It is administrative precision.

The strength of documentary pressure lies in how it redistributes burden. Direct interdiction asks the enforcing state to justify immediate coercion under conditions of incomplete information. Documentation demands ask the operator, owner, charterer, or service network to explain the transaction before the commercial chain advances. That reversal matters. It turns uncertainty into a problem for the voyage rather than only for the regulator. Trust, here, is visible in behaviour: whether documents arrive quickly, whether they align across institutions, whether explanations remain stable when repeated, whether the same names recur behind supposedly fresh corporate fronts, whether the next counterparty in line still wishes to sign. A weak file may survive rhetoric. It struggles to survive comparison.

Service denial is the second instrument, and often the sharper one. Shipping is sustained by permissions granted in fragments: bunkering, pilotage where required, port agency, repair slots, waste reception, crew changes, insurance confirmations, banking channels, technical management, cargo handling, and onward acceptance at the next node. Deny one service and the voyage may adapt. Deny enough services, or deny the right service at the right moment, and the voyage becomes commercially implausible without a single patrol craft leaving harbour. Show the mechanism. An insurer refuses to confirm cover pending clarification. A port agent steps back because documentation remains inconsistent. A yard will not commit to repairs without knowing who stands behind payment and liability. The ship still floats. Its options contract. That contraction is enforcement without spectacle.

A named example illustrates the point from the private side. After the United States designation of COSCO Shipping Tanker (Dalian) entities in September 2019, disruption spread not because warships suddenly policed every tanker lane, but because charterers, banks, insurers, and other service providers had to decide whether involvement remained tolerable. Some of the practical effect came from uncertainty: which ships were caught, which relationships were too close for comfort, which services might later be judged impermissible. The important lesson is not that ambiguity is always desirable. It is that low-visibility pressure often works by making the next commercial decision harder to take. Enforcement can travel through cancelled fixtures, withheld confirmations, and prolonged internal reviews rather than through seizure alone.

Investigative sequencing adds a third dimension. A state or coalition rarely needs to prove everything at once if it can structure inquiry in a way that gradually narrows the target's room to manoeuvre. The instinct in public debate is to demand a single decisive moment - the revelation, the detention, the conclusive interception. Real enforcement often proceeds more slowly and more intelligently. First a voyage draws scrutiny. Then information is gathered from open records, port calls, insurers, banks, agents, and service providers. Small inconsistencies are tested. One institution's question becomes another's basis for delay. A weak point in documentation becomes a reason to look more closely at ownership. An ownership anomaly becomes a reason to revisit cover. A cover problem becomes a reason for a port or terminal to hesitate. The investigation moves like a relay rather than a charge. The implication is important: sequencing allows pressure to build under conditions where each individual step may look modest, proportionate, and defensible.

This is particularly valuable when legal thresholds differ across institutions. A navy may need a strong basis before interfering directly with a vessel beyond territorial waters. A port authority may require less paperwork before granting entry. A bank may need only enough concern to freeze settlement pending review. An insurer may rely on policy wording and its own sanctions exposure to suspend confirmation. A ship manager may decide that continuing service is no longer commercially defensible. These are not substitutes for law. They are laws acting through different decision points. The enforcing state need not shoulder the entire burden if it can place the file where other institutions, each applying their own standards, begin to see the same problem.

A second named example lies in the enforcement environment around Iranian and Venezuelan oil shipping during the late 2010s and early 2020s. Public attention often settled on ship-to-ship transfers, AIS anomalies, and occasional high-profile seizures. Yet much of the actual pressure emerged through lower-visibility measures: advisories issued to insurers and traders, warning notices to shipping firms, payment scrutiny, service refusals, and the cumulative reluctance of mainstream maritime actors to carry uncertain trades. The voyage became harder not merely because a state threatened force, but because the surrounding ecosystem of commerce - to use the word concretely, not lazily - became less willing to normalise the movement. What changed first was often not the ship's course but the quality of its paperwork and the number of reputable institutions still prepared to touch it.

This quieter model has moral and strategic advantages. It tends to reduce the immediate chance of escalation because it does not humiliate a state publicly in the same way a dramatic interdiction might. It preserves more room for correction if the evidence changes. It also better matches the real structure of shipping, which is already governed through distributed approvals rather than by permanent physical coercion. A demand for additional documents can be withdrawn. A delayed payment can be released. A port can revisit a detention once deficiencies are cured. These reversibility features matter. They give calibrated pressure a degree of elasticity that direct force often lacks.

Still, a credible limitation must be faced. Low-visibility enforcement can slide into opacity, overreach, or quiet coercion untethered from clear standards. If documentation demands become endless, firms may interpret them as covert denial without due process. If service providers are pushed to act on weak or ambiguous signals, lawful trade can suffer from private fear rather than public judgement. If investigative sequencing is too murky, targeted actors may plausibly claim that they are being punished without being told the case against them. This matters because legitimacy is not an ornament added after the fact. It is part of enforcement capacity itself. Allies, firms, ports, and insurers cooperate more readily when they believe restraint and correction remain possible.

There is another limitation. Quiet pressure may avoid one kind of escalation while inviting another: market adaptation. A ship denied mainstream services may seek marginal ones. A cargo that cannot pass through ordinary banking channels may move through murkier payment structures. A manager that steps back may be replaced by one with less transparency and fewer reputational concerns. Low-visibility enforcement does not abolish trade; it can fragment it. That fragmentation may still serve the enforcing state's aims by raising costs and degrading quality, but it can also produce harder monitoring problems later. The pressure succeeds in the short term and complicates governance in the long term. That is the price of subtlety.

The answer is not to abandon calibrated pressure. It is to understand what calibrated means. It does not mean weak, hesitant, or embarrassed enforcement. It means matching instrument to evidence, objective, and political environment. A documentation request is calibrated when it seeks information genuinely needed to judge the transaction, not when it merely postpones responsibility. Service denial is calibrated when it rests on identifiable exposure or non-compliance, not when it becomes a reflex of collective fear. Investigative sequencing is calibrated when each step builds on evidence gained, rather than merely layering inconvenience until the voyage collapses under exhaustion. Precision matters. So does restraint.

The quiet motif here is the queue. Shipping depends on queues of approval: for port entry, payment release, insurance confirmation, pilot booking, cargo handling, departure clearance. Enforcement without escalation works by changing the order, length, and conditions of those queues. A vessel need not be seized to be made less viable. It may simply wait longer for answers that no credible counterparty can comfortably provide. Waiting has politics. It also has deniability. That is both the virtue and the danger of low-visibility pressure. It acts beneath the threshold of overt confrontation, yet it can still decide the fate of a voyage with remarkable force.

This is why a useful vocabulary of maritime enforcement needs more than the blunt contrast between action and inaction. It needs words for delay, conditioning, verification, sequencing, suspension, and denial. It needs to recognise that coercion can be distributed across ports, banks, insurers, managers, and documentation systems without losing its strategic purpose. It also needs to reckon honestly with the burden that such distribution places on private actors, who may tolerate uncertainty for a time but rarely forever. States may prefer quiet enforcement because it lowers the temperature. The harder question comes afterwards: when a doubtful voyage can be stopped without headlines, how much ambiguity should be accepted as the price of calm, and when does the absence of visible conflict begin to hide the absence of clear, accountable judgement?

Chapter 4

Flags, Registries, and Reflagging

A ship can change its flag faster than it can change its hull, its trading habits, or the network of people who profit from its voyages. That simple fact gives flags their peculiar force in maritime sanctions. The banner at the stern is not merely symbolic. It is an administrative address, a reputational signal, a legal attachment, and often a commercial shorthand for how closely a vessel is likely to be watched. A flag tells ports, insurers, banks, brokers, and charterers what kind of file they think they are opening before they have read very much of it. Sometimes that judgement is fair. Sometimes it is lazy. Either way, it has consequences.

The same vessel, on the same sea, can encounter a different commercial climate after a change of registry. Inspections may feel more searching. Questions may arrive earlier. Insurance conversations may lengthen. A port agent who would have accepted the appointment without fuss may pause. A charterer may decide that a nominally lawful fixture now requires more internal approvals than the freight can justify. The legal identity of the ship has altered on paper, but the deeper effect lies in how institutions interpret that paper. The flag becomes a proxy, not only for nationality in the strict sense, but for governance quality, documentary reliability, and the likelihood that problems buried in the file will be answered cleanly when asked.

The stern tells a story.

That story matters because sanctions rarely operate on certainty alone. They operate through thresholds of tolerable doubt. A mainstream registry may not guarantee clean conduct, and a lightly regarded one does not prove misconduct, yet flags compress judgement into a usable form for actors who must decide quickly whether to insure, finance, manage, or admit a vessel. Reflagging therefore becomes one of the earliest and most revealing movements in evasive behaviour. Not because a new flag erases identity - it usually does not - but because it may buy time, redistribute scrutiny, or shift the vessel into a registry where questions are asked differently, answered more slowly, or not linked as effectively to the rest of the maritime system.

That is where the moral simplifications begin to fail. Flags of convenience are easy to denounce and hard to understand properly. Shipping has long relied on registries offering commercial flexibility, lower costs, and administrative speed. Much of that activity is lawful and ordinary. To pretend otherwise would be unserious. Yet speed and opacity can serve more than one purpose. The same administrative convenience that suits a legitimate owner restructuring finance can also suit an operator trying to outrun scrutiny. The same limited transparency that lowers barriers to entry can also widen the gap between formal ownership and practical control. The issue is not whether a registry belongs on a moral blacklist by category. The issue is what kinds of behaviour become easier when rapid change meets thin disclosure.

This matters because enforcement pressure rarely ends with the flag itself. It spreads outward. A vessel pushed from a mainstream registry, or quietly steered away from one, often enters a harsher commercial weather system. Insurance becomes more fragile. Port access narrows. Service providers become more selective. The ship may still trade, but under a different discipline - one in which routine friction becomes a permanent condition of business. A flag change that looked like an isolated administrative step can trigger a chain of secondary effects. The ship is not merely registered somewhere else. It is repositioned in the hierarchy of trust that governs maritime commerce. Market discipline begins where formal registration leaves off.

That secondary pressure deserves attention because it reveals how maritime enforcement actually accumulates. States can designate, warn, and penalise, but the market decides each day how far those signals will travel. A vessel that loses the comfort of a widely accepted register may also lose easy access to reputable insurers, experienced managers, standard finance, and accommodating ports. Once that process starts, feedback loops appear. Weaker support services can make the ship look riskier. A riskier profile can push it further towards marginal providers. Marginal providers can deepen the doubts of the next institution asked to engage. The cycle is not automatic, and it is not always terminal, but it is rarely neutral.

Set against that cycle is the stubborn problem of identity. Shipping changes names, call signs, managers, owners, operators, and registries with surprising frequency. To anyone outside the trade, that fluidity can make vessels seem almost designed to escape memory. In practice, continuity is harder to break than appearances suggest. Identity in maritime investigation rests on traces that move at different speeds. Some details can be altered with comparative ease. Others persist. The work lies in comparing them without being distracted by surface novelty. A renamed vessel may still carry the same deeper administrative spine. A fresh registry entry may still sit atop an older commercial pattern. The difficulty is not only finding information. It is knowing which identifiers deserve more trust than the others when the file starts to move.

The path ahead follows that unstable surface. It begins with the practical meaning of flag choice, where a registry becomes an operating condition rather than a legal abstraction. It then turns to the ambiguities of convenience and opacity, the market consequences of exclusion and reputational downgrading, and the documentary labour required to preserve identity when names and papers shift faster than ships do. The sequence matters because reflagging never stands alone. It sits inside a wider contest over who gets to define continuity: the shipowner seeking distance, the registry offering speed, the market reading signals, or the investigator trying to hold the line of recognition together.

The deeper stakes lie in what flags do to judgement. Maritime governance depends on countless decisions taken under incomplete information by people who cannot reconstruct the whole truth every time a vessel asks to trade. Flags help them decide quickly. That is their utility and their danger. Used well, they condense governance into a workable signal. Used badly, they harden prejudice into procedure and let genuine risks hide among ordinary administrative changes. The stern tells a story, but stories can mislead when they become substitutes for inquiry rather than prompts to begin it.

That leaves a harder question than the public debate usually admits. When a vessel changes flag under pressure, what exactly has changed - its legal attachment, its commercial prospects, its exposure to scrutiny, or merely the style in which the same underlying network now presents itself? The answer cannot be read from the paint alone, and the rest of the file is rarely inclined to reveal itself without a fight.

Why flag choice matters

On 30 March 2023, the Marshall Islands registry announced that it had begun the process of withdrawing the registration of vessels linked to Sovcomflot after sanctions pressure and related compliance concerns. The immediate legal act was administrative. Its wider significance was operational. A ship can remain afloat, crewed, classed, and physically capable of trading, yet a change in flag status can still alter how ports inspect it, how insurers view it, how banks assess its transactions, and whether service providers wish to keep their names attached to its movements. The paint on the stern may change quickly. The commercial weather changes with it.

That is why flag choice matters more than casual observers often suppose. A flag is not only a matter of nationality in the formal sense. It is an organising signal inside the maritime system. It tells other actors which registry stands behind the vessel, which documentation habits they expect, how responsive the administering state may be, and how much confidence they place in the surrounding governance structure. Those expectations are not always fair. They are always consequential. A flag can shorten or lengthen an inspection, ease or complicate a financing conversation, steady or unsettle an insurer, and determine whether a port agent treats a vessel as routine business or as a file requiring early escalation.

The stern speaks first.

That small fact explains why reflagging appears so early in evasion behaviour. Before cargo is renamed, before beneficial ownership becomes harder to trace, before payment chains turn obscure, the flag offers an immediate way to alter the vessel's commercial presentation. Show the sequence plainly. A ship faces growing scrutiny because of its recent trading pattern, its ownership network, or its links to a targeted sector. Remaining under a mainstream flag may invite more questions than the operator wants to answer. A switch to a more permissive or less demanding registry can buy time, blur continuity for weaker screening systems, and change the expectations of counterparties encountering the ship anew. The concept is administrative repositioning. The implication is that flag choice affects the whole downstream life of a voyage, not just its legal paperwork.

Inspection patterns reveal this most clearly. Port state control regimes are formally built around safety, certification, manning, and seaworthiness, yet inspection is never blind to context. A flag associated with stronger oversight, cleaner records, and more responsive administration may benefit from a presumption of order, even if individual vessels under that flag still fail inspections. A flag associated with weaker governance, recent controversies, or lower confidence may attract closer scrutiny from the start. This does not mean inspectors discard evidence and operate on stereotype alone. It means institutions triage. Faced with many ships and limited time, they use flags as one of several clues about where attention may be most justified. The practical consequence is visible: more detailed document checks, more careful reading of certificates, more scepticism about recent changes in management or ownership, and a lower tolerance for inconsistencies that might otherwise be cured without much fuss.

That is where reputational risk enters. Reputation in maritime trade is often discussed as though it were a hazy moral atmosphere. In practice it appears in decisions. A charterer decides whether to nominate the ship. An insurer decides whether to continue cover. A bank decides whether the payment file clears at routine level or goes to enhanced review. A broker decides whether to circulate the candidate vessel with confidence or with caveats. A terminal decides whether the cargo booking looks ordinary enough to schedule promptly. Flag choice shapes all of these decisions because it compresses institutional memory into a portable signal. The flag is not proof of good governance, and it is certainly not proof of bad governance. Yet it often becomes a proxy for both. That may be intellectually untidy. It remains commercially real.

A named example from the Iranian sanctions environment helps make the point. When tankers linked to Iranian oil trade shifted flags, names, and management structures across the late 2010s and early 2020s, counterparties and regulators did not treat these changes as neutral housekeeping. They read them as part of a pattern. A single reflagging did not prove evasion. But reflagging combined with AIS anomalies, fresh ownership layers, unusual trading routes, or service substitutions often changed the tone of the file. Ports asked harder questions. Insurers looked more closely at exposure. Banks hesitated over payments tied to voyages whose administrative profile had recently changed. The flag mattered not because it settled the case, but because it altered the burden of explanation.

The second reason flag choice matters is access to services. Shipping survives through acceptance by others, and flags influence who remains willing to accept. A vessel under a registry widely regarded as competent and communicative may find it easier to secure agency support, insurance renewals, finance, and routine port handling. A vessel under a registry seen as opaque, politically exposed, or administratively weak may discover that nothing is formally impossible, yet everything takes longer. The port agent asks for more supporting documents. The insurer narrows cover or adds questions. The bank delays settlement. The ship manager worries about wider exposure. The service network begins to thin. The concept here is cumulative friction. No single refusal needs to be decisive. Enough small hesitations can reshape the economics of the voyage more effectively than a grand prohibition.

This explains why market actors often treat flags as shorthand for governance quality. That shorthand can be unfair, especially to vessels whose actual condition and documentation are sound despite trading under registries that attract suspicion. It can also be rational. Registries differ in how quickly they process changes, how thoroughly they check underlying ownership, how transparently they share information, how reliably they enforce standards, and how firmly they defend the credibility of their own registers. Shipping professionals know this. So do sanctions evasion networks. The same feature that makes a registry commercially attractive to lawful operators - administrative speed, low cost, flexibility, lighter bureaucracy - can make it attractive to operators seeking distance from scrutiny. The issue is not that flexibility is inherently suspect. It is that flexibility changes meaning once a vessel already sits under pressure.

A second named example returns to the Russian case. After sanctions pressure intensified following the invasion of Ukraine, vessels associated with sanctioned Russian shipping interests faced changes in flag status and registration arrangements that had clear operational consequences. The Marshall Islands decision regarding Sovcomflot-linked vessels in 2023 was instructive not because it immobilised an entire fleet by itself, but because it set off secondary effects. Reflagging or de-flagging pushed vessels towards alternative registries. Alternative registries changed how ports, insurers, financiers, and service providers viewed the ships. The formal administrative event therefore triggered a wider commercial reclassification. Once that happens, a ship does not merely carry a different flag. It occupies a different tier of maritime trust.

That trust should not be romanticised. It is built from habits of recognition, not moral purity. A mainstream flag does not cleanse a suspect voyage. Plenty of lawful ships trade under registries that outsiders disparage too casually. A credible limitation must be acknowledged here. Flags are imperfect proxies. Good vessels operate under lesser-regarded registers for legitimate reasons: cost, financing structures, corporate strategy, crewing preferences, or historical trade patterns. Bad vessels have also traded under respectable flags. Any analysis that treats flag choice as a self-sufficient explanation will make avoidable mistakes. Ports, insurers, and banks know this, which is why the flag rarely acts alone. It matters because it changes the starting posture from which the rest of the evidence is read.

That limitation, however, does not weaken the operational importance of the flag. It clarifies it. Flag choice matters not because it proves conduct, but because it alters the probability structure within which conduct is judged. A port official may inspect more carefully. A bank may escalate a payment file sooner. An insurer may ask whether recent flag changes align with shifts in ownership or trading area. A charterer may prefer a vessel whose registry history appears stable over one whose legal identity seems too recently rearranged. The flag changes the texture of commercial time. It decides whether a voyage moves through the system with relative ease or under a low but persistent hum of doubt.

That hum is precisely why reflagging becomes attractive early in evasive schemes. Changing cargo paper can be complex. Concealing beneficial ownership can take time. Restructuring finance may require multiple cooperating actors. A flag switch offers a comparatively quick administrative move that can accompany or prepare the others. It may help reset screening systems that rely too heavily on current registry data. It may create a plausible story of ordinary commercial change while deeper adjustments are underway. It may also shift the vessel into a jurisdiction less inclined to probe too deeply into beneficial ownership or trading history. Reflagging, then, is not magic. It is staging. It rearranges the scenery so that the next viewer sees the vessel under altered assumptions.

The effect is especially pronounced because maritime commerce reads continuity unevenly. A ship's hull, IMO number, and broad trading capacity change slowly. Its name, flag, manager, ownership layers, and operating narrative can change much faster. Counterparties working under time pressure often rely on the faster-changing surface cues because they are easiest to see. That creates opportunity. A newly flagged vessel approaching a fresh service provider may not look identical to the file that troubled a different institution months earlier, especially if the registry change is accompanied by a name change or management shuffle. Good investigators look through this. Not every service provider has the time or access to do so. The flag therefore matters because it sits at the boundary between durable identity and commercial first impression.

The quiet motif here is the stern, because the stern carries the signal every port, pilot, agent, and counterparties' database will see before they know much else. That signal may be accurate, incomplete, unfair, or strategic. Often it is some mixture of all four. What matters is that institutions act on it. The stern tells them which registry to query, which assumptions to bring, and how much effort the file deserves before business proceeds. Maritime sanctions do not need a perfect world to exploit that. They need only a world in which the flag continues to influence the next decision in line.

For enforcement, the deeper lesson is austere. A flag is both too little and too much. Too little, because it cannot by itself reveal who truly controls a vessel or why a trade has become suspect. Too much, because the market often loads it with reputational meaning far beyond its formal legal content. Effective analysis therefore treats flag choice as an entry point into the file, not an ending. It asks why the flag changed, what changed with it, which services became easier or harder to obtain, which inspection patterns followed, and whether the vessel's deeper identity remained far more stable than its administrative appearance.

The unresolved question comes at the exact moment reflagging is meant to influence. When a vessel changes flag under pressure, should counterparties treat that move as an ordinary commercial adjustment that still deserves the benefit of procedural neutrality, or as the earliest sign that the operator is trying to step ahead of scrutiny before the rest of the paper trail catches up? The answer cannot be read from the banner alone, yet the banner will shape who still agrees to open the file.

Flags of convenience and compliance gaps

In 1948, Liberia began developing what became one of the most consequential open registries in modern shipping. The innovation was commercial before it was polemical. A vessel owner no longer needed a deep territorial bond with the flag state in order to secure registration. Over time, other registries refined similar models, offering speed, flexibility, lower cost, and administrative ease to an industry that had already learned to distribute ownership, management, crewing, and finance across borders. The result was not a fringe practice. It became part of the mainstream grammar of shipping.

That history matters because the phrase "flag of convenience" still carries more heat than precision. It often suggests a simple moral divide between honest national registries and dubious open ones. Maritime reality is less tidy. Open registries have long served lawful trade at enormous scale. Shipowners use them for financing structures, tax planning, crewing flexibility, mortgage arrangements, and operational efficiency. Many such registries administer large fleets with serious technical systems and commercial credibility. The category itself does not prove weak governance. It merely signals a form of shipping organisation in which administrative nationality and underlying economic control need not closely match.

The paperwork moves quickly.

That is the feature that makes the subject important for sanctions analysis. Speed is not corruption. Opacity is not guilt. Yet both can be exploited. A registry that can process ownership changes, name changes, management updates, or flag transfers with unusual ease may be attractive to entirely legitimate operators who need commercial flexibility. The same capacity may also attract vessels trying to stay one step ahead of scrutiny. Show the sequence in ordinary form. A ship begins to attract unwanted attention under one flag. A new registered owner appears. The manager changes. The vessel is renamed. A different registry accepts the ship rapidly, perhaps with limited public disclosure about the deeper economic interests behind the change. None of these moves alone proves evasion. Taken together, they can create a compliance gap long enough for trade to continue while investigators, banks, insurers, and ports struggle to reconnect the file.

This is the central distinction that a serious analysis must preserve. One must separate the lawful use of administrative flexibility from the patterned use of flexibility to create delay, confusion, or plausible deniability. That separation is harder than polemic suggests because the surface forms often look similar. A legitimate owner restructures a holding company. A doubtful operator does the same. A lawful registry processes the paperwork in both cases. The concept that matters is not convenience as such, but exploitable latency: the interval in which an administrative change has taken legal effect while other institutions have not yet absorbed its meaning or tested its credibility. The implication is immediate. Sanctions pressure often fails not because the law is absent, but because the administrative tempo of some registries outruns the tempo of cross-institutional verification.

A named example helps to anchor this. During the late 2010s and early 2020s, maritime advisories issued by the United States and other authorities repeatedly warned that sanctioned shipping networks were using complex ownership and registration changes to disguise control and trading patterns linked to Iranian and North Korean sanctions evasion. The public record around these cases did not suggest that every open registry was compromised or complicit. The more interesting point was narrower. Vessels could move through combinations of renaming, reflagging, nominal ownership shifts, and documentary amendment quickly enough that some counterparties encountered only the newest surface version of the file. By the time a bank, insurer, or port reconciled that version with earlier information, the trade might already have moved on. The compliance gap was temporal before it was moral.

Transparency complicates the picture further. Registry information is only one layer of maritime identity, yet it matters because other actors rely on it as a practical entry point into the file. A port agent asked to represent a ship, a bank asked to process freight payment, or an insurer asked to maintain cover will often begin with the visible administrative record. If that record identifies only the registered owner, records changes unevenly, or makes beneficial interests difficult to trace across jurisdictions, the result is not immediate lawlessness. It is a thinner starting point for judgement. Trust, here, does not mean faith in institutions in the abstract. It appears in behaviour: whether a provider accepts the ship on routine checks, whether the file is escalated for enhanced review, whether the explanation offered for a recent change is detailed enough to preserve commercial confidence. Thin transparency makes those decisions slower, harsher, or more erratic.

A second named example sits closer to Russia-related shipping after the invasion of Ukraine. As sanctions widened and scrutiny intensified, some vessels tied to targeted interests moved away from mainstream registries or faced registry withdrawal. This did not create a universal underground fleet overnight, nor did it mean every receiving registry was inherently disreputable. The real lesson was structural. Once a ship moved into a registration environment perceived as offering faster changes and less demanding scrutiny, other institutions recalibrated their own tolerance. Ports grew more cautious. Insurers reconsidered cover. Banks read the administrative shift as a signal that wider due diligence was now necessary. The flag change did not prove wrongdoing. It altered the commercial meaning of uncertainty.

That commercial meaning is why compliance gaps matter more than registry labels. A gap appears when one institution records a change that others have not yet understood, verified, or linked to the broader pattern. Imagine a vessel that changes registered owner in one jurisdiction, moves to a new flag, appoints a different technical manager, and approaches a new service provider within a compressed period. Each move may be formally valid. The problem is cumulative. No single actor sees the whole sequence at once. The registry sees the new flag and owner. The insurer sees a request for continued or replacement cover. The bank sees changed payment instructions. The port sees a vessel whose current papers may look clean if read in isolation. The gap lies between those views. That is where evasive use of convenience thrives.

This does not mean open registries are uniquely vulnerable or uniquely culpable. National registries can also process weak filings, tolerate opacity, or fail to coordinate effectively with other institutions. A credible limitation is necessary here. Too much commentary treats "flags of convenience" as though the phrase itself solved the analytical problem. It does not. Some open registries maintain high technical and administrative standards. Some so-called traditional registries can be slow, politicised, or inconsistent. Compliance quality depends on governance practice, disclosure habits, enforcement culture, and willingness to defend registry credibility when difficult cases arise. A registry's business model matters, but it is not destiny.

Still, the limitation should not dilute the operational point. Convenience changes incentives. A registry competing on speed and ease of service must decide how much friction to impose before the business model begins to suffer. That tension is not unique to shipping, but shipping expresses it sharply because the vessel itself is mobile while the paperwork supporting it is distributed. An owner seeking a lawful and rapid commercial change may resent delays or intrusive questioning. An evasive operator seeks precisely the same administrative smoothness for different reasons. The registry sits between those pressures. If it demands too little, its records become useful to concealment. If it demands too much, it risks losing lawful clients to faster competitors. The compliance gap is born at that frontier.

The most revealing sign is often not opacity in the absolute sense, but opacity paired with velocity. A poorly transparent record that rarely changes may be frustrating but stable. A moderately transparent record changing rapidly across multiple fields can be more dangerous because it invites mistaken confidence. A new flag, a new owner, and a new name can give the impression of fresh legitimacy precisely when investigators ought to ask whether the underlying commercial network has remained largely intact. This is why careful institutions look for continuity beneath administrative novelty. They compare IMO numbers, historical management links, trading patterns, insurance history, and recurrent counterparties. Convenience becomes a sanctions problem when administrative change is allowed to masquerade as substantive transformation.

The distinction between lawful flexibility and evasion pattern can therefore be stated more clearly than the public argument usually allows. Legitimate use of registry flexibility tends to preserve coherence across the wider commercial file. The reasons for change can be explained. Supporting documents align. Payment and management structures make sense. Service providers remain willing to stand behind the vessel without unusual discomfort. Evasion patterns tend to produce a different feel. Changes cluster too tightly. Explanations become formalistic. New corporate names appear without convincing commercial purpose. Documentation arrives late or in uneven quality. Service providers agree only at the margins of the market, or after demanding unusual concessions. None of this is a neat formula. It is a matter of institutional judgement under incomplete information. Yet the pattern is real enough that experienced ports, banks, insurers, and managers often recognise it before they can prove it fully.

The quiet motif here is the registry desk. It is an ordinary image, almost disappointingly so. Yet much of maritime sanctions enforcement depends on what happens at desks: who checks which filing, how quickly a change is accepted, what supporting documents are required, whether beneficial ownership is treated as a serious question or a box to tick, whether the new information is visible enough for other institutions to act upon. The desk does not seize ships. It can still decide how difficult a ship becomes to understand. A fast desk can serve lawful commerce beautifully. A fast desk with weak inquiry can also help a doubtful vessel pass into a new administrative life before the rest of the system catches up.

That is why compliance gaps should be treated as institutional failures of connection rather than as moral stains attached to a category of registry. The decisive issue is not whether a flag is convenient. All commercial systems value convenience somewhere. The decisive issue is whether convenience outruns scrutiny so consistently that administrative validity ceases to mean much outside the registry itself. Once that happens, other actors are forced to compensate. Banks delay more files. Insurers ask harder questions. Ports treat the vessel as presumptively complicated. The burden shifts outward because confidence at the registration stage no longer travels far enough on its own.

The unresolved question returns, then, to speed. How fast should a registry be allowed to change the official story of a vessel when other institutions will bear the cost if that story proves incomplete, misleading, or strategically timed? Shipping rewards administrative efficiency. Sanctions enforcement depends on administrative memory. When the first outruns the second, the paper remains legal while the trade becomes harder to trust.

De-flagging, blacklists, and market discipline

In March 2023, the Marshall Islands registry moved to withdraw the registration of vessels linked to Sovcomflot after sanctions pressure and related compliance concerns. The administrative step looked narrow: a registry deciding that certain ships no longer belonged on its books. Yet its commercial meaning was wider. A vessel does not lose only a flag when it is pushed out of a mainstream registry. It loses a layer of credibility that countless other institutions had been using, often quietly, as a basis for routine acceptance. What appears as a clerical severance at one desk can ripple outward into insurance, port access, finance, and service provision with surprising force.

The ship still floats.

That is precisely why de-flagging matters. The vessel remains physically capable of movement, and for that reason outsiders can underestimate the depth of the disruption. Shipping does not operate on hull and engine alone. It operates on recognition. A flag state lends administrative identity. A reputable registry also lends a certain commercial presumption: that the ship has passed through a system others broadly trust to maintain records, answer questions, and defend minimum standards. When that presumption is withdrawn, the ship may still trade, but every subsequent interaction becomes harder to stabilise. The loss of flag begins as an administrative fact and becomes a market condition.

This is where sanctions and reputational discipline begin to work together. Sanctions provide formal reasons for registries, insurers, banks, and ports to reconsider their exposure. Reputational measures extend the effect beyond what law alone might compel at any given moment. Show the sequence in ordinary form. A vessel becomes associated with a designated owner, a sanctioned cargo trade, or a pattern of evasive behaviour. A mainstream registry concludes that continuing the registration threatens its own standing. The ship is de-flagged or effectively forced to seek a new home. That new search alters how other institutions read the file. The concept is secondary displacement. The implication is crucial: the real effect of de-flagging lies less in the first decision than in the chain of narrower options it creates afterwards.

Insurance often reveals this chain early. A vessel expelled from or abandoned by a mainstream registry is immediately more difficult to underwrite in ordinary commercial terms. That does not mean insurance becomes impossible. It means the ship now approaches the market under a weakened signal. An insurer asks whether the registry change was merely administrative or the exposed edge of a larger compliance problem. A port later asks whether the new insurer is acceptable. A charterer asks whether the cover remains credible enough to support the voyage. The visible behaviour is telling. Premiums rise, exclusions appear, cover narrows, renewal discussions lengthen, or the ship is pushed towards providers whose names carry less authority with ports and counterparties. Risk, here, is not a philosophical abstraction. It is a harder underwriting conversation and a thinner willingness to attach one's balance sheet to the vessel's future.

Port access follows the same logic. A port does not need to declare the vessel an outlaw in order to make life more difficult. It can require fuller documentation. It can examine insurance more closely. It can query ownership and management changes that accompanied the flag loss. It can simply take longer to decide whether entry remains acceptable. A mainstream-flagged vessel with conventional insurance and familiar management may be processed as routine business. A recently de-flagged vessel under a fresh registry, with altered service arrangements and an unusual recent history, enters a different lane altogether. The concept is administrative downgrading. The port has not banned the ship by category. It has moved the ship from ordinary throughput into exceptional scrutiny. The implication is commercial rather than theatrical: delay multiplies cost, and cost itself becomes a form of pressure.

A named example from the Iranian sanction's environment clarifies the mechanism. During the late 2010s and early 2020s, vessels associated with the Iranian oil trade frequently faced not a single decisive exclusion but a cumulative erosion of mainstream acceptance. Reflagging, insurer changes, ownership shifts, and intensified scrutiny interacted. A tanker that lost credible registry standing did not necessarily disappear from the market. Instead it often reappeared with thinner insurance, more obscure ownership presentation, and a narrower set of ports and service providers willing to touch the trade. The important lesson is not that every such case followed a uniform script. It is that de-flagging rarely acts alone. It initiates a downward movement through the hierarchy of maritime trust.

That hierarchy matters because mainstream maritime commerce is built from nested recognitions. A reputable registry encourages insurer comfort. Recognisable insurance supports port acceptance. Port acceptance supports chartering confidence. Chartering confidence sustains finance, agency support, and onward service availability. Remove one layer and the others do not collapse automatically, but they all begin to wobble. The ship becomes harder to place, harder to finance, harder to explain internally to cautious compliance teams. This is what market discipline looks like in practice. Not a single grand refusal, but a series of smaller refusals, hesitations, and price adjustments that push the vessel away from established channels and into a more precarious commercial ecology.

A second named example returns to Russia-linked shipping after the invasion of Ukraine. When sanctions pressure intensified and certain registries distanced themselves from vessels associated with targeted Russian interests, the effects were not exhausted by flag withdrawal itself. Ships pushed out of more reputable registers often had to seek alternative flags under conditions already saturated with scrutiny. That shift could change how insurers priced or even viewed the risk, how ports assessed documentary sufficiency, and whether mainstream managers or service providers wished to remain involved. The registry decision thus triggered a feedback loop. Weaker registry standing produced weaker service options. Weaker service options then deepened external suspicion, which in turn made it harder to recover mainstream standing. Market discipline often works by making reversal more difficult than descent.

The emphasis on feedback loops is essential because too much commentary still treats de-flagging as though it were a single sanction event with an immediate, measurable outcome. Maritime reality is more layered. A ship may respond to de-flagging by moving to a more permissive register, changing name, revising ownership presentation, or relying on alternative insurers and managers. At first glance, that adaptation can look like resilience. Sometimes it is. But each substitution carries its own cost. An alternative insurer may be accepted in fewer ports. A replacement registry may satisfy legal formalities while raising the suspicion of banks and charterers. A marginal ship manager may keep the vessel operating while making compliance departments elsewhere increasingly reluctant to engage. The vessel survives, but under degraded conditions. That degradation is not incidental. It is often the point.

The phrase "blacklist" also deserves careful handling. In public discourse it suggests a clear, authoritative exclusion. In practice, maritime blacklisting often mixes formal and informal processes. There are official sanctions lists, of course, and port state control blacklists or watchlists with their own safety logic. There are also softer reputational lists maintained by firms, insurers, banks, traders, and intermediaries who never publish them as law but nevertheless act on them as internal discipline. A vessel may be fully legal in one narrow sense and still effectively blacklisted by mainstream commerce because too many actors have decided the file is no longer worth carrying. Trust leaves the room quietly. The implication is powerful: market discipline can exceed formal law without becoming lawless, though it can also blur into overreach if not checked by evidence and procedural seriousness.

A credible limitation must be faced. De-flagging and reputational pressure do not necessarily immobilise targeted shipping. Parallel markets emerge. Alternative registries accept vessels mainstream systems reject. Insurance can sometimes be arranged through state-backed, captive, or marginal providers. Ports with different incentives or political alignments may remain open. A ship pushed out of one commercial universe may continue trading in another. This matters because analysis becomes self-congratulatory when it mistakes movement into murkier channels for disappearance. A vessel that has lost respectable standing may still carry cargo. The trade may persist under worse documentation, weaker safety assurance, and narrower service support. That is not full success. It is displacement.

Still, displacement is not trivial. It changes both cost and quality. A ship reliant on marginal service providers faces more friction, less flexibility, and greater vulnerability to further disruption. Insurance disputes become harder to resolve. Port options shrink. Spare parts and technical support may become less reliable. Crew recruitment may grow more difficult. Freight negotiations may involve larger discounts or unusual commercial terms to compensate for the stigma attached to the vessel. These visible adjustments are precisely what market discipline produces when it cannot produce total exclusion. The ship becomes commercially burdensome. Burden is often enough to alter trade patterns, even when it does not halt them.

The deeper question is how such discipline maintains legitimacy. A registry has reasons to protect its name. An insurer has reasons to protect its book. A port has reasons to protect its administrative integrity. Yet if de-flagging and blacklisting drift too far from evidence and become habits of reputational contagion, lawful shipping can suffer collateral damage. A vessel may be treated as toxic not because the case is strong, but because no one wishes to be the first institution to say yes after others have begun saying no. The feedback loop then becomes self-fulfilling. That danger is real, especially where information is patchy and administrative changes cluster for reasons not wholly related to sanctions evasion. Market discipline gains force from shared caution. It can also inherit the errors of shared caution.

That is why one must look closely at the structure of descent. A vessel's expulsion from a mainstream registry matters most when it coincides with other weakening signals: insurer substitutions, unclear beneficial ownership, recent management changes, service refusals, narrowed route options, and increasingly defensive documentation. The pattern, not the label, does the analytical work. A de-flagged ship with coherent new arrangements, credible alternative cover, and explainable commercial logic presents one problem. A de-flagged ship surrounded by hurried administrative change and thinning service quality presents another. The task is not to romanticise mainstream registries or demonise every replacement. It is to understand how exclusion changes the probability that the next institution in line will still agree to touch the file.

The quiet motif here is the ladder. A vessel does not fall out of mainstream commerce in a single dramatic plunge. More often it descends rung by rung. The registry withdraws. The insurer hesitates. The port asks more questions. The bank delays. The charterer looks elsewhere. The manager changes. The new service providers are less trusted than the old ones. Each rung alone may look survivable. Together they mark a shift into a lower tier of maritime life. That shift is the real substance of de-flagging under sanctions pressure.

The wider lesson is austere. Maritime sanctions often succeed not by preventing every voyage but by changing the grade of commerce available to the targeted ship. A vessel may continue moving while losing the comforts of ordinary market acceptance. It trades with worse paper, dearer money, thinner cover, fewer ports, and less margin for error. Feedback loops matter because they turn one loss of recognition into several more. Yet the system never becomes simple. Every rung lost by the targeted vessel may create demand for new marginal providers, and those providers can in time become more organised than the architects of sanctions intended.

That leaves a harder question than the language of blacklists usually allows. When a ship has been pushed out of mainstream registration and down through successive layers of market acceptance, should that be read as proof that the system is working, or as evidence that trade has merely been professionalised into darker channels where visibility is lower and the next crisis will be harder to manage?

Document trails and identity continuity

In May 2020, the United States Departments of State, Treasury, and Coast Guard issued a sanctions advisory warning about deceptive shipping practices, including the manipulation of vessel identifiers, documentation, and ownership structures. The advisory did not reveal a hidden truth so much as restate a stubborn one: a ship can change its name, its flag, its registered owner, and even its manager without ceasing to be the same ship in the eyes of anyone patient enough to follow the record. Maritime identity is not a single label. It is a layered file. That is why renaming a vessel so rarely achieves what public imagination assumes it should.

A new name can alter the first impression. It cannot rewrite steel.

This distinction matters because sanctions enforcement and evasion both depend on the unequal speed of administrative change. Some details move quickly. A vessel can be renamed, reflagged, or assigned to a freshly incorporated owner with relative ease. Other details move more slowly or persist altogether: the IMO number, the hull's build history, the sequence of port calls, the pattern of insurers and managers, the physical characteristics recorded across technical and commercial databases, the recurring counterparties who continue to orbit the ship after each paper transformation. Continuity is established by comparing what changes against what stays stubbornly the same. The work is less dramatic than seizure and more revealing.

Show the problem at the level where it actually arises. A tanker appears under a new name in a port file. Its registry information has been updated. The registered owner is unfamiliar. The call sign is different. A casual reader might treat the file as a new beginning. A more disciplined reader asks narrower questions. Does the IMO number match an older vessel already known to have traded in higher-risk corridors? Do the technical particulars align with earlier records? Is the new manager genuinely new, or merely a nominal replacement linked through addresses, officers, or service providers to the prior structure? Did the insurance and classification history change in a way that makes commercial sense, or did the paper alter faster than the surrounding support network? The concept is identity continuity. The implication is practical: investigation depends on finding the slow variables beneath the fast ones.

The IMO number sits at the centre of that effort because it was designed precisely to outlast changes in name and flag. Once assigned, it generally remains attached to the hull for the life of the vessel. That persistence gives investigators, ports, insurers, and banks a comparatively stable anchor in an otherwise fluid administrative environment. A ship's name can change. Its paint can change. Its legal owner can change several times. The IMO number usually does not. This does not make the system foolproof. Records can be entered poorly, systems can lag, and human users can still search carelessly. Yet the basic point remains. Maritime identity rests less on what the ship is called this month than on which enduring identifier binds today's paperwork to yesterday's conduct.

Call signs occupy a more ambiguous place. They matter operationally and administratively, but they can change more readily with flag and registration updates. That makes them useful but insufficient. A call sign can help corroborate continuity across port records, radio logs, and service documents, yet it can also contribute to confusion if analysts treat it as more stable than it really is. The same is true of registered ownership. Ownership disclosures are indispensable, but they are also contingent on jurisdictional rules, filing discipline, and the willingness of legal structures to reveal genuine control. A fresh owner on paper may reflect a real sale, a financing restructure, a family succession, a merger, or an attempt to place distance between the vessel and its prior trading history. The visible behaviour that matters is not the mere existence of change, but its pattern, timing, and coherence across other records.

A named example clarifies this. During the late 2010s and early 2020s, maritime advisories and public reporting repeatedly pointed to vessels involved in sanctions-sensitive oil trades that changed names and flags while maintaining trading patterns or network relationships suggesting substantial continuity. The lesson was never that a name change itself proved evasion. The more instructive point was that renaming seldom erased the deeper identity record. IMO numbers, hull particulars, historic port calls, repeated management links, and insurance histories continued to connect the vessel to its earlier life. The new name functioned as surface novelty; the record beneath it remained stubbornly intelligible to anyone willing to compare across datasets rather than reading only the newest entry.

This comparison across datasets is where document trails become more than clerical residue. A port log records a call under one name. An insurance record refers to the same IMO number under another. A classification database shows survey history that spans both identities. Corporate filings connect successive owners through shared addresses or officers. AIS histories, though imperfect, suggest continuity in voyage patterns. None of these fragments is sufficient alone. Together they create a chain. The concept is evidentiary stitching. Each record is a piece of cloth cut for its own purpose, and the investigator's task is to stitch them into a continuous garment strong enough to bear scrutiny. The implication follows naturally: continuity is not discovered in a single document; it is built by comparison across documents that were never designed to tell one complete story.

That is why time matters so much. Different parts of the file update at different speeds. A registry may record a name or ownership change quickly. Commercial databases may lag. Port systems may preserve the older identity for some time. Insurers and financiers may hold internal records that still connect the ship to prior structures even after public-facing details have been refreshed. This asynchronous movement creates both danger and opportunity. Danger, because a counterparty relying on only one updated system may mistake administrative freshness for substantive novelty. Opportunity, because discrepancies in update timing often reveal the continuity an evasive actor hoped to blur. A vessel that looks new in one system and old in another is not necessarily suspicious, but it is certainly not self-explanatory. The file needs work.

A second named example lies in the many vessel renamings associated with oil trades linked to Iran and Venezuela during the sanctions-heavy years around 2019 to 2023. Public tracking by maritime analysts, regulatory advisories, and enforcement actions repeatedly showed that names and registries shifted while the same hulls continued to serve familiar commercial functions. The important lesson was procedural rather than sensational. Effective monitoring did not depend on dramatic discoveries. It depended on patient cross-referencing: build details, IMO records, flag histories, ownership changes, insurer information, port calls, and recurring counterparties. Renaming did not fail because the tactic was foolish. It failed when enough institutions looked past the most recent label and recognised the ship's longer documentary spine.

A credible limitation deserves emphasis. Identity continuity can be harder to establish than this account may seem to suggest. Databases contain errors. Transliteration across languages introduces variation in names, companies, and addresses. Ownership structures may involve lawful complexity that looks suspicious to the untrained eye. Corporate services firms, nominee directors, and shared registered offices can create misleading associations. Different ships can have similar names. Historical records are not always complete. Even the strongest identifiers can be entered incorrectly or omitted in certain records. This matters because the temptation to force continuity where only coincidence exists is real. Investigators and compliance teams must guard against confirmation bias just as firmly as they guard against concealment.

That limitation does not weaken the method. It defines its discipline. Establishing continuity requires more than spotting one recurring identifier and declaring victory. It requires testing whether the apparent link survives contact with independent records. Does the build year match? Do the tonnage and dimensions align? Does the classification history fit the same hull? Do old and new ownership structures share meaningful ties beyond generic corporate services? Do service providers recur in ways that are commercially plausible? Does the route pattern remain consistent with the supposed transformation in ownership or purpose? The aim is not to produce a dramatic narrative quickly. It is to produce a defensible chain slowly enough that it can survive a challenge later.

This is why document trails matter even when they look mundane. Maritime enforcement often turns on paperwork not because paper is somehow superior to physical evidence, but because shipping is itself an industry of recorded relationships. Ships cannot trade seriously without registration, certificates, insurers, agents, ports, payments, service bookings, and management instructions. Each of those leaves traces. An evasion network may try to alter the visible front of the file, but it often cannot reconfigure every supporting relationship at the same speed. The classification society may remain the same a little longer. The manager may persist through a nominal ownership change. The bank account may shift, but the address of the corporate vehicle may recur. The bunker supplier, the crewing pattern, the technical superintendent, the route logic - each may disclose continuity even when the vessel's public-facing identity has been refreshed.

Trust, in this setting, becomes measurable in the willingness of institutions to rely on the continuity they can establish. A bank processing a payment wants to know whether the vessel before it is merely renamed or substantively transformed. An insurer wants to know whether a new owner brings new governance or only a cleaner surface. A port wants to know whether yesterday's concerns remain alive under today's paperwork. Efficiency also becomes visible. A strong compliance system does not drown in every name change. It builds routines for comparing stable identifiers against recent administrative events. That may sound pedestrian. It is often the difference between meaningful scrutiny and mere information overload.

The quiet motif here is the spine. A vessel's administrative surface may change repeatedly, but the file still has a spine if one knows where to look. The IMO number, the build characteristics, the historic service record, the continuity of management and commercial behaviour - these are the vertebrae holding the record upright when the softer tissue of names and flags shifts around them. A weak investigation stares at the skin. A stronger one feels for the bones. That is why renaming a vessel so rarely severs the underlying identity record. It changes the introduction, not the body.

The broader significance extends beyond any one sanctions case. Maritime governance depends on the ability of multiple institutions to recognise the same ship across time even when administrative change is legitimate, frequent, and sometimes strategically timed. If continuity cannot be maintained, every renaming becomes a partial amnesty, every ownership shift a chance to outrun institutional memory. If continuity is pursued too aggressively, lawful commercial restructuring starts to look guilty by form alone. The balance is delicate. It requires scepticism without paranoia, technical patience without fetishising data, and an awareness that the strongest evidence often lies in the alignment of ordinary records rather than in any single revelatory document.

That leaves a harder question than the mere mechanics of tracking ships. When a vessel's current paperwork is facially valid but its deeper documentary spine suggests continuity with a problematic past, how much weight should institutions place on the history they can reconstruct against the administrative present they are formally asked to recognise? That question never disappears. It only gets sharper as names change faster than memory and the next file arrives asking to be treated as new.

Chapter 5

Beneficial Ownership and Corporate Veils

How can a ship be perfectly documented and still remain obscure? That question sits at the centre of maritime sanctions more firmly than many legal texts admit. A vessel may have a registered owner, a flag, a manager, a charterer, an insurer, and a bank account that all appear on paper. Yet none of those labels, taken alone, settles the hardest question. Who actually controls the trade? Shipping has long organised itself through layered companies, delegated authority, and carefully distributed liability. Those structures are neither exotic nor automatically suspect. They are also exactly what make sanctions enforcement so difficult when pressure turns from the vessel to the interests behind it.

The complication begins with a simple commercial truth. Ships are expensive, risky, mobile assets. Owners have good reasons to separate financing from operation, operation from management, and liability from the wider corporate group. A holding company may own the vessel. A different company may manage it. Another may charter it. Another may receive revenue or arrange crewing. Nominee directors may appear for reasons of convenience, confidentiality, or legal form. None of this proves concealment. It does, however, mean that the person who benefits from a voyage, the person who directs it, and the person whose name sits on the registry extract may not be the same. The signature can mislead.

That is the central tension. The corporate veil in shipping serves ordinary commerce and extraordinary evasion with many of the same tools. The very arrangements that allow lawful fleets to manage tax exposure, financing, and operational risk also create room for sanctioned interests to hide behind layers of formal distance. Public debate often treats transparency as though it were a moral preference frustrated by bad actors. The harder reality is institutional. Ownership transparency is difficult because maritime trade is designed to divide functions across entities, jurisdictions, and service relationships that do not update at the same speed or disclose at the same depth. The problem is not merely secrecy. It is structure.

This matters because sanctions do not attach only to names on lists. They also depend on determining who benefits, who directs, and who pays. A vessel may continue trading under a registered owner that appears innocuous while control has shifted through management contracts, financing arrangements, or informal influence that never appears neatly in public filings. A payment may clear to one company while the commercial advantage flows elsewhere. A manager may be changed without a sale, quietly altering the vessel's banking, crewing, and operational ecosystem. These are not side issues. They decide whether an investigation finds the person the paperwork wishes to display or the network that actually runs the trade.

The stakes are therefore higher than corporate tidiness. If beneficial ownership cannot be established with enough confidence, sanctions either miss their real target or spread too widely in compensation. That is when lawful trade begins to absorb the cost of institutional uncertainty. Banks hesitate because names half-match and cannot be resolved quickly. Insurers narrow appetite because the file contains too many unverifiable assertions. Ports, managers, and charterers become more cautious because they cannot tell whether a benign-looking vehicle is a normal shipping structure or a liability buffer designed to absorb scrutiny for someone else. Risk, here, is visible in behaviour: delayed payments, refused cover, longer internal reviews, requests for fresh attestations, and the quiet refusal to take the next step until the corporate story sounds less rehearsed.

A second stake follows close behind. Access to data does not solve the problem by itself. Maritime enforcement now lives in a world dense with corporate registries, sanctions screening tools, vessel databases, and open-source records. That abundance can create a false sense of mastery. A database may contain names, addresses, directors, and ownership links, yet still fail to answer the practical question of control. Records go stale. Identifiers vary. Transliteration creates duplicates or disguises continuity. Common addresses can suggest false connection; nominee arrangements can disguise real connection. The investigator's burden becomes interpretive before it becomes legal. The file is fuller. The certainty is not.

This is why the distinction between owner, operator, charterer, and manager matters so much. Those are not merely industry terms. They describe different forms of power over the same ship. One party may hold title. Another may decide the trade. Another may provide the crew and pay the suppliers. Another may control the money. The legal owner may be important and still not be the decisive actor. A compliance system that cannot distinguish among these roles will either chase the wrong entity or ask the right entity the wrong question. Corporate veils are powerful not because they create perfect invisibility, but because they encourage people to stop their inquiry at the first plausible answer.

The argument ahead follows that distributed control as it moves through paper and institutions. It begins with the ways layered companies separate ownership from decision-making, then moves into the contested terrain of beneficial ownership verification, the shifting roles of managers and operators, and the quieter but no less dangerous problem of poor data quality masquerading as insight. The sequence matters because the difficulty is cumulative. A single obscure company can often be understood. A ship that sits inside several lawful but opaque layers, administered across multiple jurisdictions by records of uneven quality, asks much more of the institutions expected to judge it quickly.

The deeper friction is not between transparency and secrecy in the abstract. It is between the speed of commerce and the speed of verification. Shipping rewards structures that divide liability, preserve flexibility, and make assets tradable across borders. Sanctions enforcement rewards continuity, clarity, and records that can survive comparison under pressure. Those two logics do not naturally align. The same corporate veil that protects legitimate enterprise can also protect strategic concealment until someone insists on looking past the first layer and then the second. The signature can mislead again.

That leaves a harder question than the language of shell companies usually captures. When a ship's paperwork presents several lawful entities performing several lawful roles, at what point does complexity cease to be ordinary commercial architecture and become evidence that the real controller has been placed just far enough behind the glass to avoid being named?

Layered companies and control rights

On 21 December 2001, the United States Treasury designated the shipping interests of the Saudi businessman Yassin al-Qadi, including assets tied to maritime commerce through layered corporate arrangements spread across jurisdictions. The case belonged to an earlier sanctions era, yet it exposed a feature that has only become more important since: a ship can be perfectly well owned on paper and still be directed, financed, and economically enjoyed by someone standing several legal steps away from the registered owner. The legal shell is not always false. It can still be strategically placed.

That matters because shipping has never been a trade of simple ownership. A single vessel may sit inside a holding company incorporated for financing reasons, operated by another company under a management agreement, chartered by a third, insured through arrangements negotiated by a fourth, and serviced through banks and suppliers that see only fragments of the whole. None of this is exotic. Much of it is ordinary. The veil becomes dangerous not when structure exists, but when structure outruns explanation. The signature is not enough.

This is the first point worth stating without moral fog. Layered companies are not an aberration in shipping; they are one of its standard operating forms. Ships are expensive, mobile, and exposed to accident, arrest, tax complexity, mortgage enforcement, environmental liability, and jurisdictional variation. Owners use special-purpose vehicles and holding companies to contain risk, isolate assets, facilitate finance, and ease sale or transfer. A fleet may be split across multiple one-ship companies not because the owner is hiding, but because lenders, insurers, and lawyers all prefer clean asset separation. The concept is liability partitioning. The implication is important. Corporate layering in itself cannot serve as proof of sanctions evasion, because lawful shipping has too many commercial reasons to use it.

And yet the same architecture creates room for concealment. Show the problem in practical terms. A vessel's registered owner is a company with no staff, little public footprint, and directors provided by a corporate services firm. That is not unusual. The technical manager sits in another jurisdiction. The commercial manager sits in a third. Freight revenue flows through accounts associated with yet another entity. The charterer is genuine, the cargo real, the voyage commercially plausible. Then a sanctions question arises. Who, exactly, is the relevant person for enforcement purposes? The concept is separation of title from control. The implication is that sanctions investigators cannot stop at "Who owns the ship?" They must ask harder and more commercially grounded questions: who benefits, who directs, who pays?

Those questions are distinct because ownership and control are not the same legal or practical relation. A holding company may possess title while day-to-day operational control sits with a manager under contract.

A nominee director may sign formal papers while strategic decisions come from a beneficial owner or financier behind the corporate structure. A charterer may not own the vessel but may dictate employment patterns so completely that the ship functions as part of the charterer's network. A lender may not manage the ship but may exercise rights that profoundly shape who can sell it, where it can trade, and under what conditions default changes effective control. This is why control rights matter. They are the means by which influence survives without appearing as straightforward ownership.

Nominee directors illustrate the ambiguity particularly well. In some corporate environments, nominee arrangements are routine and lawful, used to preserve privacy, manage governance across borders, or provide local administrative presence. The existence of a nominee does not prove that the true principal is suspect. But nominees also buffer scrutiny. They create an extra layer between the person signing formal documents and the person whose interests those documents serve. Investigators therefore learn to read nominations not as incriminating in themselves, but as prompts for further inquiry. Who gave the instructions? Who receives the economic return? Who can replace the director? Who pays the services firm supplying the nominee? Paper authority is one thing. Decision authority is another.

Management contracts create a second and often more revealing divide. A shipowner may outsource technical management, crewing, procurement, regulatory compliance, and even commercial employment to specialist firms. That is common practice and often sensible. Yet a management contract can also move the practical centre of the vessel away from the registered owner without changing title at all. The visible behaviour shifts. New crew suppliers appear. Payments begin running through different banks. Insurance correspondence is handled by a different office. Ports, agents, and vendors start hearing from unfamiliar names. The ship looks owned by one company and directed by another because, in practice, it is. The concept here is delegated control. The implication is straightforward: operational influence can migrate through contract faster than public ownership records can explain it.

A named example clarifies the stakes. During the later phases of sanctions pressure on Iranian shipping, public advisories and enforcement actions repeatedly pointed to one-ship companies, nominee arrangements, and management changes used in ways that complicated the tracing of sanctioned interests. The lesson was not that every special-purpose company in shipping suddenly became suspicious. It was that the same lawful instruments that protect investors and structure finance can also be assembled to place sanctioned control behind several layers of apparently ordinary commercial distance. Investigators did not succeed merely by identifying a shell company. They succeeded by reconstructing the chain of benefit, direction, and payment running through the shell.

That chain matters because money often tells the truth faster than formal ownership does. The question "Who pays?" sounds almost crude beside the more elegant language of beneficial ownership, yet it is often the sharper investigative tool. A registered owner with no meaningful cash activity beyond formal maintenance of corporate status may tell us less than the company paying crew wages, insurance premiums, agent fees, and emergency repair invoices. A nominee director with signing authority may matter less than the account from which recurring operating costs are settled. Freight revenue may be booked through an intermediary, but the pattern of who receives net benefit, repatriates value, or absorbs loss can still reveal the real economic centre of the venture. Payment is not identity, but it is evidence of relationship.

Who directs matters just as much. Shipping is full of arrangements in which the legal owner does not make the commercially decisive choices. Someone must decide employment, approve significant technical expenditures, negotiate management agreements, appoint service providers, authorise route changes, and bear the political or legal risk of continuing certain trades. Those decisions usually leave traces: emails, management instructions, contract amendments, recurring representatives at negotiations, bank mandates, insurance contacts, operational meetings, and service appointments. Investigators look for those traces because direction is rarely abstract. It appears in the behaviour of institutions and the permissions they extend. A person who never appears on a registry extract may nevertheless keep turning up wherever consequential choices are made.

A second named example comes from the post-2022 sanctions environment around Russian maritime trade. Public reporting and advisory material increasingly described how vessels, commodity flows, and service relationships were reorganised through networks of newly formed companies, management transfers, and changed intermediary structures. Not every rearrangement concealed sanctioned control. Some reflected ordinary market shock, urgent restructuring, or lawful adaptation to altered trading conditions. Yet the difficulty lay precisely there. Operational continuity could persist beneath a new registered owner. A management transfer could change banking and crewing relationships while leaving the same commercial interests effectively in command. The legal paper moved. The strategic hand sometimes did not.

A credible limitation must be faced squarely. Complex corporate structures are not exclusive to bad actors, and reducing them to red flags can lead to damaging false positives. A one-ship company may exist because a lender insisted on it. A management agreement may reflect efficiency rather than concealment. Nominee directors may be routine in a jurisdiction without implying hidden sanctions risk. Even recurrent service providers may indicate industry concentration rather than covert continuity of control. This matters because a sanctions system that mistakes normal maritime finance for proof of wrongdoing will impose broad costs on lawful shipping while missing the more careful evasive actors who understand how to mimic legitimate form.

That limitation does not weaken the method; it disciplines it. The task is not to treat complexity as guilt, but to distinguish commercial architecture from strategic obscurity. Investigators therefore compare several questions at once. Does the structure have a commercially intelligible reason? Do the parties involved behave like genuine independent actors or like placeholders? Are the flows of money, authority, and operational instruction aligned with the story the corporate chart is telling? Do changes in management, ownership, or service provision occur in a pattern that reflects normal commercial adaptation, or do they cluster suspiciously around moments of regulatory pressure? The answer rarely lies in one record. It emerges from coherence, or the lack of it.

This is why the language of "beneficial ownership" sometimes misleads by sounding too settled. In practice, beneficial ownership is not a single fact waiting patiently in a database. It is often an inference built from overlapping signs of benefit, direction, and payment. A person may not own the shares directly yet still receive the economic upside, appoint the real decision-makers, and control the core service relationships. Another may hold formal title and still function mainly as a liability buffer. Ownership in law, benefit in economics, and control in practice do not always point to the same person. The corporate veil becomes powerful when institutions are forced to choose which of those realities should govern their next decision.

The quiet motif here is the hand. Not the hand that signs the registry paper, but the hand that moves the vessel through commerce by authorising payments, appointing managers, selecting routes, accepting freight, and deciding whether a doubtful trade will proceed. Shipping corporate structures are full of gloved hands - lawful, ordinary, sometimes necessary. The problem for sanctions enforcement is not that the hand is covered. It is that several gloves may appear at once, and the wrong one is often the easiest to see. A registered owner may be visible. The directing hand may sit one contract further back.

For banks, insurers, ports, managers, and investigators, the practical lesson is harder than the slogans suggest. They are not being asked to pierce every veil in every transaction. They are being asked to know when the veil matters enough to justify deeper scrutiny. That threshold depends on evidence, timing, and exposure. A file with a plausible commercial structure may proceed. A file in which title, direction, and payment drift apart without convincing explanation demands more. The difference is not ideological. It is operational. Shipping lives by distributed roles. Sanctions enforcement must decide which role actually governs the voyage before the voyage is too far gone for the answer to matter.

That leaves the unresolved question at the centre of every layered structure. When a ship is owned by one company, managed by another, financed through a third, and commercially directed through a fourth, which of those relationships should count most when a sanctioned interest may be benefiting from the arrangement without ever appearing plainly on the surface? The legal answer is often narrower than the commercial one. The commercial answer is often easier to feel than to prove.

Beneficial ownership as an enforcement battleground

In April 2016, the Panama Papers exposed how offshore companies and nominee structures could obscure the real people behind assets moving through the global economy. Shipping was not uniquely implicated, but it was impossible to miss how well the sector fit the architecture that had been revealed. A vessel can be registered under one company, managed by another, financed through a third, and commercially directed through a fourth, all while the person or network that truly benefits remains difficult to place with confidence. The problem was never only secrecy. It was verification.

That distinction matters because beneficial ownership sounds simpler than it is. The phrase suggests a factual answer waiting in a file somewhere, obscured perhaps, but ultimately recoverable through enough persistence. Maritime sanctions practice rarely enjoys that clarity. A registry extract may identify a legal owner. A corporate filing may list shareholders. A bank may hold onboarding documents. A sanctions screening tool may attach names to related entities. Yet none of those records, by itself, guarantees that the person who benefits, directs, or pays has been identified correctly. The record can be present and still be wrong. The record can also be absent for ordinary reasons. The paper says less.

This is why beneficial ownership becomes an enforcement battleground rather than a mere compliance checkbox. Show the ordinary scene. A bank receives payment instructions linked to a vessel trading in a sanctions-sensitive corridor. The registered owner appears clean. The ship's management company is incorporated elsewhere. The beneficial ownership declaration on file says that no designated person holds control or economic interest. The bank's database search, however, turns up adjacent names, variant spellings, stale addresses, and a recent ownership amendment that has not yet propagated across all systems. Nothing here settles the question. The concept is contested legibility. The implication is severe. An institution must decide whether the declared owner is enough, whether the anomalies justify escalation, or whether the commercial timeline will run out before certainty arrives.

That is the first reason verification is so difficult across jurisdictions and registries: records do not mature at the same speed. Some registries update rapidly. Others lag. Corporate filings may reflect a change in legal ownership before beneficial ownership declarations are refreshed, or the reverse. Shipping databases may preserve historic names and structures longer than public corporate records do, or fail to capture them with enough precision to be trusted. Port systems may continue using familiar ship names after the legal paperwork has changed. This asynchrony creates a practical weakness in enforcement. A vessel or company does not need perfect invisibility. It only needs enough time between administrative change and institutional recognition to keep the trade moving. Transparency, in other words, is not just about what is disclosed. It is about when disclosure becomes usable.

Stale records are the most familiar failure point because they produce a false confidence that can be more dangerous than admitted ignorance. A beneficial ownership register that has not been updated after a sale, management transfer, or intra-group restructuring may still look authoritative. A bank or insurer under time pressure may rely on it because it exists in official form. Yet stale data do not merely leave gaps. They misstate the present in the language of certainty. Show the effect in practice. A charterer screens a vessel and sees a legally registered owner with no obvious sanctions exposure. The beneficial ownership record behind that owner remains months old. In the meantime, control has shifted informally through financing, management, or share transfer structures that have not yet been reflected. The ship proceeds because the official record looked complete. The failure lies not in the absence of transparency, but in the age of it.

Inconsistent identifiers create a second, subtler battleground. Names do not travel well across jurisdictions, alphabets, and corporate filing systems. A beneficial owner may appear under multiple transliterations. Addresses may be abbreviated differently. Directors may be listed with and without middle names, patronymics, or local formatting. Corporate service firms may reuse office addresses across dozens of entities, creating misleading connections. Identical or similar names may belong to entirely different people. The same vessel management company may be shortened one way in port records, another in insurance correspondence, and a third in banking files. The concept here is matching risk. The implication is that false positives and false negatives are built into the work. A system that matches too aggressively may entangle innocent actors. A system that matches too cautiously may miss the continuity that matters.

A named example clarifies the problem from the regulatory side. After sanctions pressure intensified on Russian shipping and energy-linked trade following the 2022 invasion of Ukraine, compliance teams across banks, insurers, ports, and maritime service firms faced repeated difficulty distinguishing between officially non-sanctioned corporate fronts and deeper beneficial interests that might still connect to designated persons or politically exposed networks. Public ownership shifts, management changes, and new intermediaries could be recorded quickly in one jurisdiction and unevenly in others. The challenge was not simply that some actors wished to conceal the truth. It was that even diligent institutions struggled to reconcile fragmented records quickly enough to make confident decisions. Beneficial ownership became a moving target because the supporting data moved unevenly.

Unverifiable attestations form the third major weakness. Many compliance systems still depend heavily on declarations supplied by the customer or intermediary: signed statements of beneficial ownership, certified corporate charts, letters from lawyers or corporate service providers, and similar documents intended to establish who ultimately owns or controls the asset. Such attestations have obvious value. They create a formal basis for inquiry and a record of what was claimed at the time. Yet they also reveal the limits of paper. An attestation may be complete in form and thin in substance. A company may declare that no sanctioned interest exists while relying on a level of corporate layering that renders outside verification difficult or impossible without cooperation from several jurisdictions. The visible behaviour that follows is familiar: banks escalate, insurers narrow appetite, ports ask for more, and yet the underlying question remains suspended because the declaration cannot be tested with confidence.

This is why transparency should be framed as a capacity problem, not simply a policy preference. Public debate often treats beneficial ownership transparency as though governments need only decide to want it strongly enough and the problem will yield. The harder truth is institutional. Registers must be designed well, kept current, cross-checked, searchable, and linked to identifiers that survive routine changes in names and structures. Firms must have the staff, language capability, data discipline, and legal authority to compare records across jurisdictions. Regulators must be able to distinguish a technically complete filing from a credible account of control. Without that capacity, calls for transparency amount to moral aspiration without operational weight. The file grows longer. The answer does not.

A second named example comes from the repeated use of one-ship companies and layered offshore structures in sanctions-sensitive oil trades linked to Iran during the late 2010s and early 2020s. Public advisories from United States authorities warned that ownership and management structures were being used to disguise sanctioned interests. The lesson was not merely that bad actors lie. It was that even when records existed, they were often fragmented across registries, company service providers, flag administrations, and maritime databases that did not speak to one another cleanly. A beneficial ownership declaration could appear facially satisfactory while key surrounding records remained stale, incomplete, or technically mismatched. Enforcement therefore turned less on access to a single decisive source than on the institutional ability to compare multiple imperfect sources without mistaking administrative neatness for truth.

A credible limitation should be stated plainly. Beneficial ownership is not always hard to verify because someone is trying to cheat. Lawful shipping is structurally complex. Lenders may require one-ship companies. Joint ventures may divide economic interest in ways that do not fit simple percentage thresholds. Family-controlled groups may use layers for succession planning or tax neutrality rather than concealment. Corporate restructurings can create temporary confusion without any sanctions motive at all. Even high-quality registries and compliance teams can struggle to map real control where legal rights, financing covenants, management contracts, and economic benefit do not point neatly to one person. This matters because a sanctions system that treats complexity as guilt will generate noise, alienate lawful operators, and eventually drown in its own false alarms.

That limitation does not weaken the central argument. It sharpens the discipline required. The relevant question is not whether the structure is complex, but whether the explanation for the structure remains coherent across time, records, and institutions. Does the beneficial ownership declaration align with who pays operating costs, who appoints managers, who receives freight income, who negotiates financing, and who appears when difficult operational choices are made? Are changes in ownership or control explained before regulators and banks discover them, or only after questions arrive? Do identifiers remain stable enough to allow the same person or entity to be recognised across filings, or does every layer introduce just enough variation to frustrate comparison? Transparency becomes meaningful only when records are good enough, fresh enough, and linked enough to answer these practical questions.

This is where data quality overtakes data access. A firm with access to several databases can still reach the wrong conclusion if the underlying records are old, duplicated, mistranscribed, or improperly matched. A poor search query can generate the illusion of a sanctions link where only a common surname exists. A hasty analyst can miss a true link because the decisive corporate vehicle was incorporated under a variant spelling or because the beneficial ownership filing sits in a registry not covered by the firm's usual tools. Quality shows itself in behaviour. Good teams pause over mismatched identifiers, compare histories rather than snapshots, and resist the urge to treat a signed declaration as closure when the surrounding pattern remains unstable. Bad teams either believe too quickly or distrust too indiscriminately. Both errors distort enforcement.

The quiet motif here is the file. Not the file as a stack of paper, but the file as an institutional object that must travel between banks, insurers, ports, regulators, and service providers without losing the thread of who actually matters. A file can look thick and still be weak. It can contain registry extracts, declarations, addresses, corporate charts, and screening results while leaving the central question unanswered. The strength of the file lies not in its volume but in its coherence. Can the same person or controlling interest be recognised across the changing forms in which the trade presents itself? Can the institution explain why it trusted, distrusted, or escalated the record at the time it acted? That is what beneficial ownership enforcement finally tests.

The broader lesson is austere. Maritime sanctions do not fail only because transparency is politically resisted. They also fail because verification is administratively hard. Jurisdictions disclose differently. Records age at different speeds. Identifiers slip. Attestations outrun proof. Private firms and public agencies alike must decide under time pressure whether the file before them is good enough to justify moving money, admitting a vessel, continuing cover, or refusing service. Beneficial ownership sits at the centre of that decision because it asks institutions to determine not merely what the paperwork says, but whose interest the paperwork is actually serving.

That leaves the unresolved question every serious enforcement system must confront. When the declared beneficial owner appears clean, the surrounding records are incomplete, and the commercial timeline demands an answer before the data can fully settle, should the institution trust the declaration because verification capacity is limited, or distrust it because limited capacity is precisely what layered corporate veils are designed to exploit?

Ship managers, operators, and liability buffers

In September 2019, when sanctions pressure disrupted shipping linked to COSCO Shipping Tanker (Dalian), many market participants discovered that the most important question was not simply who owned a vessel. It was who was still willing to manage it, insure it, crew it, pay for it, and instruct it. Ownership sat on the registry. Operational reality sat elsewhere. A ship could remain legally owned by one company while the practical network that made it tradable shifted around it in days.

That distinction is easy to miss because shipping encourages a visual mistake. We see a ship and assume a unitary enterprise: one asset, one owner, one chain of command. Maritime commerce almost never works that way. A vessel may be owned by a single-purpose company, commercially employed by a charterer, technically supervised by a ship manager, crewed through another firm, financed through a lender with strong control rights, and insured through still other institutions. Each actor holds a different kind of power over the same hull. None of those powers is merely decorative. The desk decides at sea.

That is why the difference between owner, operator, charterer, and manager matters so much for sanctions compliance. The legal owner holds title. The charterer acquires some right to use the vessel's carrying capacity under agreed terms. The operator, depending on context and contract, may organise the vessel's commercial employment or voyage pattern. The manager handles the daily mechanics that keep the ship lawful, crewed, classed, supplied, and technically viable. These roles overlap in practice, and industry language can shift between sectors, but the analytical point remains clear. Control at sea is distributed. The implication is immediate: when sanctions seek to identify who is responsible for a voyage, formal ownership is often only the beginning of the file.

Show the sequence in ordinary commercial terms. A tanker is legally owned by a one-ship company with little public footprint. Its technical management is outsourced to a specialist firm that appoints crew, arranges maintenance, handles classification interactions, manages procurement, and communicates with insurers and port agents. The vessel's commercial employment is directed through a separate operator or chartering entity. Freight flows through banking channels chosen by yet another part of the corporate group. If a sanctions issue arises, which relationship matters most? The concept is functional control. The answer depends on which actor actually keeps the ship moving. A name on a registry tells us who holds title. It does not tell us who makes the voyage happen.

This is where liability buffers enter the picture. Shipping has valid commercial reasons to separate risk. A fleet owner may prefer one-ship companies so that an accident or arrest involving one vessel does not automatically imperil others. A specialist manager may deliver technical competence more cheaply and effectively than an in-house team. A charterer may want tonnage without owning steel. A lender may want security without day-to-day operational responsibility. None of this is suspicious by default. Yet these same separations can also absorb scrutiny. When a sanctions question arrives, each actor can point to another. The owner says the manager handled operations. The manager says the charterer directed the trade. The charterer says the owner represented the vessel as compliant. The banking channel says it only processed payment. Liability becomes distributed precisely where enforcement seeks concentration.

That distribution is one reason management contracts matter more than public debate usually admits. A management transfer can alter the practical identity of a vessel without any sale, mortgage discharge, or headline-grabbing corporate event. Crew wages may start being paid through different accounts. Procurement shifts to different suppliers. Insurance correspondence moves to a new office. Port agents begin hearing from unfamiliar names. Compliance teams at banks and insurers notice changed contact details, amended payment instructions, new email domains, or different documentary habits. The ship has not changed owner. It may have changed world. The concept is operational migration. The implication is that sanctions exposure can shift materially through contract rather than title.

A named example makes this concrete. In the Iranian sanctions environment of the late 2010s and early 2020s, regulatory advisories repeatedly warned that vessels involved in sensitive trades could be moved through changed managers, altered ownership fronts, or reconfigured operating structures without any neat sale visible to casual observers. The lesson was not that management changes always conceal something improper. The more careful point was that management is where compliance often becomes real. The manager knows who pays crew, who orders bunkers, which ports are being approached, which insurers are being used, and which certificates are being maintained. A change in manager therefore changes more than stationery. It changes the institution that mediates between the ship and the wider compliance system.

Ship managers are especially important because they occupy the seam between legal structure and daily reality. A legal owner with no in-house capability depends heavily on the manager to keep the vessel classed, crewed, certificated, and technically defensible. The manager chooses service providers, pays bills from designated accounts, handles surveys, arranges repairs, oversees safety systems, and often becomes the practical face of the vessel to ports, insurers, and suppliers. Trust, in this setting, is not an abstract idea about corporate reputation. It is visible in decisions: whether a port agent still accepts appointment, whether an insurer still treats the file as routine, whether a bank accepts amended payment instructions, whether a supplier extends credit, whether the next crew change can be arranged without extra review. Once the manager changes, all those relationships may be reopened.

Charterers matter differently. They may not own or technically manage the vessel, yet they can exert strong control over employment. Under some charter structures, the charterer decides where the ship goes, what cargo it carries, and how commercially exposed it becomes, while the owner or manager remains responsible for technical condition and crewing. This division is lawful and commercially efficient. It is also useful to anyone trying to place controversial cargo into a structure where responsibility looks blurred. The charterer can say the ship was merely hired tonnage. The owner can say the commercial itinerary was not theirs. The manager can say it only kept the vessel seaworthy. The concept here is divided agency. The implication is that sanctions investigators must map decisions, not just contracts. Who selected the cargo? Who instructed the route? Who approved counterparties? Who kept earning from the trade after the file became difficult?

A second named example lies in the Russian shipping adjustments that followed the 2022 invasion of Ukraine. Public reporting and compliance guidance increasingly described how vessels, operators, and service structures were rearranged under pressure. Some management roles shifted. New intermediary firms appeared. Banking and insurance relationships changed or narrowed. Not every such alteration concealed sanctioned interests; many reflected genuine commercial disruptions. But the enforcement lesson was clear. A ship could remain in nominally lawful hands while the surrounding operational network reconstituted itself in ways that altered who actually carried the risk and who actually sustained the voyage. The registry might show continuity. The compliance reality might not.

This is why owner, operator, charterer, and manager should be treated as different questions rather than different labels for the same entity. The owner question asks who holds title. The operator question asks who organises commercial employment. The charterer question asks who has acquired the right to use carrying capacity under specified conditions. The manager question asks who keeps the vessel administratively and technically alive. These are all forms of power. They do not map neatly onto one another. A sanctions system that does not distinguish them will often end up asking the wrong party for the wrong explanation. An owner may not know the immediate commercial counterparty selected by a charterer. A charterer may not know the full chain of technical vendors used by a manager. A manager may not know the deepest beneficial owner behind the holding company but may know exactly who now pays crew and spares.

The banking consequences of management transfer show how operational control can shift quietly. A new manager often brings new signatories, new payment routines, new invoice addresses, and new relationships with crewing agencies, suppliers, and service firms. To a compliance analyst, those changes may look administrative. In fact they are clues about who now exercises real influence over the ship's daily life. A vessel whose management changes from a well-known firm to a newer or less transparent one may immediately encounter more questions, even if its registered owner has not changed at all. A bank sees amended instructions. An insurer sees changed points of contact. A port sees altered local representation. The file thickens without a sale ever occurring. This is how liability buffers work: they shift operational responsibility through contracts that are less publicly legible than title transfers but often more consequential.

A credible limitation needs to be stated plainly. Management changes and divided roles are not themselves badges of misconduct. Shipping depends on outsourcing and role separation for ordinary, often sensible reasons. Owners change managers because of cost, performance, geography, fleet strategy, mergers, or dissatisfaction. Charterers use independent tonnage because owning every ship would be commercially irrational. Operators appear and disappear with market cycles. A compliance system that treats every management transfer as presumptive evasion will overreach badly and punish normal commerce. This matters not just for fairness but for accuracy. Too much suspicion produces noise, and noise makes the real patterns harder to see.

That limitation does not undercut the central point. It refines it. The relevant issue is not whether roles are divided, but whether the division remains commercially coherent under scrutiny. Does the management transfer make operational sense? Do the banking and crewing shifts line up with the stated explanation? Are new service providers credible and proportionate to the vessel's needs, or do they look like hurried substitutions designed to keep a controversial trade moving? Does the charter structure reflect ordinary market practice, or does it seem engineered to leave every actor with just enough distance from the difficult part of the voyage? The answers emerge from pattern, timing, and behaviour, not from any single title on a document.

The quiet motif here is the desk. Not because shipping is sedentary, but because each role in this structure controls a different desk from which the voyage can be moved or stopped. One desk signs title papers. Another fixes employment. Another pays crew. Another confirms insurance. Another authorises purchases. Another receives freight. When sanctions pressure rises, the question is rarely which desk officially owns the ship. It is which desk can still make the next consequential instruction. Liability buffers matter because they are built precisely to prevent all those instructions from appearing to come from one place.

For investigators and compliance teams, the deeper lesson is sobering. Maritime control is often contractual before it is proprietary. A vessel can change operational character while remaining legally in the same hands. A manager can become the decisive sanctions actor because it controls the practical relationships through which compliance is lived. A charterer can drive exposure without holding title. An owner can remain formally central while being operationally distant. Good enforcement therefore asks not only who owns, but who instructs, who pays, who appoints, who can replace whom, and who bears the commercial consequences when a voyage is slowed or stopped.

That leaves the unresolved question at the heart of every difficult file. When a ship's legal owner appears clean, but the manager, charterer, and operator have shifted into a pattern that changes money flows, crewing, and service relationships without any sale at all, which of those actors should count as the true locus of compliance responsibility - the one on the title, or the one behind the desk that still makes the ship move?

Data quality, not just data access

In April 2016, the Panama Papers seemed to promise a new age of clarity. Corporate records, nominee arrangements, offshore vehicles, and hidden linkages suddenly appeared searchable, discussable, and morally vivid. Yet one of the quieter lessons was less flattering to the modern appetite for data. A larger pile of documents did not automatically produce a cleaner picture of ownership or control. Investigators still had to decide whether two similar names referred to the same person, whether a familiar address indicated meaningful connection or merely a corporate services office, and whether a document's formal completeness said anything trustworthy about the reality it claimed to describe.

That remains the hard truth of maritime sanctions work. Access is not understanding. A compliance team may hold subscriptions to vessel databases, corporate registries, sanctions screening tools, leaked archives, beneficial ownership filings, and open-source trade records, yet still be wrong about the central question in front of it. The file may be thick, the search results abundant, and the conclusion fragile. More data can sharpen judgement. It can also amplify error. The search box lies easily.

This is why data quality matters more than the rhetoric of transparency sometimes allows. Show the ordinary scene. An analyst screens a vessel owner and finds a director's name that resembles a name on a sanctions list. The registered office matches an address used by several other companies in the same maritime cluster. A sister company appears in one database but not in another. The beneficial ownership filing is technically complete, though not recently updated. The analyst now faces two equal and opposite dangers. The first is a false positive: treating a weak resemblance as proof of a prohibited connection. The second is a false negative: treating formal neatness as evidence that no deeper link exists. The concept is data ambiguity. The implication is immediate. Corporate records do not interpret themselves.

False positives arise because corporate and personal identifiers are far less stable than compliance systems pretend. Names shift under transliteration, local naming conventions, abbreviations, patronymics, and inconsistent input habits. One system may record a middle name; another may omit it. A company incorporated in Cyprus may appear with one spelling in banking files, another in registry extracts, and a third in maritime databases curated by private vendors. Addresses behave no better. A corporate services firm may host dozens or hundreds of entities at the same address. Shared office space may imply nothing beyond administration. Yet to a hurried analyst, repeated appearance of the same address can create the glow of conspiracy. The visible consequence is over-escalation: payments delayed, cover withheld, port agents warned off, and ordinary business treated as suspect because a search result felt too persuasive.

False negatives are usually more dangerous because they masquerade as certainty. A record appears clean. No sanctioned name is visible. The beneficial ownership declaration exists and bears the right signatures. The company chart is tidy enough to satisfy the first pass. The analyst moves on. What remains hidden is not necessarily hidden by genius. It may simply sit beyond the reach of the specific datasets being queried, or under a variant name that the search logic did not catch, or in a stale filing whose legal validity outlasts its factual accuracy. The concept here is administrative innocence. The implication is that a clean result can mean either true absence of risk or merely the absence of data capable of showing it. Institutions that do not distinguish those possibilities become vulnerable to actors who understand how easily formal order can satisfy procedural appetite.

A named example makes the point from the regulatory side. In May 2020, the United States Departments of State, Treasury, and Coast Guard issued a sanctions advisory warning maritime actors about deceptive shipping practices, including the use of complex ownership structures and false documentation. The advisory mattered not because it revealed that bad records exist, but because it recognised a deeper problem: the practical limits of matching identity across fragmented datasets. A vessel's paperwork might look compliant in one system while surrounding corporate records remained stale, inconsistent, or strategically incomplete elsewhere. The real challenge was not obtaining any data at all. It was deciding which data deserved confidence and which merely satisfied the appearance of due diligence.

This is why matching names, entities, and addresses is less a technical step than an interpretive act. Consider names. A director appearing in several offshore companies may be a nominee professional with no meaningful control over any of them. The same director may also be the reliable sign of a corporate network designed to conceal one principal's interest across jurisdictions. The database cannot settle that distinction alone. It can only present the recurrence. Meaning comes from context: who paid the service firm, whether the director appears alongside the same lawyers or managers, whether the vessel trading pattern changed when the director appeared, whether the companies share more than a postbox. Good investigators compare. Poor ones merely collect.

Entities generate similar traps. A company may look new because it has only recently appeared in a particular registry feed, yet in fact it may sit within a longer corporate history visible elsewhere. Another may appear well established because it has a historic name, even though its beneficial ownership shifted quietly months earlier. A one-ship company may be perfectly ordinary in maritime finance. A cluster of one-ship companies with near-identical naming patterns, shared service providers, and synchronised management changes may signal something else entirely. The concept is relational quality. One corporate record gains meaning only in relation to other records, and those relations are often weakly represented in commercial screening tools built for speed rather than inference.

Addresses are especially treacherous because they look factual. An address feels like a hard point in the world, something that can anchor investigation. Yet maritime corporate structures frequently use service addresses, registered offices, management addresses, trading addresses, and correspondence addresses that serve different functions. A company sharing an address with twenty others may be part of an evasion network. It may also simply be a client of a routine incorporation service used across the shipping sector. The visible danger is not just analytical error but behavioural distortion. A bank or insurer may treat the address match as strong evidence and escalate unnecessarily. Another institution, having learned that many such matches are benign, may dismiss a genuinely meaningful address cluster too quickly. Data quality problems teach contradictory habits at once.

A second named example lies in the sanctions-heavy response to Russian shipping and related trade after 2022. Compliance teams across banks, insurers, ports, and maritime service firms were forced to screen new companies, new intermediaries, and changing management structures at speed. Publicly available records often existed. The problem was that they differed in freshness, formatting, and scope. A corporate vehicle could appear benign in one database because beneficial ownership had not yet been updated. A vessel manager's name could be entered slightly differently across registries, obscuring a link obvious to a human reader but invisible to automated screening. An address associated with a professional services firm could either dilute real signal or point to an entire cluster of reconfigured entities tied to the same trade. The challenge was less about secrecy in the cinematic sense and more about the uneven quality of ordinary records under pressure.

This is where the distinction between raw access and usable quality becomes decisive. Access tells us that a record can be retrieved. Quality asks harder questions. When was it last updated? Who supplied the information? For what purpose was it created? Is the identifier stable across systems? Does the record preserve history or merely the latest filing? Can the same entity be matched independently through banking, insurance, registry, and vessel data, or is the apparent link resting on one unstable field such as a name spelling or office address? A strong compliance system asks these questions almost instinctively. A weak one confuses database visibility with institutional knowledge.

A credible limitation must be admitted. Data imperfections do not always point to manipulation. Shipping remains a multilingual, multi-jurisdictional industry administered through systems never designed to produce perfect interoperability. Clerical errors happen. Legacy systems truncate names. Transliteration varies for entirely innocent reasons. Corporate groups change addresses after mergers, sales, or restructuring. Records can be incomplete because local law requires less, because filings are delayed, or because the reporting threshold was never crossed. An analyst determined to find misconduct can weaponise these imperfections into a story they do not support. That risk matters because false positives impose real costs: lawful shipments delayed, relationships severed, ports made hesitant, insurance narrowed, and whole classes of clients treated as radioactive because the data trail was merely untidy.

That limitation does not diminish the warning. It sharpens the method. Reliable conclusions do not emerge from a single database hit, however authoritative the platform may appear. They emerge from comparison across differently generated records. Does the name match the same birthdate, nationality, or corporate role elsewhere? Does the address recur with meaningful commercial relationships, or merely with service-company administration? Does the beneficial ownership filing line up with who pays crew, who receives freight, who appoints managers, and who interacts with insurers? Do historic records show continuity hidden by a recent filing change? The goal is not certainty in the abstract. It is disciplined confidence built from converging indicators strong enough to justify the next institutional decision.

The quiet motif here is the ledger. Not the old paper ledger of romantic commerce, but the larger idea of an account that must balance. A name in one column, an address in another, a payment trail elsewhere, a management contract in a different file, a vessel history in yet another. When the ledger balances across sources, confidence grows. When it does not, caution becomes rational. The problem is that many modern systems show the columns separately and flatter the user into thinking the total has already been computed. It has not. Someone still has to read across the page.

This is why cautious interpretation is not timidity. It is operational seriousness. A port deciding whether to admit a vessel, a bank deciding whether to clear funds, an insurer deciding whether to confirm cover, and a manager deciding whether to continue service all depend on more than access to data. They depend on judging whether the data are current enough, linked enough, and specific enough to support action without turning ordinary corporate untidiness into a quasi-criminal narrative. Good compliance work therefore looks slower than technological marketing suggests. It measures before it concludes. It checks history, not just snapshots. It distrusts both the too-perfect record and the too-convenient match.

The broader lesson for sanctions enforcement is austere. Corporate transparency fails not only when information is hidden, but when visible information is too weak, too stale, or too loosely matched to bear the weight institutions place upon it. False positives distort commerce and waste enforcement capacity. False negatives let sanctioned interests travel under the shelter of formally neat but substantively empty records. The battle is therefore not merely for more data. It is for better data, better linkage, and better habits of interpretation. Without those, access becomes theatre.

That leaves a difficult question at the centre of every corporate file. When the database returns a plausible match, a plausible non-match, and just enough surrounding noise to support either story, what should an institution trust more: the availability of records, or its own disciplined suspicion that records without quality are often the cleanest disguise of all?

Chapter 6

Insurance, Classification, and P&I Dependence

How can a ship be free to sail and yet unable to trade? That question sits at the heart of modern maritime sanctions more sharply than any image of interdiction at sea. A vessel may be seaworthy, crewed, loaded, and technically capable of completing its voyage. None of that settles whether it will be welcomed into port, accepted by a canal authority, financed by a bank, fixed by a charterer, or trusted by the counterparties whose signatures turn movement into commerce. The answer often lies not in force, but in recognition.

That recognition is rarely granted by the state alone. It is distributed across insurers, P&I clubs, classification societies, and the claims processes that follow when something goes wrong or merely begins to look doubtful. These institutions do not govern the sea in the grand constitutional sense. They do something quieter and often more consequential. They decide whether risk will be named, priced, shared, certified, investigated, or left to the vessel and its owner to carry alone. A ship without those recognitions does not become physically impossible. It becomes commercially awkward, administratively suspect, and increasingly difficult to touch.

The certificate opens doors.

That is why insurance and classification occupy such a strange but decisive place in maritime power. They are not regulators, yet they behave like gatekeepers. Insurance determines whether a port, charterer, lender, or canal authority is prepared to tolerate the liabilities surrounding the voyage. Classification determines whether the ship's technical legitimacy remains persuasive enough for other institutions to rely upon. P&I clubs, with their collective structure and sensitivity to predictable conduct, add another layer: they reward ships that remain legible, documentable, and governable, and they become uneasy when a vessel begins to drift towards opacity. None of this looks like sanctions enforcement in the cinematic sense. Much of it functions exactly that way in practice.

The tension lies in the fact that these institutions were not built primarily to carry geopolitical burdens. They were built to make maritime risk manageable. Insurers calculate exposure. P&I clubs socialise liabilities across members who have a common interest in avoiding surprises. Classification societies test technical standards so that ports, financiers, insurers, and owners do not need to reinvent those judgements from scratch every time a ship appears. Yet once sanctions pressure intensifies, these same institutions become the points through which legal uncertainty turns into operational consequence. A policy exclusion can bite harder than a speech. A class question can travel further than a naval warning. A claims investigation can freeze a voyage more efficiently than a dramatic interception.

This matters because maritime trade depends on borrowed confidence. A charterer does not usually inspect the entire ship from first principles. A port does not independently recreate the entire technical and ownership history of every arriving vessel. A bank does not physically verify each cargo movement it finances. They rely on the work already done by others. Insurance says that liabilities are, within limits, carried by a recognisable market. Classification says that technical compliance has been assessed by a body whose judgement others are willing to trust. P&I says that the vessel sits within a mutual framework that values order, disclosure, and claims discipline. If those assurances weaken, each downstream institution must decide whether to replace them with its own scrutiny or to step back. Most step back.

The stakes are therefore practical before they are doctrinal. When cover narrows, or a club withdraws, or a class society raises concerns, the ship does not simply lose a service. It loses a portion of the commercial language that allows other actors to say yes. Ports ask harder questions. Charterers seek alternatives. Service providers demand payment in advance or decline altogether. Claims become more frightening because they invite deeper scrutiny. The burden does not remain with the insurer or the class society alone. It radiates outward through the voyage plan, changing the behaviour of institutions that may never mention sanctions at all while nevertheless acting under their shadow.

That radiation is especially important because it shows how enforcement can proceed without overt state choreography. A government may designate, warn, or prohibit. The decisive movement often occurs later, when insurers begin reading a class of voyages as too uncertain, when P&I clubs treat gaps in documentation as signs of conduct outside acceptable norms, when classification decisions become harder to separate from the political environment around the ship, and when claims handlers start asking questions whose answers lead beyond the casualty itself and into cargo origin, management relationships, or counterparty identity. Even a delay can be enough. A claim not yet denied may still become commercially decisive if the waiting unsettles charter performance, financing, or port acceptance.

The argument ahead follows that chain of recognition where it is most exposed. It begins with insurance as an enabling condition of trade, moves through the collective discipline of P&I, then into the technical authority of classification, and finally into the investigations that claims and disputes can trigger once doubt has entered the file. The sequence matters because each layer relies on the others. A ship whose cover is questioned may find class newly significant. A class issue may alter insurer appetite. A claims process may force both insurance and classification to revisit assumptions they had previously treated as routine.

The deeper friction is not hard to state. States want private maritime institutions to amplify sanctions pressure because these institutions can shape behaviour at the points where trade is actually enabled. Those same institutions want to remain recognisable as technical, commercial, and mutual bodies rather than undeclared ministries of foreign policy. The distinction is unstable. If they refuse too little, they risk becoming conduits for transactions others now find intolerable. If they refuse too much, they may distort legitimate trade, undermine their own procedural credibility, or drive business towards thinner and less trusted alternatives. The certificate opens doors again, and it can close them just as quietly.

That leaves the harder question this chapter must face. When insurance, P&I, and classification start acting as the practical conditions of market access, where exactly does prudent risk management end and indirect enforcement begin - and what happens to maritime legitimacy when the institutions most relied upon for technical judgement are asked to carry political weight they did not originally exist to bear?

Insurance as permission to trade

In September 2019, when the United States designation of COSCO Shipping Tanker (Dalian) entities disrupted tanker markets, the most revealing question was not whether the affected ships could still float or even whether cargoes still existed to be moved. It was whether the vessels remained insurable in ways that ports, charterers, banks, and service providers would recognise as good enough. The legal measure came from Washington. Its force travelled through insurance screens in London, Singapore, and elsewhere, where underwriters and compliance teams had to decide whether continuing cover would expose them to a risk they could no longer price or defend. Steel had not changed. Permission had.

That is why insurance matters so much more than the public imagination usually grants it. Maritime insurance is often described as financial protection after the fact, a back-office cushion against collision, pollution, cargo claims, or crew liabilities. In practice it functions much earlier and much more sharply. A ship without acceptable insurance may still be seaworthy, crewed, and technically ready to sail, yet it can become commercially unusable. Ports may refuse entry or hesitate over berthing. Canal transits may become difficult or impossible. Charterers may decline to fix the vessel. Banks and traders may refuse to attach their own names to the movement. No policy, no passage.

This is the first point that must be kept in view: insurance in shipping is not merely compensation. It is a condition of legitimacy. Show the ordinary sequence. A vessel is nominated for a cargo. Before the fixture becomes real, the charterer checks whether the ship carries cover acceptable to its internal compliance standards and to the counterparties likely to touch the voyage. A port agent wants to know whether local authorities will accept the vessel's liability arrangements. A canal or terminal asks for evidence that claims arising from transit or handling can be met. None of these institutions needs to regulate the ship in the sovereign sense. They only need to decide whether the liabilities attached to the ship will be carried by someone they trust. The concept is delegated permission. The implication is decisive: insurers become gatekeepers not because the law explicitly appoints them as such, but because maritime commerce cannot function without their recognisable assent.

That assent works through several visible behaviours. A policy may be issued without controversy, and the voyage proceeds as ordinary trade. Or questions may begin. The underwriter wants fuller information on cargo origin, counterparties, routing, recent management changes, or ownership connections. Certain ports are excluded. Certain perils are narrowed. Sanctions clauses are read more aggressively. Premiums shift. Renewal becomes less certain. A policy that exists on paper may cease to serve as a persuasive passport in practice. This is what turns insurance into a form of enforcement without open proclamation. Pricing can discipline conduct.

Exclusions can make routes commercially unattractive. Refusal can leave a vessel technically afloat but economically stranded.

The important feature is that insurers do not need to prove a sanctions violation in the courtroom sense before they alter behaviour. They need only conclude that the file can no longer be understood well enough to support the risk. That threshold matters because shipping operates under time pressure. A charterer cannot wait indefinitely for underwriters to resolve doubts. A port cannot suspend all operational judgement while ownership and cargo narratives are reconstructed from fragments. An insurer's hesitation therefore acquires practical force long before any state actor boards a ship. Trust, here, is not a mood. It is visible in whether the cover note is accepted without argument, whether the voyage is fixed, whether the port says yes, and whether the next institution in line still believes the liabilities are safely placed.

A named example from the Russian energy sphere shows the mechanism clearly. After the United States sanctioned Arctic LNG 2 in November 2023, the legal act did not itself stop every possible voyage connected to the project. What it did was force surrounding institutions, including insurers, to ask whether supporting those voyages remained commercially and legally tolerable. The decisive question was not merely whether gas could be produced or loaded. It was whether vessels, cargo interests, ports, banks, and service providers could still assemble a chain of cover and confidence sufficient for trade to proceed in recognisable form. Insurance became an early and often decisive point of friction because it translated geopolitical risk into operational hesitation.

That translation is one reason insurance can function as enforcement while remaining formally commercial. A state may prohibit certain dealings, designate certain entities, or warn against particular deceptive practices. The insurer then internalises those moves as exposure. An underwriter does not need to become a foreign ministry. It needs only to ask whether a claim arising from this voyage would be payable, defensible, and survivable in its own regulatory and reputational environment. Once the answer becomes unstable, the ship's commercial life narrows. The concept is risk internalisation. The implication is broader than insurance law. Maritime sanctions succeed partly because insurers, acting to protect themselves, reduce the number of ships, routes, and cargoes that can still pass as ordinary business.

This is most evident when one considers port entry and canal passage. Ports and transit authorities are not usually content with a vessel owner's verbal promise that liabilities will be met if something goes wrong. They want evidence of cover from a source they know how to recognise. The requirement can sound procedural. It is in fact structural. A vessel carrying obscure or disputed insurance may face extra questions, slower treatment, demands for additional security, or outright refusal. The insurer's name, standing, and sanctions posture therefore influence maritime access without any need for overt political theatre. The port does not have to announce a geopolitical stance. It can simply say that the liabilities are not acceptably arranged.

Charter contracts reveal the same dynamic in a more commercial idiom. A charterer fixes a vessel not merely on freight and availability, but on the confidence that the ship will remain employable throughout the voyage. Insurance sits inside that confidence. A vessel whose cover might be challenged at a load port, discharge port, canal, or by cargo interests is less attractive even if its freight looks competitive. The charterer prices not only the cost of the ship, but the risk of interruption, dispute, and reputational spillover. That is why insurers become quiet authors of the voyage plan. Their willingness to cover, question, exclude, or step back reshapes who can trade, where, and on what terms.

A second named example lies in the long-running sanctions pressure around Iranian oil shipping during the late 2010s and early 2020s. Public advisories repeatedly warned insurers about deceptive shipping practices, including manipulated documentation, opaque ownership structures, and ship-to-ship transfers designed to obscure cargo origin or destination. The practical effect was not simply the withdrawal of some policies. It was the broader weakening of market willingness to treat certain voyages as intelligible enough to insure with confidence. Alternative cover could sometimes be found. But alternative cover was often less credible to ports, traders, and financiers. The legal rule thus travelled through an insurance market that did not need to be commanded in every detail to produce constraining commercial effects.

A credible limitation must be admitted. Insurance withdrawal or narrowing does not automatically end trade. Ships can and do seek alternative arrangements, including cover from less established providers, state-backed mechanisms, or structures designed mainly to satisfy minimum formal requirements rather than to command broad market trust. In some cases, politically important trade continues under such conditions. This matters because sanctions analysis becomes lazy when it treats mainstream insurance loss as equivalent to immobilisation. A vessel can keep moving after losing widely recognised cover. It simply moves under degraded conditions: fewer acceptable ports, more suspicious counterparties, reduced creditworthiness, and greater vulnerability when something goes wrong.

That limitation sharpens rather than weakens the central claim. The power of insurance lies not in perfect exclusion, but in the distinction between trading with mainstream confidence and trading under a permanent cloud. Mainstream cover makes a voyage easier to berth, finance, charter, service, and defend. Marginal cover may preserve motion while hollowing out those surrounding recognitions. The vessel survives, but with thinner commercial oxygen. Risk pricing illustrates the point. When insurers perceive elevated sanctions exposure, the cost is not merely monetary. Higher premiums signal that the voyage belongs to a category of trade others may also wish to avoid. Price becomes narrative. Narrative affects access.

Coverage exclusions work even more directly. An insurer may continue some form of relationship with the vessel while carving out particular routes, ports, cargoes, counterparties, or sanctions-related exposures. The result can be commercially devastating without looking dramatic. A ship whose policy excludes the very trade it is supposed to undertake is not effectively insured for that movement, whatever the certificate says in broader terms. A charterer reading such exclusions does not need legal metaphysics to grasp the problem. Nor does a port considering whether it wishes to receive the ship. Exclusions therefore function as finely tuned enforcement tools even when they arise from ordinary underwriting caution rather than explicit state instruction.

This is also why evasion networks dislike claims. A claim invites documentation, investigation, and re-reading of the voyage. It asks where the cargo came from, who instructed the route, which counterparties were involved, what the ownership structure really looked like, whether declarations were accurate, and whether the policy responded at all. Even if the insurer does not immediately deny liability, the process itself can expose contradictions that make future trade harder. The visible cost is delay. The deeper cost is scrutiny. Insurance, then, is not only permission at the start of the voyage. It is a continuing test of whether the voyage's story can withstand official curiosity once money is at stake.

The quiet motif here is the policy slip, because this modest piece of paper carries a surprisingly large share of modern maritime order. It does not merely record that insurance exists. It tells ports, charterers, banks, and service providers that someone recognisable has agreed to stand behind the vessel's liabilities under defined conditions. If that agreement weakens, the whole surrounding chain becomes more cautious. The policy slip opens doors. It also teaches the market which doors should remain closed.

The wider lesson is austere. Insurance functions as permission to trade because maritime commerce depends on liabilities being placed within institutions others are willing to trust. Sanctions exploit that dependence not always by banning ships directly, but by making insurers ask whether certain risks still deserve to be carried at all. Once that question turns from technical underwriting to reputational and regulatory exposure, cover begins to govern access. The insurer is not a regulator. It may still decide the fate of the voyage more effectively than many regulators can.

That leaves the harder question at the centre of maritime sanctions practice. When a ship still has some form of cover, but not the kind that ports, charterers, banks, and service providers regard as fully credible, should that count as lawful continuation of trade under altered market conditions, or as proof that insurance has already done the real enforcing long before any state says the ship may not move?

P&I clubs and collective risk

In February 2024, the International Group of P&I Clubs issued guidance on compliance and sanctions exposure that, in form, looked routine: cautious language, procedural emphasis, no flourish. Yet the commercial meaning was sharper than the prose. Protection and indemnity cover is not a decorative add-on to shipping. It is one of the ways a vessel proves to ports, charterers, terminals, and counterparties that the liabilities surrounding it belong to an intelligible system of collective responsibility. When that assurance weakens, the ship does not merely lose insurance. It loses a portion of its claim to normal trade.

That is because P&I is built on a distinct institutional idea. Hull and machinery insurance may answer for physical loss to the ship itself. P&I clubs exist to mutualise the wider liabilities that shipping generates: pollution, cargo claims, crew matters, collision liabilities beyond hull cover, wreck removal, and a host of other exposures that can become financially ruinous if they are carried alone. The club is not simply selling a product. It is managing a pool of shared vulnerability among members whose continued participation depends on the confidence that others in the pool are acting predictably, documenting properly, and not inviting unbounded trouble. Mutuality disciplines quietly.

This is the first fact that matters for sanctions analysis. A P&I club does not behave like a neutral vending machine that dispenses cover to any vessel meeting a minimal formal threshold. It is a collective system that depends on trust in other members' conduct. Show the ordinary sequence. A shipowner enters a club and gains cover recognised across the maritime world. Ports accept the club's standing. Charterers assume the vessel sits within a claims-paying framework whose habits are familiar. Canal authorities and terminals know what sort of liability machinery stands behind the ship. That recognition flows not only from legal rules, but from the club's accumulated reputation for dealing with claims, policing documentation, and distancing itself from conduct that could endanger the whole pool. The concept is collective credibility. The implication is plain: when a club withdraws or hesitates, the ship loses more than an insurer. It loses a piece of borrowed legitimacy.

That borrowed legitimacy has direct operational consequences because P&I cover functions as a passport to ordinary maritime interaction. A port may technically admit a vessel without asking about the finer structure of its liabilities, but serious commercial actors rarely behave as though liability arrangements are irrelevant. A charterer wants to know whether cargo claims can be handled through a club whose processes it recognises. A port wants confidence that pollution or wreck removal exposure will not become a local fiscal nightmare. A terminal wants assurance that a damaged berth, contaminated cargo, or injured worker will not be met with an opaque or undercapitalised response. The club, therefore, becomes a gatekeeper without being a regulator. It says no by refusing the mutual promise that others have learned to trust.

The mutual structure explains why predictable conduct matters so much. P&I clubs do not merely price isolated risks one voyage at a time. They depend on members behaving in ways that make liabilities legible and manageable across the whole system. Documentation matters because claims handling depends on reconstructing what happened, who knew what, what was declared, and whether cover applies. Predictability matters because a mutual system cannot absorb large pockets of strategically hidden conduct without weakening confidence among all participants. This is why sanctions-sensitive shipping sits so awkwardly inside the P&I world. It often comes wrapped in the very features clubs dislike: unstable ownership presentation, unusual routing, opaque cargo origin, inconsistent records, rapidly changing managers, and heightened risk of later dispute over legality or disclosure. The file begins to look expensive before the casualty has even occurred.

A named example clarifies the point. After sanctions pressure intensified on Russian maritime trade following February 2022, one of the practical questions for many vessels was not merely whether some form of insurance could be found, but whether International Group club cover would remain available and, where unavailable, what sort of replacement the market would regard as credible. This mattered because club cover is embedded in ordinary maritime expectations. A vessel relying on a less recognised or politically improvised alternative might still move. Yet ports, charterers, and service providers would read the change as a signal that the ship had moved outside the most trusted circle of collective liability management. The difference was not theoretical. It appeared in extra questions, narrowed opportunities, and a general thickening of commercial doubt.

That doubt is where reputational spillovers become decisive. A P&I club protects not only against direct liability but against the reputational consequences of uncertainty by standing as a known institution with known claims behaviour. Remove that club from the picture and surrounding actors begin to reassess far more than insurance. If the club no longer wishes to carry the vessel, what does that imply about the underlying file? Has ownership changed in a way the club found uncomfortable? Has the trading pattern become too exposed? Are documentation and disclosure habits slipping? The port agent may not know the full answer. Neither may the charterer. Both may still infer that a credible institution has seen enough to hesitate. Reputation travels by inference. This is why club withdrawal or non-renewal can alter market access far beyond the formal boundaries of the policy.

Alternatives do exist, and a serious account must acknowledge them. State-backed arrangements, smaller mutuals, fixed-premium providers, captive structures, or less globally familiar insurers can step into gaps left by mainstream clubs. Some politically important trades continue precisely because such alternatives are assembled. This matters because sanctions analysis becomes self-flattering when it assumes that loss of mainstream P&I automatically immobilises the vessel. It does not. Trade adapts. The ship can still float, cargo can still move, and some ports or counterparties may remain willing to engage. Yet the quality of recognition changes. An alternative provider may be legally sufficient while commercially weak.

It may offer a certificate without offering the wider market the same confidence that claims will be handled predictably, funded reliably, and defended through procedures others already understand.

That distinction between formal availability and practical credibility is central. P&I cover is not merely a piece of paper confirming that some institution has assumed some liabilities. It is a social fact in maritime commerce. The best-known clubs benefit from shared habits of claims handling, correspondence networks, legal experience, and a long record of standing behind members in ways other actors can price into their own decisions. When a vessel loses access to that world, it often discovers that the replacement market imposes higher cost, tighter limits, more suspicion, or less acceptance by ports and commercial counterparties. The concept here is degraded substitutability. The implication is that alternative cover may preserve motion while sharply reducing the quality of the ship's integration into mainstream trade.

A second named example comes from the sanctions environment around Iranian oil shipping during the late 2010s and early 2020s. Public advisories repeatedly warned maritime actors about deceptive practices and the insurance implications of engaging in such trades. The effect was not simply that mainstream insurers and P&I providers feared direct legal exposure. They also feared being drawn into claims connected to voyages whose documentation, ownership, and cargo narratives might later unravel under scrutiny. A mutual system dislikes surprises of that kind because every disputed claim tests not only policy wording but the discipline of the member's disclosures. Clubs are built to mutualise risk, not to mutualise strategic ambiguity. Once that distinction sharpens, the ship begins to look like a bad member even before it has become a bad claim.

Claims culture is crucial here. P&I clubs live close to claims. They do not merely underwrite from afar; they coordinate correspondence, legal defence, evidence gathering, and settlement across jurisdictions and incident types. That proximity makes them unusually sensitive to the future cost of doubt. A vessel that trades through opaque structures, inconsistent documentation, or sanctions-sensitive cargo chains may generate liabilities that are difficult to investigate, hard to defend, or reputationally damaging to the club, even if technically within some arguable form of cover. The visible result is not always immediate expulsion. It may be tighter questioning at renewal, reduced appetite for ambiguities that once would have been tolerated, demands for fuller disclosure, or decisions to step back from particular trades. Enforcement enters through the claim's imagination: the club asks what kind of file it may later have to defend and decides whether it still wishes to be attached to it.

A credible limitation deserves candour. Clubs are not infallible moral instruments, nor are they designed to adjudicate geopolitical truth. They can become over-cautious. They can contribute to collective overreaction, treating uncertainty as contamination and pushing legitimate trade into unnecessary difficulty. They also depend on the same imperfect information environment that troubles banks, ports, and insurers more broadly. A club may hesitate because records are incomplete, not because misconduct is established. That can produce collateral harm. Lawful operators with complex but innocent structures may find themselves burdened by the same heuristics used to detect real evasion. Reputational spillovers do not distinguish neatly between guilty opacity and ordinary commercial complication unless evidence is handled with discipline.

That limitation does not weaken the central argument. It clarifies the balance P&I clubs try to strike. A mutual system must remain open enough to ensure ordinary shipping in all its structural untidiness, yet selective enough to protect the pool from members whose conduct or concealment threatens disproportionate loss. This balancing act becomes harder under sanctions because the risks are not merely actuarial. They include regulatory exposure, reputational damage, payment disruption, and the possibility that a claim will force the club into a politically charged reconstruction of the voyage. That is why clubs care so much about predictable conduct and documentation. They do not need members to be pure. They need them to be knowable.

The quiet motif here is the membership card. A vessel does not carry it in the theatrical sense, yet maritime commerce reads the presence or absence of reputable club cover in much the same way. Membership signals that the ship sits inside a collective discipline of disclosure, claims handling, and mutual obligation that others are prepared to trust. Lose that signal and every subsequent interaction becomes slightly more strained. The port asks more. The charterer hesitates. The service provider worries about who will answer if something goes wrong. The vessel has not been banned by the sea. It has been moved down a rung in the hierarchy of commercial confidence.

This is why reputational spillovers shape compliance so powerfully. A club's withdrawal or visible discomfort tells the market something, even when the precise internal reasoning is not public. It suggests that the file no longer sits comfortably within a system designed to reward order and punish surprise. Other actors, each with their own narrower perspective, take that cue. They may not know whether the issue lies in ownership, cargo origin, route, disclosure, or some combination of all four. They still react. Mutuality becomes signalling. Signalling becomes discipline.

The deeper lesson is austere. P&I clubs help govern maritime sanctions not because they were created to do so, but because collective risk cannot tolerate too much unpriced uncertainty. The vessel that remains within a reputable club enjoys more than cover. It enjoys a presumption that its liabilities can be managed through a known institutional language. The vessel that falls outside that world may still trade, but it does so with thinner credibility and a weaker claim on the patience of mainstream ports, charterers, and service providers. The mutual promise contracts, and the market notices.

That leaves a harder question than the language of alternatives usually captures. When a ship loses mainstream club cover and replaces it with something formally sufficient but commercially doubted, has the market merely adjusted to a new insurance provider, or has the vessel already crossed an invisible line from ordinary trade into a more precarious world where every subsequent claim, port call, and counterparty must decide how much of the old collective trust still attaches to the paper now presented?

Classification societies and technical legitimacy

In March 2022, major classification societies began reviewing or withdrawing services from parts of the Russian shipping market in response to sanctions pressure and the wider legal risks that followed the invasion of Ukraine. The visible event looked technical: survey relationships altered, certificates came under question, established institutional ties loosened. Yet the commercial force was larger than the paperwork suggested. A ship may still float when class support weakens. It may still even sail. What it loses is something harder to replace quickly: technical legitimacy that other actors have learned to trust without recreating it for themselves from the keel up.

That is the first thing classification does in modern shipping. It does not merely inspect steel. It translates technical condition into a form usable by others. Ports, insurers, banks, charterers, terminals, and flag administrations all rely, to varying degrees, on the fact that a recognised society has surveyed the vessel, maintained records, and certified compliance against standards they are not equipped to reproduce independently for every voyage. Classification is therefore not only technical supervision. It is a language of reassurance. The certificate speaks before the ship does.

This is why classification societies matter so much to sanctions enforcement even though they are not sanctions authorities. Their decisions shape market access because technical legitimacy is one of the enabling conditions of normal trade. Show the sequence plainly. A vessel seeks charter employment, insurance, port access, and ordinary service relationships. Each counterparty assumes that the technical condition of the vessel has already been filtered through a classification system whose methods and reputation it broadly accepts. If that filter disappears, the counterparty must choose between performing more of the technical judgement itself or refusing the exposure. Most choose refusal, or something close to it. The concept is delegated trust. The implication is practical: a class society can restrict a vessel's trading life without issuing a political statement or taking any direct state action at all.

The significance becomes clearer when one notices how classification is actually used in commerce. A charterer does not normally send its own naval architects to inspect every candidate ship in exhaustive detail. A port does not independently reconstruct the vessel's maintenance history from raw engineering records. An insurer does not begin from first principles every time it considers cover. These institutions compare, inquire, and verify where needed, but they do so against the background assumption that class offers a reliable baseline. Classification therefore compresses technical complexity into an administratively usable form. The certificate is not the whole truth about the ship. It is the socially accepted shorthand for where technical trust begins.

That shorthand turns class into a gatekeeper precisely because it remains narrower than law and broader than engineering. A class society is not deciding whether a cargo is morally acceptable or geopolitically desirable. It is deciding whether the ship remains within the technical and documentary regime it is prepared to stand behind. Yet once that support weakens, market effects follow immediately. A port asks whether entry remains prudent. An insurer asks whether cover still makes sense. A charterer asks whether fixing the ship is worth the uncertainty. A service provider asks whether the vessel is drifting outside the circle of recognisable shipping. Technical legitimacy becomes commercial permission by indirection.

A named example from the post-2022 sanctions environment illustrates the point. As mainstream class societies reduced or withdrew services from vessels tied to certain Russian interests, the question was not merely whether alternative classification could be obtained. In some cases, it could. The harder question was whether the replacement carried the same weight with ports, insurers, financiers, and charterers. Often it did not. The vessel might remain legally documented and physically operable while sliding into a different tier of market recognition. This is what matters operationally. Class withdrawal does not need to immobilise the ship completely in order to reshape its commercial world. It needs only to weaken the confidence others place in the ship's technical paper.

That confidence rests on more than survey competence. It also rests on institutional reputation: how the society handles rules, deficiencies, records, continuity, and difficult cases. Reputation matters because classification is relational. A certificate from a society others regard as demanding and procedurally serious carries more force than a certificate from an organisation seen as politically exposed, newly improvised, or insufficiently independent. This is not always fair to newer or smaller providers, and it should not be romanticised as an infallible hierarchy of virtue. But it remains commercially decisive. Trust, here, is visible in behaviour. The charterer fixes or declines. The port admits or hesitates. The insurer renews or asks harder questions. The class certificate may look like a technical document. It is also a market signal.

This is why alternative classification is not a simple substitute when mainstream societies step back. A vessel can obtain a certificate from another society and still discover that the surrounding market treats the replacement as thinner cover for a thicker problem. Ports may scrutinise more closely. Insurers may narrow appetite. Service providers may worry about future claims and surveys. Banks may take the altered class relationship as one more sign that the file has moved into higher-risk territory. The concept here is asymmetric substitutability. The implication is that class can be formally replaceable and commercially irreplaceable at the same time. That tension gives classification decisions their quiet force as tools of indirect enforcement.

A second named example lies in the longstanding importance of classification to tanker, bulk, and LNG trades where technical standards are bound tightly to chartering and insurance expectations. When class issues arise - whether because of overdue surveys, unresolved recommendations, or changes in society - commercial consequences can arrive before any state intervenes. A ship may lose a fixture, fail to secure cover on ordinary terms, or face questions at the port that delay the voyage enough to alter its economics. The larger lesson is not confined to any one sanctions regime. It is structural. Classification matters because many maritime actors have organised their own risk management around the assumption that class provides a reliable first screen. Once that assumption weakens, the whole chain stiffens.

This is where safety oversight and geopolitical pressure begin to rub against one another. In principle, class societies exist to evaluate technical condition, not to carry foreign policy. In practice, they operate within legal and commercial environments shaped by sanctions, export controls, reputational risk, and the exposure of their own offices, personnel, and relationships. A society withdrawing from a sanctions-sensitive client may describe the move in legal or compliance terms. The market still reads a geopolitical signal into it. That creates a real tension. If classification becomes too visibly political, its technical authority risks looking instrumentalised. If it ignores geopolitical realities entirely, it may expose itself to legal penalties and reputational damage severe enough to undermine its broader credibility. The boundary is unstable because the ship itself sits at the intersection of safety, law, and commerce.

A credible limitation needs to be faced directly. Class is not a perfect measure of seaworthiness, nor is loss of class always a reliable proxy for sanctions risk. Ships with proper class can still be poorly governed, and ships shifting between societies are not automatically engaged in evasion. Operators change class for cost, service, strategic, or regional reasons that may be commercially legitimate. A sanctions system that treats every class change as presumptively suspect will generate serious false positives. That matters because maritime trade depends on not turning every technical adjustment into political evidence. Over-reading classification changes can burden lawful trade and encourage more actors to seek marginal technical support simply because mainstream channels feel too quick to stigmatise them.

That limitation, however, does not weaken the central claim. It makes the necessary distinction sharper. The issue is not whether classification decisions prove wrongdoing. The issue is whether classification determines which ships remain easy for the mainstream market to trust. When class support becomes unstable, a vessel's technical status stops being background and becomes the foreground of every commercial interaction. A charterer may still use the ship, but only after more checks. An insurer may still cover it, but with more conditions. A port may still accept it, but after a delay. The certificate's weakening does not end trade automatically. It raises the cost of every yes that follows.

This is why classification works as a form of indirect enforcement, even when no one sets out to use it that way. A state imposes sanctions or legal risks. A class society reassesses whether it can continue standing behind certain ships or owners. Market actors read that reassessment as a change in technical legitimacy. The vessel finds itself pushed towards narrower service markets and less patient counterparties. No warship has moved. No customs officer may yet have acted. The ship's operating space has still contracted. Enforcement happens through credibility as much as through command.

The quiet motif here is the certificate, because it captures the strange modesty of the whole mechanism. A single document, or a set of linked documents, carries far more than a record of survey compliance. It carries the accumulated willingness of others to rely on a society's judgment instead of reproducing that judgment themselves. The certificate opens commercial doors precisely because it saves time, transfers trust, and reduces the need for every port, insurer, or charterer to start from zero. Once the certificate loses force, time returns, trust thins, and every decision becomes more difficult. A ship can survive that. It cannot ignore it.

The broader lesson is austere. Classification societies confer technical legitimacy, and technical legitimacy is one of the conditions under which maritime trade looks ordinary rather than exceptional. Sanctions exploit this not always by commanding societies explicitly, but by changing the legal and reputational environment in which societies decide what they are willing to certify, continue, or defend. The result is a form of market restriction that feels technical while carrying unmistakable political effect. That dual character is precisely what makes it powerful and uneasy at once.

The unresolved question comes when the two logics press hardest against each other. When a classification society steps back from a vessel partly because the legal and reputational environment has changed, should the market treat that move as a neutral technical judgment, as a prudent compliance decision, or as a quiet geopolitical act whose consequences reach far beyond the survey report itself?

Claims, investigations, and the cost of doubt

On 23 March 2021, the container ship *Ever Given* grounded in the Suez Canal and turned a navigational casualty into a global legal and commercial drama. The accident itself was spectacular enough, but what followed is more instructive for sanctions analysis than the images of stranded traffic. Claims began. Liability questions multiplied. Cargo interests, insurers, correspondents, lawyers, surveyors, and authorities all demanded documents, timelines, and explanations. A voyage that had seemed routine was suddenly required to account for itself in exhausting detail. Once the claim file opened, the ship's story could no longer remain casual.

That is the crucial point. Claims do not merely ask who will pay. They ask what really happened, who was involved, what was declared, what was omitted, and whether the transaction behind the casualty can survive formal scrutiny. In ordinary trade, this can be burdensome enough. In sanctions-sensitive trade, it becomes dangerous. A voyage that has been kept commercially afloat through ambiguity, thin documentation, or carefully distributed responsibility may function well enough until nothing goes wrong. The claim changes the weather.

Paper becomes evidence fast.

This is why claims handling matters so much in maritime sanctions even though it sounds, at first glance, like a downstream issue. A sanctions regime may concentrate public attention on designations, ports, payment rails, or ship-to-ship transfers. The more revealing pressure can emerge later, when a casualty, cargo dispute, pollution incident, damage claim, delay claim, or contractual fight forces the trade into a documented, adversarial process. Show the ordinary sequence. A vessel suffers damage, a cargo arrives contaminated or late, a terminal alleges loss, or a third party claims pollution exposure. The insurer or P&I correspondent opens the file. Surveyors are appointed. Statements are taken. Bills of lading, charter terms, notices, logs, crew accounts, port records, cargo documents, and payment trails are assembled. The concept is forensic activation. The implication is clear: a claim turns ordinary commercial records into a structured test of truth.

This is precisely what evasive networks try to avoid. They do not merely dislike paying claims. They dislike what claims compel. A ship can often pass through commerce with imperfect documents so long as no institution has reason to compare every layer against every other. A claim creates that reason. An insurer asks whether the voyage was covered at all. A club asks whether the member disclosed material facts accurately. A cargo insurer asks whether origin and handling were correctly described. Lawyers ask who controlled the vessel, who directed the route, who knew what, and when. Ports and terminals revisit service records. Banks and traders may be drawn in if the commercial chain behind the cargo begins to matter. The claim becomes a lever for broader investigation without ever announcing itself as sanctions enforcement.

The difference between a claim and a denial matters here. Public commentary often imagines the decisive moment as a refusal to pay. In practice, delay can be enough. A claim under review may be commercially harmful long before anyone reaches a formal coverage decision. A charterer's cash flow tightens. A cargo owner cannot settle onward obligations. A shipowner faces mounting port costs, security demands, or legal fees. A bank sees the transaction move from routine settlement into dispute. A port agent becomes reluctant to continue exposure. Trust, in this setting, is visible in speed: how quickly institutions still move when doubt enters the file. Once that speed collapses, the voyage may have effectively failed even if the policy is never repudiated outright.

A named example from the sanctions-adjacent world helps clarify the mechanism. After the *Ever Given* grounding in 2021, the dispute over salvage compensation, detention, and cargo consequences illustrated how claims processes force maritime actors to reconstruct events through documents, technical evidence, and contractual relationships rather than through broad narrative alone. The case was not a sanctions matter, and it should not be bent into one. Its value lies elsewhere. It showed how quickly a maritime casualty opens a dense evidentiary environment in which formal records, operating decisions, insurance arrangements, and contractual roles are placed under pressure. A sanctions-sensitive voyage entering that environment would face not merely financial exposure, but a level of scrutiny its paper trail might not survive.

This is why claims handling changes the economics of concealment. Before a claim arises, opacity may be commercially useful. After a claim arises, opacity becomes expensive. An insurer deciding whether a casualty falls within cover wants to know who the assured really is, whether routing and cargo declarations were accurate, whether sanctions clauses were implicated, whether vessel management had shifted, and whether the underlying voyage remained lawful and disclosed. A P&I club wants to know whether the member's conduct stayed within the bounds of predictable, documentable risk. A hull underwriter wants to know whether the casualty narrative aligns with logbooks, reports, and survey evidence. The concept is the reversal of advantage. Ambiguity that once protected the trade now destabilises it.

Cargo origin becomes especially sensitive in this setting. A voyage carrying a commodity whose provenance may matter for sanctions, customs, or contractual reasons can often survive on ordinary paperwork if no one has an incentive to question it too deeply. A cargo claim, contamination dispute, delay claim, or delivery problem changes that incentive. Now the claimant, insurer, and often the court or arbitral process want to know what the cargo was, where it came from, how it was handled, what representations were made, and whether those representations were accurate. The visible behaviour shifts. Certificates are re-read. Bills of lading are compared against purchase contracts and manifests. Intermediate transfers that looked commercially routine begin to look evidentially awkward. A relabelled cargo may travel well. It litigates badly.

The same is true of counterparties. A sanctions-evasive structure often depends on fragmentation: one company appears in the charter, another in the bill of lading, another in the payment chain, another in vessel management, another in beneficial ownership declarations. Claims processes do not tolerate fragmentation politely. They ask who had authority, who owed duties, who received instructions, who can be served, who can settle, and who must disclose more. A company that was useful as an intermediary in trade may become a weakness in litigation if it has no real operational role, no documents beyond boilerplate, or no coherent explanation for why it sat in the chain at all. The claim forces the structure to account for itself, not merely to exist.

A second named example lies in the repeated maritime advisories issued by the United States and partner authorities during the late 2010s and early 2020s concerning deceptive shipping practices tied to sanctions evasion. These advisories consistently emphasised documentation, ownership opacity, AIS manipulation, and cargo obfuscation. What they implied, even when not stated in claims language, was that a formal dispute or casualty would expose these practices harshly. The real danger for evasive trade was not only interdiction. It was discoverability. A ship could avoid a boarding. It might not avoid the disclosure burden triggered by a pollution incident, cargo claim, collision, detention dispute, or insurance review. The threat of claims scrutiny, therefore, indirectly reinforces sanctions by making some voyages too evidently risky to handle through mainstream institutions.

This helps explain why delays are often commercially decisive even without a coverage denial. Maritime claims sit inside a time-sensitive world. Cargoes spoil, financing windows close, berths are missed, substitute tonnage must be found, counterparties grow impatient, and legal costs accumulate. A claim under investigation can freeze reimbursements, delay letters of undertaking, complicate port release, and disrupt the onward contractual chain. The insurer may simply be doing its job. The effect can still resemble enforcement. A doubtful voyage, once pushed into formal review, begins to encounter costs that no rhetorical assurance can cancel. The question is not only whether the claim will be paid. It is whether the voyage can survive the waiting.

A credible limitation should be faced directly. Claims processes do not exist to serve sanctions strategy, and it would be a mistake to romanticise them as neutral truth machines. They are shaped by institutional incentives, legal tactics, uneven evidence, and the financial interests of parties seeking to minimise liability or maximise recovery. A poorly documented but innocent voyage can suffer badly in claims handling. So can a lawful operator whose records are incomplete for mundane reasons of language, system mismatch, or commercial haste. Delay is not proof. Nor is scrutiny. A sanctions analyst who treats every claim as a hidden enforcement victory will misunderstand both insurance practice and maritime law.

That limitation, however, sharpens rather than weakens the core argument. The importance of claims lies not in their perfection, but in their structure. They create occasions on which institutions must gather documents, test narratives, compare records, and assign responsibility under conditions less forgiving than ordinary commercial flow. A weakly evidenced file may pass through routine trade because no one has time to fully interrogate it. The same file may fail once a casualty or dispute obliges formal questioning. Claims expose the difference between a voyage that merely looked acceptable and a voyage that can withstand reconstruction. That difference is central to sanctions enforcement because evasion so often depends on the assumption that reconstruction will never become necessary.

This is also why reputational effects spread beyond the immediate dispute. A ship or trading network drawn into a claim marked by inconsistencies, unclear ownership, unstable cargo narratives, or doubtful disclosures may find future dealings harder even if the formal legal outcome remains unresolved. Insurers remember troublesome files. Clubs read patterns. Charterers and ports ask who handled the last dispute and what it revealed. Banks notice counterparties that repeatedly generate evidentiary headaches. The claim's direct financial cost may be manageable. Its indirect market cost may be larger. Doubt, once documented, tends to travel.

The quiet motif here is the file drawer. Before the claim, documents can remain dispersed across desks, inboxes, service providers, and assumptions. After the claim, they are pulled into one place and asked to speak to one another. That is when contradictions begin to matter. The file drawer does not moralise. It compares. A date that looked harmless in isolation now clashes with a port call. A cargo certificate no longer sits comfortably beside the payment trail. A manager's role becomes inconsistent with the owner's representation. A sanctions clause that once seemed boilerplate suddenly governs the entire dispute. The file drawer is where commercial ambiguity loses its room to breathe.

For that reason, evasive networks prefer clean passages, quiet transfers, and low-drama trading patterns. They value routes and practices that minimise the chance of casualties, disputes, or claims large enough to trigger serious inquiry. This is not because they dislike operational inconvenience in the abstract. It is because claims invite institutions with money at risk to ask disciplined questions. An enforcement authority may miss a voyage. A claims handler may stumble into it by following liability. That accidental rigor is one of the quiet strengths of the maritime system. It does not replace sanctions law. It often makes sanctions law more dangerous to evade.

The unresolved question is therefore not whether claims reveal truth perfectly. They do not. It is whether a voyage whose paperwork has been designed to survive routine movement can also survive the slower, colder logic of a formal claims process once money, liability, and institutional memory all demand the same answer at once.

Chapter 7

Bunkering, Repairs, and Maritime Services

How does a ship get stopped without being stopped? That question matters more than any dramatic image of interdiction. A vessel can remain physically free to sail while becoming commercially immobile because the ordinary services that make a voyage possible begin to thin, hesitate, or disappear. Fuel is not delivered. A repair slot is not confirmed. A crew change becomes awkward. A manager asks one question too many. An accounts team refuses to release payment without cleaner documents. The voyage survives in theory and weakens in practice.

This is where maritime sanctions become most intimate. They move away from law in the abstract and into the service routines that hold a ship together between departure and arrival. A voyage does not rely only on hull, cargo, and route. It relies on credit, fuel quality, spare parts, technical expertise, trained seafarers, local agents, accountants, and managers who can still persuade others that the ship remains acceptable to touch. These are not supporting details. They are the working tissue of trade. Once pressure reaches them, enforcement begins to feel less like a public act of state and more like a gradual tightening of the service environment around the vessel.

The invoice matters first.

That is the central tension of this chapter. Maritime services are mundane enough to look apolitical and indispensable enough to become powerful under pressure. A bunker supplier does not need to act like a regulator to alter the fate of a voyage. A repair yard does not need to issue a geopolitical statement to make delay expensive. A crewing firm does not need to know every detail of a sanctions regime to decide that a last-minute change, a difficult payment route, or an unstable management structure is no longer worth the trouble. Outsourced managers and service companies become enforcement actors precisely because they were built to keep ships moving efficiently, and efficiency depends on refusing files that no longer cohere.

That matters because service provision is one of the places where maritime trade reveals its true dependency. Fuel supply rests on contracts, credit, port access, and trust in counterparties. Repairs and spare parts depend on skilled labour, technical records, and yards willing to expose their own name to the vessel's condition and ownership history. Crewing depends on certification, travel, vetting, payroll, and the confidence that the ship will not strand the people sent aboard it. Management firms control documents, invoices, vendors, and the daily administrative metabolism of the voyage. Once any one of these functions begins to doubt the file, the others tend to notice. Friction spreads quietly.

The stakes are especially high in harsher waters, where options are fewer and the cost of improvisation rises quickly. A bunker dispute in a crowded southern corridor may be expensive and still recoverable. A bunker problem near the edge of an Arctic season can rewrite the voyage. Deferred maintenance that might be tolerable for a time in gentler service becomes far more consequential when ice, cold, and distance punish weakness. A crewing issue that looks administrative in a temperate port can become operationally serious where specialist competence is harder to replace. Northern trade therefore turns ordinary services into concentrated leverage points. Geography makes the service file heavier.

Yet this is not simply a story of state pressure flowing downward through obedient firms. Maritime service providers have their own interests, fears, and thresholds. A bunker supplier worries about payment, documentation, and reputational exposure. A repair yard worries about liability, delay, and whether a difficult vessel will bring scrutiny or losses. A crewing agent worries about the safety, legality, and recoverability of the placement. A ship manager worries about every one of these at once. Firms internalise sanctions not as abstract moral commitments, but as operational risks that can damage their balance sheet, client base, insurance, or licence to carry on ordinary business. That is why service denial can look so restrained and still bite so hard.

The path ahead follows the ship through these dependencies rather than around them. It begins with fuel, where contracts and customer screening turn bunkering into a natural checkpoint. It then moves into repairs, spares, and cold-weather maintenance, where technical need narrows the field of acceptable providers. From there it turns to crewing, training, and certification, where human competence becomes a hidden fault line in evasive trade. It ends in the outsourced management offices where invoices, documents, and vendor relationships quietly determine whether the vessel remains governable enough for others to keep saying yes.

The deeper friction lies in what these services are being asked to become. Bunker suppliers, yards, crewing firms, and managers are not customs authorities, coast guards, or sanctions ministries. They are commercial actors with specialised tasks. Yet their decisions increasingly shape which voyages can still proceed in recognisable form. That creates a difficult balance. If they apply too little scrutiny, they risk becoming conduits for trade others now find intolerable. If they apply too much, they can distort lawful commerce, raise safety risks, and push ships towards thinner, less transparent service markets. A vessel denied mainstream repairs does not always stop trading. It may simply begin trading in worse condition and with a worse company.

That is why this chapter sits so close to the living centre of maritime sanctions. The most consequential forms of pressure often arrive not through seizure, but through withheld routine: the missing bunker nomination, the delayed spare part, the crew list that no longer satisfies, the manager who decides the accounts are no longer clean enough to defend. The invoice matters again because it is where law, commerce, and technical necessity meet in the least glamorous and most decisive way. The harder question is not whether a ship can still move after one service provider steps back. It is how many ordinary services can begin to doubt the voyage before movement itself becomes a fiction sustained only on paper.

Fuel supply as a compliance node

In May 2020, the United States Departments of State, Treasury, and Coast Guard issued a sanctions advisory that drew unusual attention to a mundane truth of shipping: fuel does not arrive by magic, and the act of supplying it creates one of the clearest compliance checkpoints in the voyage. A vessel can conceal ownership through layered companies, rename itself, alter its management, and route through thinner oversight. It still needs bunkers. That need forces the ship back into contracts, counterparties, invoices, port arrangements, and credit decisions that somebody must be willing to defend.

Fuel tells the truth.

Not always the whole truth, and not always immediately. But enough of it. A bunker stem requires a supplier, a buyer or intermediary, a payment route, a delivery location, a nominated vessel, and documentary confidence that the transaction will not later become a regulatory or financial liability. The ship may be physically at sea, yet the fuel supply chain drags it back into administrative visibility. This is why bunkering matters so much to sanctions enforcement. It is not merely a technical necessity. It is a commercial event that forces the voyage to explain itself.

That is the first claim worth making plainly. Fuel supply is a compliance node because it combines three things that sanctions regimes exploit well: dependency, documentation, and timing. Show the sequence in ordinary terms. A vessel approaching a bunkering port or arranging offshore delivery needs quantity agreed, specifications confirmed, credit or prepayment settled, and port or local service permissions in place. A supplier will want the vessel's name, IMO number, flag, ownership or management details, intended payment route, and often some comfort about cargo, itinerary, or counterparties if the file already looks difficult. The concept is transactional exposure. The implication is immediate. A supplier does not need to prove an entire sanctions case before saying no. It only needs to decide that the risk of saying yes has become too awkward to carry.

This is why bunker suppliers increasingly resemble gatekeepers even when they are acting from ordinary commercial instincts rather than public policy fervour. Fuel is expensive, margins can be narrow, and delivery creates not only credit exposure but regulatory and reputational exposure. If a stem later appears connected to a sanctioned voyage, a deceptive shipping network, or a payment chain that should have raised alarms, the supplier may face consequences far beyond an unpaid invoice. That risk changes behaviour. Trust, in this setting, is visible in whether the supplier extends credit, accepts the named buyer, recognises the insurer, clears the payment structure, and feels comfortable enough with the documentation to send the bunker barge alongside. Once that confidence weakens, the ship's room for manoeuvre narrows quickly.

A named example helps anchor the point. During the late 2010s and early 2020s, repeated United States and partner advisories concerning Iranian and Venezuelan oil sanctions highlighted deceptive shipping practices that implicated not only cargo and ownership, but the wider service chain supporting vessels engaged in such trade. Bunkering firms were part of the intended audience because the delivery of fuel could no longer be treated as a morally neutral act detached from the vessel's broader commercial profile. The practical lesson was not that every supplier suddenly became a sanctions investigator. It was that the ordinary act of selling fuel had become a place where counterparties, documentation, and payment arrangements had to withstand more disciplined scrutiny than before.

That scrutiny tends to begin with customer screening, but it does not end there. Screening can catch a designated name, a familiar vessel, or an obviously problematic ownership link. Harder cases lie in the grey space between clean and prohibited. A vessel may not itself be designated. The registered owner may look harmless. The trading history may be ambiguous rather than damning. Yet other features create discomfort: a recent flag change, a new manager, a payment request routed through an unfamiliar intermediary, documentation that arrives late or in strangely uneven quality, or a request to supply in a location whose commercial logic feels thinner than its geographical convenience. The concept is cumulative doubt. The implication is that bunker compliance often turns on patterns rather than on one decisive red flag.

This is where documentation demands become operationally important. A supplier can ask for more than the basic stem request: confirmation of ownership and management, evidence of insurance, beneficial ownership statements, cargo details, routing explanations, sanctions compliance certifications, advance payment, or stronger counterparty guarantees. None of these requests needs to look political. They are contractual and credit decisions with compliance implications. Yet each extra demand alters the economics of the voyage. A ship that thrives on opacity pays a price when fuel can be obtained only by producing cleaner paper. A network that relies on speed and fragmented counterparties suffers when suppliers start slowing the process down. Documentation becomes friction. Friction becomes deterrence.

This dynamic is even sharper in remote or harsh environments, where bunkering options are fewer and the cost of being refused is higher. A ship operating in ordinary dense trade lanes may recover from a supplier's refusal by turning to another port or another bunker provider. A ship in more remote waters, or one running close to seasonal limits, may not enjoy that luxury. Geography magnifies the compliance function of bunkering because fuel denial travels further when there are fewer substitutes. That is why cold-water and peripheral trades deserve attention here. They do not simply make bunkering more logistically complex. They make every fuel decision more consequential.

Remote refuelling arrangements become attractive under these conditions for reasons that are commercially understandable and compliance-relevant at the same time. A vessel that wants to avoid close scrutiny at a major port may prefer delivery offshore, at anchorage, or through less visible arrangements where the number of institutions involved is smaller, and the documentary expectations may be thinner. The appeal is not mysterious. Fewer formal touchpoints mean fewer chances for someone to compare ownership, routing, payment, and cargo narratives against one another. The concept is reduced exposure. The implication is unsettling but clear: remote refuelling can serve lawful logistical convenience and strategic opacity at once, which is why disciplined inference matters more than moral panic.

A second named example lies in the wider trade patterns that developed around sanctioned oil movements through waters near Fujairah, the eastern Mediterranean, and parts of East and Southeast Asia during the late 2010s and early 2020s. Public reporting and regulatory notices repeatedly suggested that vessels connected to sanctions-sensitive cargoes sought to reduce exposure through altered routing, ship-to-ship transfers, and service arrangements that kept them away from the most demanding commercial checkpoints. Bunkering sat inside that pattern. A vessel that can fuel without passing through an institutionally thick port environment preserves more ambiguity around its wider trade. What mattered was not that remote or offshore fuelling was inherently illicit. It was that, in the context of already difficult voyages, it could reduce the number of records and relationships available for later comparison.

This does not mean bunker suppliers are omnipotent. A credible limitation is necessary. Fuel markets are varied, incentives differ across jurisdictions, and suppliers do not all possess the same compliance infrastructure, risk appetite, or access to information. Some will screen carefully and demand substantial documentation. Others will rely on narrower checks, particularly where margins, local practice, or political exposure differ. A vessel denied by one supplier may still obtain fuel elsewhere, perhaps on worse commercial terms, through a less transparent intermediary, or from a provider more willing to absorb uncertainty. Sanctions analysis becomes lazy when it assumes that refusing bunkers at one node equals immobilising the ship. It may instead mean displacement into murkier channels.

Still, displacement is not trivial. A vessel forced away from mainstream bunkering markets often pays in more than money. It may lose flexibility in route planning. It may accept inferior credit terms. It may become more dependent on intermediaries whose own documentation weakens the file. It may need to coordinate fuel around less convenient anchorages or riskier timing. Those are not cosmetic inconveniences. They alter the voyage's resilience. A ship operating under uncertain fuel arrangements has less room for delay, detour, or unexpected inspection. Bunkering pressure therefore works even when it does not achieve perfect exclusion. It narrows operational margin.

The role of credit is especially important here because fuel supply is rarely a simple cash-on-delivery affair in major commercial practice. Credit terms reflect trust in the buyer, the vessel, the corporate structure behind the trade, and the likelihood that disputes can be pursued through recognisable institutions if things go wrong. Once sanctions pressure rises, credit becomes harder to obtain. A supplier may insist on prepayment, reject certain banks, refuse certain intermediaries, or require documentation that effectively reopens the whole compliance file. Risk, then, is visible in whether the bunker stem remains ordinary trade or turns into a quasi-investigation before the first tonne is delivered. A cautious supplier does not need to deny the stem outright. It can make the conditions of supply heavy enough that the trade no longer looks worth doing.

This is why bunkering often functions as a better compliance checkpoint than more dramatic tools. It is routine, recurrent, and unavoidable. A ship can sometimes avoid a port call, delay a repair, change its management, or rearrange its paperwork. It cannot run indefinitely without fuel. That dependence gives suppliers a practical influence disproportionate to their public visibility. They sit close enough to the voyage to ask difficult questions, and far enough from sovereign coercion to exercise leverage through ordinary commercial discretion. The bunker stem is not a courtroom hearing. It is often where the voyage first learns whether its story still works under pressure.

The quiet motif here is the invoice. Fuel itself is physical, but the enforcement significance of bunkering lies in the paper and promises wrapped around delivery: who ordered, who paid, who guaranteed, who received, where delivery occurred, under what terms, and with which supporting declarations. The invoice records a transfer of commodity and a transfer of confidence. A clean invoice in a mainstream bunkering chain says that several institutions found the trade intelligible enough to touch. A difficult invoice says the opposite. The ship may still receive fuel. It receives it under a shadow that tends to travel with the next transaction.

For maritime sanctions, the wider lesson is austere. Fuel supply matters not because bunker firms are substitute coast guards, but because shipping depends on recurring moments where commercial actors must decide whether a voyage remains acceptable enough to provision. These moments are rich in documentation, sensitive to counterparty risk, and tied to geography in ways that can sharpen enforcement pressure. Remote refuelling may offer evasive networks temporary relief by thinning the institutional audience. Yet even that relief usually comes at the price of higher cost, greater operational strain, and a weaker paper trail when something later goes wrong.

The unresolved question is not whether fuel can still be bought somewhere. It usually can. The harder question is when a ship's need for bunkers stops being an ordinary procurement problem and becomes the point at which too many suppliers, ports, and payment channels begin to decide that the voyage is no longer worth the paperwork required to keep it moving.

Repairs, spares, and ice-class maintenance

In March 1989, the *Exxon Valdez* struck Bligh Reef in Prince William Sound, Alaska, and turned a navigational casualty into a lasting lesson about what harsh waters do to ships, institutions, and public tolerance for avoidable risk. The disaster was not a sanctions case, and it would be foolish to pretend otherwise. Its value here lies in something colder and more structural. In northern and sub-Arctic environments, mechanical weakness does not remain a private inconvenience for long. Wear, delay, misjudgement, and deferred attention can move quickly from technical defect to political problem. Steel remembers the route.

That memory matters because cold-water trade imposes a different tempo of maintenance. Ice, low temperatures, heavy weather, remote operations, and long distances between reliable support points place unusual strain on hull, machinery, auxiliary systems, deck equipment, and the administrative machinery that proves the ship remains fit to operate. A vessel in easier service may absorb minor delay or imperfect planning with manageable consequences. A vessel working at the edge of season or in demanding ice conditions has less room for bravado. Repairs are not a side issue. They are part of the voyage's legal and commercial credibility.

Maintenance grows teeth fast.

This is why repairs, spare parts, and specialist yard access matter so much to sanctions enforcement. A ship can often survive political pressure longer than it can survive unresolved technical dependency. Show the sequence in ordinary terms. A vessel operating in cold waters needs a particular component, a drydock slot, class-related work, a survey, or specialist labour familiar with its operating profile. The number of providers able and willing to do the work is small. The transaction therefore becomes a checkpoint. A yard asks who owns the vessel, who will pay, whether insurers remain comfortable, whether sanctions exposure exists, whether export controls affect the parts, whether servicing the ship will bring regulatory or reputational trouble. The concept is concentrated capability. The implication is decisive: where technical support is scarce, service denial carries far more force than it would in a dense, forgiving maritime market.

That force is often indirect. No authority needs to seize the vessel. No dramatic public refusal is required. A supplier can simply decline to provide a part. A yard can refuse a booking. A service company can delay acceptance pending clarifications that never become satisfactory. A classification-related survey can become harder to arrange. The vessel still exists, the route may still be open, and the cargo may still be waiting. Yet the operational chain begins to fail because a ship in cold-water service cannot improvise indefinitely around technical need. Risk, here, is visible in the most practical decisions imaginable: whether a yard offers a slot, whether a procurement team places an order, whether a superintendent can still obtain the part before the next weather window closes.

Ice-class maintenance sharpens this dynamic because specialised ships rely on specialised confidence. One need not descend into engineering minutiae to see the institutional point. A vessel intended for ice service is not merely another hull with a different trade pattern. It sits inside a denser web of expectations about structural condition, machinery reliability, survey discipline, and operational limits. That means the providers who maintain, inspect, and support such vessels are not easily replaceable. A mainstream commercial cargo vessel may find multiple yards or workshops able to perform equivalent work across several regions. A cold-water or ice-class vessel often cannot. Technical support concentrates. Enforcement pressure, once it reaches that concentration point, becomes more potent precisely because alternatives are few and often visibly inferior.

A named example from the Russian Arctic makes the mechanism plain. The specialised carrier fleet built around projects such as Yamal LNG depended not merely on ice-capable hulls, but on a continuing ecosystem of technical support, survey confidence, spare parts logistics, and service relationships able to sustain demanding northern operations. Once sanctions pressure intensified around related Russian Arctic trade after 2022, the crucial question was not only whether ships could still sail or cargoes still existed.

It was whether the surrounding support lattice could be maintained at a level recognised by insurers, charterers, ports, and technical overseers. The lesson is wider than one project. Cold-water shipping is sustained less by heroic vessel design than by ongoing access to competent repair and maintenance structures. Interrupt those, and the voyage's future narrows quickly.

The importance of spare parts is often underestimated because they sound too mundane to carry geopolitical weight. Yet maritime sanctions repeatedly demonstrate that small things matter most when they are not truly substitutable. A single specialist part, a software update, a certified component, or a service visit from a trusted technician can decide whether a vessel remains within the envelope of acceptable operation. Show the everyday reality. A superintendent identifies a fault or rising wear trend. The ship can continue for a time, but not indefinitely. Procurement begins. The vendor asks questions. Export restrictions, sanctions exposure, payment routes, ownership opacity, or the destination of the vessel make the sale awkward. Delay begins. The concept is technical bottleneck. The implication is not merely inconvenience. The vessel's operational margin shrinks while the paper trail thickens around the unresolved defect.

This is where commercial caution and safety pressure start to align without becoming identical. A yard or supplier may refuse involvement because sanctions exposure looks unmanageable. A manager or owner may respond by postponing non-urgent work in the hope of avoiding scrutiny, preserving cash flow, or simply keeping the vessel trading until a more permissive opportunity appears. Deferred maintenance is not always sinister. Shipping is full of imperfect timing, temporary workarounds, and cost discipline. But in cold-water service, the meaning of deferral changes. The environment punishes optimism. A decision to delay can migrate from commercial expediency into safety degradation more quickly than many shore-based decision-makers admit. The ship can keep moving while becoming less governable.

That risk deserves plain treatment without sensationalism. Vessels under pressure may defer repairs because every yard visit is also an encounter with records, class oversight, service providers, insurers, and ports. A ship entering a reputable facility invites scrutiny of certificates, management, ownership, payment, and technical condition all at once. A manager seeking to preserve optionality may prefer to keep the ship away from those touchpoints for as long as possible. The resulting behaviour can look deceptively disciplined from a distance: fewer major stops, fewer formal interventions, fewer opportunities for outsiders to ask difficult questions. The reality may be more brittle. Work accumulates. Small deficiencies become linked. Routine maintenance becomes a future casualty's pre-history.

A second named example comes from the wider adjustments in Russian-linked shipping after the invasion of Ukraine. As access to mainstream technical services, parts, and recognised support structures became more difficult for some vessels and projects, the market did not simply stop. It adapted unevenly. Alternative yards, suppliers, and service pathways emerged or were sought. Some vessels continued trading. The important lesson is not that maintenance denial produces immediate paralysis. It is that it often pushes ships towards thinner technical ecosystems whose quality, transparency, and international acceptance may be weaker. A vessel can remain active under such conditions. It rarely remains as commercially or operationally comfortable as before. That decline in comfort is part of the enforcement effect.

Still, a credible limitation must be faced. Not every delay in repair or shortage of spares reflects sanctions pressure. Maritime maintenance is often messy for ordinary reasons: yard congestion, procurement delays, weather, financing strain, labour shortages, or the strategic scheduling decisions owners make in all markets. Cold-water ships are not uniquely sanctimonious about planning. They too operate under commercial pressure, imperfect information, and conflicting priorities. A sanctions analyst who attributes every deferred repair to evasion or coercion will misread the trade badly. There are lawful reasons why work slips. There are innocent reasons why parts arrive late. The file must be read against wider operational reality.

That limitation does not soften the central argument. It refines the method. The relevant question is not whether delay exists, but what sort of pattern it forms. Does maintenance deferral coincide with ownership opacity, insurer unease, shifting management, marginal service providers, or routes that avoid major scrutiny points? Do alternative repair arrangements make commercial and technical sense, or do they look like expedients chosen mainly because more reputable providers would ask harder questions? Does the ship's paper remain coherent as the technical story becomes more strained? The answer emerges not from one missed yard booking, but from the relationship between technical necessity and the shrinking set of institutions willing to engage with it.

This is why capable providers matter so much. A specialist northern yard or trusted service company does more than perform work. It lends confidence through its own standards, records, and reputation. Ports, insurers, charterers, and financiers understand what it means when a vessel is maintained inside that kind of ecosystem. They also notice when the ship leaves it. The movement from recognised technical support to more marginal arrangements changes how the vessel is read. Trust, in this setting, becomes visible in whether a provider signs the work order, whether a class-related issue can be resolved cleanly, whether the next port accepts the maintenance history without deep discomfort, and whether the insurer still believes the risk remains understandable.

The quiet motif here is the wrench. Not as a romantic image of labour, but as a reminder that maritime sanctions often turn on physical maintenance performed by institutions that must decide whether they still want to touch the ship. A wrench in a reputable yard implies records, standards, invoices, known personnel, and a paper trail that can later be examined. A missing wrench implies something else: deferred work, improvised support, or a ship trying to stay outside the frame long enough to complete one more voyage. The difference is operational before it becomes symbolic.

For sanctions enforcement, the deeper lesson is austere. Technical dependency can be more constraining than legal prohibition because it reaches the ship where rhetoric cannot help it. A vessel under pressure may still find fuel, cargo, or even a willing port. Finding credible maintenance support in harsh service conditions is often harder. That is especially true in cold waters, where the number of capable providers is small and the consequences of poor upkeep are enlarged by geography. Service denial therefore works not by proving every allegation in advance, but by forcing difficult ships into a harsher trade-off between scrutiny and deterioration.

That leaves the hardest question where it belongs: not in abstract law, but in the sequence of decisions made before a casualty occurs. When a vessel under sanctions pressure begins deferring maintenance because reputable yards, suppliers, or service firms will no longer engage easily, at what point does ordinary commercial adaptation become a form of technical self-erosion that the wider maritime system can neither safely ignore nor easily police before something goes wrong?

Crewing, training, and certification

In March 2020, as pandemic border closures spread across ports from Singapore to Rotterdam, crew changes became one of the clearest demonstrations of a truth shipping often hides in plain sight: a vessel does not trade on steel alone. It trades through people whose documents must be accepted, whose travel must be arranged, whose certificates must be recognised, and whose presence on board must satisfy not only safety rules but the comfort of insurers, managers, ports, and counterparties. When crew movement stalled, ships that remained technically serviceable still drifted into operational strain. The human chain had tightened.

That episode was not a sanctions story. Its value lies elsewhere. It showed how crewing depends on a lattice of permissions that can harden suddenly and unevenly. Visas, endorsements, flag approvals, airport transit, agency coordination, payroll, training records, medical clearances, and shore-side vetting do not sit outside maritime enforcement. They form one of its quieter fault lines. A vessel may change owner, manager, or route on paper and still discover that the decisive question is simpler: who can actually be put on board, with which documents, through which jurisdictions, under whose name? The passport matters first.

This is why crewing deserves more attention than sanctions analysis often grants it. Human labour at sea is not merely an employment issue attached to the voyage after the real commercial decisions have been made. It is part of the voyage's legal and operational architecture. Show the ordinary sequence. A ship requires licensed officers and certified ratings in numbers and combinations suited to its trade. The manager or crewing firm must source them, verify certificates, arrange travel, secure sign-on approvals, pay wages through accepted banking channels, and reassure ports, insurers, and flag administrators that the vessel remains properly manned. The concept is personnel dependency. The implication is direct: any trade operating under sanctions pressure must still survive a series of human-documentary tests that are harder to improvise than a name change or a new invoice.

Training and certification sharpen this dependency because maritime labour is not infinitely interchangeable. One need not descend into technical manuals to see the institutional point. Certain trades, especially those involving harsh weather, specialised cargoes, or remote routes, depend on seafarers whose credentials and experience carry more than formal value. Employers, insurers, and authorities do not merely want a warm body in the right rank. They want a person whose training record can be trusted, whose endorsements align with the vessel and route, and whose presence does not create further regulatory or operational fragility.

A crewing problem, therefore, becomes a compliance problem the moment the ship needs people who cannot be replaced casually.

This is where sanctions pressure enters through vetting rather than drama. Crewing agencies and ship managers increasingly screen seafarers, counterparties, managers, and payment routes not because they aspire to police geopolitics, but because the costs of getting the file wrong have become too high. A crewing firm placing officers on a vessel with opaque ownership, unstable management, doubtful insurance, or a difficult sanctions profile may worry about more than regulation. It may worry about unpaid wages, blocked payroll, stranded personnel, reputational exposure, and the possibility that it has placed people aboard a ship that will later prove hard to service, insure, or relieve. Trust, here, is visible in practical decisions: whether the crewing agency accepts the order, whether the payroll route still clears, whether the visa support letter is issued, whether a travel plan is built with confidence or with caveats.

A named example clarifies the broader mechanism. The crew change crisis that intensified after March 2020, recognised by the International Maritime Organization and labour organisations as a severe operational problem, demonstrated how quickly ships become vulnerable when crew travel, certification recognition, and relief planning fall out of alignment. Again, the crisis was not born of sanctions. Yet it revealed the same institutional structure on which sanctions pressure later acts: crew movement depends on states, ports, managers, insurers, medical clearances, visa systems, and wage channels all accepting the underlying voyage as normal enough to facilitate. Once that normality is in doubt, human logistics become a point of leverage rather than a background function.

This matters especially in sanctions-sensitive trades because crewing is often more revealing than ownership paper. A ship can acquire a fresh registered owner quickly. It is harder to replace an entire competent crew, build new crewing relationships, and stabilise training and payroll systems without leaving traces. Last-minute crew changes are particularly telling. They do not prove misconduct, and many lawful reasons explain them: illness, family emergency, visa trouble, contract expiry, fatigue management, or operational necessity. Yet in a file already troubled by opaque ownership, unusual routing, or unstable service arrangements, sudden crew substitutions can signal broader instability. The concept is human discontinuity. The implication is that counterparties read rapid personnel turnover as a clue about whether the ship remains governable.

That reading is commercially rational. A port agent notified of hurried crew changes may ask whether immigration and certification documents remain in order. An insurer may wonder whether operational discipline is slipping. A bunker supplier or repair yard may infer that the ship is working through difficulties not fully captured in its formal paperwork. A bank or cargo interest may conclude that the vessel is entering a more fragile phase of management. None of these actors needs proof of wrongdoing. They need only decide that the cumulative discomfort now exceeds the ordinary patience of trade. The crew list, in such moments, becomes part of the compliance file.

A second named example lies in the broader restructuring of Russian-linked shipping after the invasion of Ukraine in 2022. As ownership, management, insurance, and service patterns shifted, crewing arrangements also came under pressure from banking difficulties, travel restrictions, altered port appetites, and the reluctance of some service providers to remain involved. Not every adjustment was evasive. Many were lawful and unavoidable responses to a disrupted environment. Yet the operational lesson was clear. A ship whose corporate profile changes under pressure often discovers that its crewing chain changes too: new agencies, different payroll pathways, altered embarkation ports, unfamiliar visa support, and greater dependence on narrower labour pools. Operational control migrates through human logistics just as surely as it does through contracts.

This is one reason certification matters beyond formal compliance. A certificate is not only evidence that a seafarer once passed an examination or completed training. It is part of the wider claim that the ship remains professionally manned in a way others can trust. That claim becomes fragile when the vessel sits inside an evasive or marginal network. A crewing firm may have difficulty verifying endorsements from unfamiliar channels. A port state control officer may look more closely at documentation when the vessel's wider file already appears unstable. A manager relying on improvised crewing solutions may find that what was formally sufficient on paper does not reassure insurers, charterers, or ports. The certificate opens doors only when the institutions seeing it still believe the rest of the ship's story.

This is particularly acute in cold-water or specialist operations, where competence cannot be treated as a generic commodity. Harsh environments magnify the consequences of fatigue, poor communication, uneven familiarisation, or rushed relief planning. The question is not simply whether officers possess valid papers. It is whether the crewing arrangement itself demonstrates stability, planning, and recognisable oversight. A ship working in ice, remote waters, or demanding seasonal routes with last-minute crewing fixes invites a different kind of attention. The risk becomes visible in behaviour: managers shorten handovers, agencies scramble for replacements, travel routes grow more improvised, and the vessel begins to depend on a narrower set of acceptable people. Human resilience becomes thin.

A credible limitation must be admitted. Crewing disruption is common in ordinary shipping, and not every difficult crew change carries sanctions meaning. Maritime labour markets are global, fragmented, and frequently messy. Visa delays, medical issues, family emergencies, wage disputes, geopolitical crises unrelated to sanctions, and simple poor planning all produce sudden changes that can look suspicious from afar. A sanctions analyst who over-reads crew movement will generate false alarms and risk mistaking maritime reality for evidence of concealment. Lawful vessels also suffer rushed reliefs, uneven paperwork, and frayed personnel systems. The sea is administratively untidy even before politics makes it worse.

That limitation does not undercut the larger argument. It defines the pattern that matters. Crewing becomes a compliance signal when personnel instability aligns with other forms of institutional strain: altered ownership, hurried management changes, unclear payment channels, unusual route choices, thinner insurance, or more marginal service providers. A single late crew substitution proves little. A cluster of last-minute changes, unresolved documentation, awkward travel arrangements, and altered payroll pathways suggests something more. The task is not to moralise the crew list. It is to ask whether the human system around the vessel still looks like ordinary commercial administration or like a ship losing access to the mainstream structures that usually keep seafarers moving safely and lawfully.

The hidden vulnerability for evasion schemes lies exactly there. Paper companies can be incorporated quickly. Flags can be changed. Cargo descriptions can be softened. Human logistics resist such speed. A crewing agency needs names, documents, travel plans, wage arrangements, and confidence that the ship will not become a stranded liability. Seafarers themselves need assurance that they will be paid, relieved, and able to disembark in ports that still recognise the vessel as legitimate enough to handle. A network trying to avoid scrutiny may discover that its hardest problem is not concealing the ship from systems, but persuading enough human institutions to place real people aboard it under their own name.

The quiet motif here is the passport, because crewing turns enforcement into a series of human permissions. A passport must be stamped, a visa honoured, a certificate recognised, a crew list accepted, a flight booked, a wage paid. Each of these steps forces the voyage back into a world of ordinary institutions that can still say no without looking geopolitical. The passport is not a metaphor from a distance. It is the practical document by which the vessel proves, again and again, that its operations remain acceptable enough for others to help staff them.

This is why crewing should be seen as a leverage point rather than a welfare footnote. Human labour is where sanctions pressure meets operational continuity in the least glamorous and often the most revealing form. A ship can survive rumours about ownership longer than it can survive a breakdown in competent manning. Last-minute crew changes, unstable certification trails, or brittle travel arrangements may not prove evasion, but they can tell counterparties that the vessel's wider support system is fraying. Once that conclusion spreads, the next refusal becomes easier.

The unresolved question is therefore not whether a ship can still find seafarers. It usually can. The harder question is when the effort required to source, vet, move, certify, and pay those seafarers becomes so improvised, so compressed, or so dependent on marginal channels that the crew list itself begins to reveal what the ownership papers still struggle to say plainly.

Ship management services and outsourcing

In September 2019, when sanctions pressure hit COSCO Shipping Tanker (Dalian) entities, the most consequential decisions were not made only in ministries, courts, or boardrooms. They were made in management offices: in the accounting teams that decided whether an invoice would be paid, in the operations desks that chose whether a bunker order would be placed, in the crewing departments that judged whether a relief plan still looked defensible, and in the compliance staff who had to decide whether the ship's paper could still be carried through ordinary commerce. The sanctions list named companies. The management office translated that fact into movement or stoppage.

That is the hidden force of outsourcing in shipping. A vessel may be legally owned by one company and commercially directed by another, yet its daily life often runs through a network of specialist firms handling technical management, accounting, procurement, crewing, safety administration, insurance coordination, and voyage support. These firms are not decorative. They are the operators of the paper engine. When sanctions pressure rises, it is often outsourced management - not only the registered owner - that decides whether the ship can still function as a recognisable commercial object. The inbox governs the voyage.

This is why outsourcing should be understood as an enforcement pressure point rather than as administrative background. Show the ordinary sequence. A shipowner appoints an external management company to run the vessel's technical operations, arrange crew, pay vendors, handle class and certification matters, coordinate with insurers, and manage procurement. Another service firm may process accounts or act as a commercial intermediary. A travel provider handles relief planning. A logistics office manages spares and stores. On paper, these arrangements look like efficiency. In practice, they concentrate operational control in institutions that touch almost every document and payment required to keep the ship moving. The concept is delegated gatekeeping. The implication is decisive: when management firms refuse, delay, or question, they can immobilise a voyage without ever appearing to act politically.

The reason is simple. Outsourced managers control paperwork at the points where other institutions are most vulnerable. They prepare or transmit invoices. They confirm vendor identities. They coordinate bunker stems, repair orders, and port agency appointments. They submit payroll instructions. They liaise with insurers and class. They maintain certificates, crew records, and technical files. They answer the calls when something goes wrong. In sanctions-sensitive trades, this makes them far more than clerks. They become the place where law, commerce, and practical seamanship meet in a stream of ordinary decisions. A ship whose manager no longer believes the file can survive scrutiny will begin to slow even before any port or bank formally objects.

That slowdown can start with something as unglamorous as an invoice. A bunker supplier submits a bill. The management company must decide whether the counterparty remains acceptable, whether the payment route is still usable, whether the fuel order itself fits the vessel's authorised trading pattern, and whether sending the money may later become impossible to explain. A crewing agency asks for confirmation of wages and travel. The manager must consider whether payroll can still move through ordinary banks and whether visa support letters remain prudent. A repair yard wants assurance of payment and ownership clarity before accepting the booking. The manager has to decide whether the vessel's profile will survive the yard's due diligence. None of these are grand strategic acts. Together they decide whether the ship is still a functioning participant in mainstream trade.

This is why management firms become compliance gatekeepers even when they were hired for efficiency rather than enforcement. They see enough of the transaction to recognise when the story begins to fray. A port may see only arrival. A bank may see only payment instructions. An insurer may see only the risk file placed before it. The manager sees the chain: the owner requesting a route, the bunker supplier asking for confirmation, the crew change becoming difficult, the insurer asking sharper questions, the spare-part order routed through a new intermediary, the invoice address suddenly changing, the management agreement itself perhaps amended in a way that alters who can instruct what. The concept is cumulative visibility. The implication is that managers are often the first institutions to notice when a vessel's commercial life has become too awkward to defend.

A named example from the Iranian sanctions environment makes the mechanism plain. During the late 2010s and early 2020s, public advisories repeatedly emphasised that deceptive shipping practices involved not only vessels and cargoes, but the surrounding service network: shell owners, changing managers, dubious documentation, and shifting intermediaries. The crucial lesson was that management changes were not merely formal rearrangements. They affected who handled banking, who paid suppliers, who arranged crew, who corresponded with insurers, and who answered due diligence questions. Once management moved to thinner or less transparent firms, the vessel's relationship with mainstream commerce often weakened even if title remained unchanged. Outsourcing had become the real front line of legitimacy.

Accounting support illustrates this especially well because payments are where administrative neatness is most severely tested. A ship manager or outsourced accounts team may pay crew wages, fuel invoices, class fees, agent disbursements, spares suppliers, and emergency service providers from a set of approved banking relationships. If sanctions pressure unsettles those relationships, the file must be reworked quickly or the voyage begins to stall. A bank refuses a payment. A correspondent relationship becomes unusable. An invoice from a familiar vendor must be routed differently. A new payee appears. The accounting office now becomes a compliance office whether it likes the role or not. Risk, in this context, is visible in held transfers, revised signatory chains, requests for additional documentation, or the sudden insistence on prepayment where credit once sufficed.

This is also why management transfers can be so revealing. A ship may be sold without changing manager, or remain under the same owner while changing manager entirely. From a sanctions perspective, the latter can matter more. A new manager often means new bank accounts, new payroll systems, new crewing agencies, new purchasing channels, new safety administration, new email domains, new signatories, and a different internal appetite for risk. The ship may appear unchanged to an outsider following only registry data. Internally, its operational metabolism may have been rebuilt. The concept here is administrative reconstitution. The implication is that control can migrate without a sale, and compliance responsibility migrates with it.

A second named example lies in the restructuring that followed sanctions pressure on Russian-linked shipping after February 2022. As owners, operators, insurers, and registries adjusted, management arrangements also shifted. New service firms appeared, payment routes changed, and the practical burden of keeping vessels supplied and documented moved into offices forced to decide, line by line, whether the trade could still be serviced. Not every change concealed misconduct. Many reflected lawful commercial adaptation. Yet the operational lesson was unmistakable. A ship's ability to remain in mainstream commerce depended not only on legal ownership, but on whether recognisable management firms, accounts teams, and logistics providers were still prepared to attach their own processes and reputations to it.

That dependence becomes even sharper in harsher operating environments. Northern routes, specialist cargoes, and technically demanding ships require more from management firms than ordinary trades do. Procurement must be tighter. Crew planning must be more credible. Repair and spare-part logistics must be handled with less margin for error. Insurance and class relationships require more attentive maintenance. In such contexts, outsourcing does not merely save costs. It centralises operational intelligence in a small number of offices. If those offices decide the ship's paperwork, payments, or vendor relationships are no longer defensible, the vessel's room for manoeuvre contracts very quickly. The manager's refusal travels farther because the environment is less forgiving.

A credible limitation should be stated plainly. Outsourcing is not suspicious in itself. Commercial shipping would function far less efficiently without specialist management, accounts handling, crewing support, procurement firms, and technical service providers. Many owners, including entirely reputable ones, lack the scale or desire to run these functions in-house.

Outsourcing often improves compliance because specialist firms know how to maintain records, deal with regulators, and operate disciplined vendor networks. A sanctions analyst who treats every outsourced function as a red flag will misunderstand the industry and burden lawful trade unnecessarily. Delegation is ordinary. Sometimes it is prudent.

That limitation does not weaken the central point. It clarifies where attention should fall. The issue is not whether management is outsourced, but how the outsourced structure behaves under pressure. Does the manager maintain coherent records across payments, crew, suppliers, and technical support? Do accounting arrangements remain stable and explainable? Are vendor selections commercially sensible, or do they suddenly shift towards marginal providers when scrutiny intensifies? Does the service firm answer due diligence questions with specificity, or with formulaic distance from the voyage it is supposedly managing? The answers reveal whether outsourcing is serving efficiency, concealment, or some unstable combination of both.

This is why outsourcing often works as a lever for indirect enforcement. States may not directly control management firms, accountants, or logistics providers. They do not need to. Those firms respond to their own exposures. They fear unpaid invoices, blocked transfers, reputational damage, insurance problems, regulatory attention, and the possibility that one awkward ship will contaminate wider client relationships. As a result, they become selective. They may refuse new mandates, terminate old ones, demand stronger paperwork, reroute payments only within defensible limits, or insist on more intrusive client screening. These are commercial decisions. Their cumulative effect can rival direct legal prohibitions in practice.

The quiet motif here is the inbox. Shipping still depends on steel, but the steel moves through instructions, attachments, vendor forms, payroll files, purchase orders, certificates, and payment confirmations. The inbox is where those documents gather, contradict one another, or finally align. A ship with clean outsourcing support produces an inbox that looks ordinary: routine approvals, recognisable vendors, stable banking, predictable answers. A ship moving into evasive or marginal territory produces something else: late amendments, new intermediaries, awkward payment requests, unexplained management changes, suppliers asking harder questions, compliance teams copying more people into each thread. The inbox records the erosion of confidence before the voyage visibly fails.

For maritime sanctions, the broader lesson is austere. Outsourced management services matter because they control the documentary and financial circulation without which the vessel cannot function as legitimate trade. These firms are not merely administrative assistants to the real actors. They are among the real actors. They decide whether money moves, whether documents are credible enough to send onward, whether vendors are engaged, whether crews are paid, and whether the ship still looks like something a mainstream institution can serve without later regret. To miss that is to misunderstand how modern maritime coercion actually works.

That leaves the harder question at the centre of this service economy. When a vessel's legal owner remains unchanged but the outsourced managers, accounts teams, and logistics providers begin to hesitate, withdraw, or demand ever more paperwork, should that be read as mere administrative friction - or as the point at which the voyage has already lost the practical consent on which normal trade depends?

Chapter 8

Port Access and Cargo Documentation

How does a voyage become real? Not when the ship clears the horizon, and not even when cargo is loaded. A voyage becomes real when a port agrees to treat its paperwork, liabilities, and explanations as good enough to admit. That decision rarely arrives as a grand political gesture. More often it takes the form of routine administration: a berth window confirmed, an insurance certificate accepted, a manifest deemed coherent, a bill of lading treated as credible, a customs filing allowed to stand. The gate does not need to clang shut to change the fate of the trade. A pause can do it.

That is why ports matter so much in sanctions enforcement. They are not merely places where goods move between ship and shore. They are sorting systems. A vessel approaching port asks for more than physical entry. It asks to be recognised by a dense coalition of authorities and service providers who each bring their own reasons for caution. Law matters. So do safety, insurance, local procedure, commercial reputation, and the practical fear of becoming the institution that admitted a cargo whose story later collapsed under scrutiny. Ports do not need to moralise the voyage. They only need to decide whether its documents still hold.

The stamp carries weight.

That small fact gives ports an unusual form of power. A state may struggle to act cleanly on the high seas. A port can ask for one more certificate, one clearer origin statement, one explanation for a discrepancy, one insurance confirmation that actually matches the ship before it. In that setting, denial often appears in gentler clothing. A vessel is not refused in dramatic terms. It is delayed for administrative non-compliance. A cargo is not denounced as illicit. Its documentation is treated as insufficient. The result is often the same. Trade depends on acceptance by routine.

This matters because cargo identity is not a natural fact waiting in a hold to be discovered. It is built through documents. Bills of lading, manifests, certificates of origin, customs declarations, storage records, terminal data, and commercial invoices all contribute to the official story of what the cargo is, where it came from, who owns it, and where it is meant to go. That story can be honest and still fragile. It can also be manipulated without looking obviously theatrical. A description becomes broader. An intermediary is added. A blended shipment acquires a cleaner narrative than any one component would have carried alone. Integrity, in this setting, is visible not as virtue but as consistency across forms that were created by different actors for different reasons.

The stakes rise because ports sit where legal and commercial tolerances meet. A weak document trail does not simply create evidentiary inconvenience. It changes incentives for everyone involved in the call. The terminal asks whether unloading the cargo is worth the risk. The port agent wonders whether local authorities will revisit the decision later. The insurer re-reads the cover. The bank worries about settlement timing. The buyer asks whether the shipment will retain value if its origin becomes contested after discharge. What looks like a paperwork issue is often a question of who will carry the cost of being wrong. Ports tend to answer that question cautiously.

Storage sites, free zones, and transhipment terminals complicate the matter further because they can turn geography into administrative distance. Cargo handled through a reputable hub may inherit a kind of borrowed respectability even when the underlying trail has grown thinner. A relabelled shipment, a mixed consignment, or a cargo shifted between legal owners and logistical operators may emerge from storage looking cleaner on paper than it would have at the point of origin. That is why sanctions enforcement so often migrates towards terminals and logistics firms. By the time the ship reaches the final port, the most revealing work may have happened earlier in warehouses, tank farms, and transfer points where ownership, identity, and destination become harder to separate neatly.

Yet ports rarely want to play the role of theatrical enforcer. Their preference is for ordinary procedure, and there are sound reasons for that. Dramatic refusals invite political attention, legal challenge, and commercial retaliation. Administrative friction, by contrast, can be defended as part of normal governance. A longer berthing decision, additional documentary checks, extra certifications, or a request for clearer origin support can change voyage economics without requiring the port to pronounce on every geopolitical question hidden inside the cargo file. This is not weakness. It is the practical language of selective access. Friction often disciplines more effectively than spectacle.

The path ahead follows that language where it becomes most decisive. It begins at the port gate itself, where law, insurance, safety practice, and commercial discretion converge in the seemingly modest act of entry control. It then moves into the paper by which cargo becomes legible, through the intermediate sites that can blur or launder that legibility, and finally into the politics of delay, denial, and negotiated compliance that ports use when they do not wish either to wave the ship through or to start a public confrontation. The sequence matters because each layer tests a different version of the same question: whether the trade can still be explained well enough for the next institution to accept it.

The deeper friction is not between open commerce and closed ports in any simple sense. It is between the desire for fluid movement and the need for documents sturdy enough to bear scrutiny. Ports are asked to keep trade moving while also absorbing the consequences when weak paperwork turns into a customs dispute, an insurance fight, a sanctions breach, or a diplomatic incident. Innocent trade can be caught in that caution, which is why delay carries political cost as well as deterrent value. A port that asks too little may become a conduit for concealment. A port that asks too much may turn itself into a bottleneck for lawful commerce.

That leaves the harder question standing at the quay. When a ship arrives with papers that are plausible but not quite reassuring, and every institution involved can see enough to worry without seeing enough to prove, what should count as sufficient for entry: the formal completeness of the documents, or the port's colder judgement that the story they tell may not survive the next round of comparison?

Ports as selective gateways

On 4 July 2019, authorities in Gibraltar detained the tanker *Grace 1* on suspicion that it was carrying Iranian crude oil to Syria in breach of European Union sanctions. The episode drew global attention because it looked like a hard case of maritime coercion: a vessel stopped, a cargo contested, states trading accusations. Yet the more durable lesson lies in something less theatrical. The ship became vulnerable where maritime movement had to pass through legal authority, insurance scrutiny, local procedure, and administrative judgement at close range. The port did not merely receive the voyage. It tested whether the voyage deserved to be received.

That is why ports matter so much in sanctions enforcement. A port is not only a place of physical transfer. It is an institutional filter made up of harbour authorities, terminal operators, pilots, agents, customs officials, insurers, compliance staff, and local service providers who each ask whether the vessel and cargo remain acceptable enough to touch. The answer rarely arrives in grand language. It arrives in paperwork. An entry request is held. A certificate is queried. A berth window is delayed. A cargo description is treated as insufficiently clear. The file thickens. A ship can be refused without anyone needing to stage a refusal.

The gate closes quietly.

This is the first point worth stating plainly. Ports are selective gateways because entry is never governed by law alone. Show the ordinary sequence. A vessel approaches a commercial port seeking berth, discharge, bunkers, pilotage, agency support, and onward commercial legitimacy. The port authority asks whether the ship satisfies local legal requirements. The terminal asks whether insurance and cargo documentation are acceptable. The harbour master considers safety and traffic management. Customs and other officials examine declarations. The local agent and service firms worry about their own exposure. The concept is layered discretion. The implication is decisive: port access depends on several institutions making overlapping judgements, and sanctions pressure travels through those judgements far more effectively than public debate often admits.

That layered discretion gives ports a special advantage over more dramatic forms of maritime enforcement. A state trying to stop a ship at sea may face immediate questions of legal basis, diplomatic escalation, and evidentiary sufficiency. A port acts in a denser environment. It already has established powers to require documents, inspect conditions, sequence arrivals, and ensure compliance with safety, customs, and operational standards. This means that a doubtful voyage can be slowed through ordinary procedure rather than extraordinary force. The concept is administrative conversion. What looked offshore like a difficult geopolitical problem becomes, at the quay, a file with deficiencies that must be resolved before the ship can proceed normally. The implication is that ports often enforce by asking the ship to satisfy standards it would have faced anyway, only now under less generous assumptions.

Insurance is part of this conversion because ports do not treat liability as an abstract concern. They want to know who stands behind pollution risks, collision exposure, cargo damage, wreck removal, and the host of consequences that can follow an incident in confined waters. A ship arriving with cover from a recognised source usually passes this checkpoint without much drama. A ship whose insurance is unclear, politically exposed, or carried by an unfamiliar provider enters a different lane. The visible behaviour shifts. Extra confirmations are requested. Entry timing becomes less certain. The berth decision stretches. Commercial discretion begins to speak in the language of administrative caution. Trust, here, is not a moral feeling. It is the willingness to let the ship alongside without first trying to protect the port against future regret.

Safety checks function similarly, though they should not be collapsed into sanctions analysis too casually. Port state control and local safety procedures exist for their own reasons. A ship can be sanctions-compliant and still unsafe. It can be politically controversial and technically sound. Yet ports do not experience these categories in isolation. A vessel already marked by ownership opacity, unusual routing, or difficult documentation is more likely to attract patient scrutiny of its certificates, crew records, maintenance history, and insurance. This is not hypocrisy. It is institutional risk management. A port deciding whether to expose its waters, infrastructure, and officials to a doubtful vessel will rarely choose the narrowest imaginable reading of the file. The implication is practical: safety review can become the point at which broader sanctions discomfort acquires a defensible administrative form.

A named example from a different register shows how this works. In July 2022, the cargo vessel *Zhibek Zholy* became the subject of dispute when it approached the Turkish port of Karasu with grain alleged by Ukraine to have been taken from occupied territory. Turkey faced a difficult decision at the level where ports live: not in pure geopolitical abstraction, but in the space where legal claims, cargo documents, local procedure, and diplomatic consequences meet. The port question was not simply whether the allegations were serious. It was whether the administrative basis for detention, delay, or acceptance was strong enough to act upon. That is the port condition in its starkest form. Visibility does not settle responsibility. Procedure does.

This is why ports often prefer standard procedures to dramatic refusals. They can deny by refusing to find the file complete. They can delay by insisting on clarifications that may be routine in form and severe in effect. They can require fresh insurance confirmations, fuller cargo descriptions, revised ownership information, or additional safety documentation. They can sequence berthing decisions so that uncertainty becomes expensive.

The concept is procedural friction. The implication is not only deterrence but deniability. A port can say, with some truth, that it is enforcing ordinary compliance standards rather than wading openly into geopolitical contest. That stance protects the port as much as it pressures the voyage.

Commercial discretion matters here because ports are not purely public-law machines. Terminals depend on throughput. Agents depend on business. Local service providers weigh future relationships as well as present exposure. A port may hesitate to stage a visible refusal that could alienate customers or attract retaliation. Administrative non-compliance offers a narrower path. The ship is not condemned. It is simply not ready. The cargo is not denounced. Its paperwork remains incomplete. This distinction is more than cosmetic. It allows ports to exert selective pressure without claiming powers they may not wish to defend politically in broader terms. Denial becomes a condition rather than a proclamation.

A second named example returns to the *Grace 1* case. What made Gibraltar such an important setting was not only its strategic location, but the fact that the vessel's problem became actionable at a jurisdictional and administrative edge. Once the voyage entered a space where local authority, documentary scrutiny, and legal process could converge, the port environment transformed suspicion into concrete measures. This is what ports do best. They force a trade to stand still long enough for competing records and claims to be compared. A ship in motion can live on momentum. A ship seeking entry must live on paperwork.

A credible limitation must be faced directly. Ports are not all-powerful, and they are not always aligned. Some ports have greater administrative capacity than others. Some are more commercially dependent on throughput or more politically reluctant to absorb controversial cases. Some may prefer not to ask questions they are not eager to answer later. A vessel refused or delayed in one port may find another more tolerant or less well resourced. Sanctions analysis becomes lazy when it assumes that port authority on paper translates automatically into consistent port behaviour in practice. It does not. Ports are institutional actors with varying appetites, legal cultures, and thresholds for discomfort.

That limitation, however, clarifies rather than weakens the main point. Port power works best not as universal prohibition, but as differential scrutiny. The ship does not need to be excluded everywhere to feel the force of selectivity. It need only find that more reputable, better connected, and commercially central ports are less willing to process its file routinely. That change alone can alter voyage economics. Longer waits, fewer options, more document requests, and a shrinking set of acceptable terminals all raise cost and narrow flexibility. The ship may still move. It moves on less favourable terms and with thinner patience from everyone involved.

This is why ports are best understood as places where several kinds of legitimacy are tested at once. Legal authority asks whether entry is permissible. Insurance asks whether liabilities are acceptably placed. Safety asks whether the ship can be tolerated operationally. Commercial discretion asks whether the file is worth the trouble. A vessel may satisfy one of these tests and fail another. Port decisions are shaped by the combined result, not by any single abstract principle. The port does not need to say that the voyage is geopolitically intolerable. It need only conclude that the ordinary standards of acceptable entry are no longer comfortably met.

The quiet motif here is the stamp, because a port's power so often appears in that modest form. The stamp clears, delays, conditions, or withholds. It marks the point at which a ship's story is no longer told mainly by itself but judged by institutions whose tolerance for ambiguity is lower than the sea's. A stamped acceptance lets the voyage become ordinary commerce again. A missing stamp turns time into pressure, and pressure into discipline.

The broader lesson is austere. Ports serve as selective gateways not because they were invented for sanctions, but because modern trade already depends on their ability to filter ships and cargoes through law, insurance, safety practice, and commercial judgement. Sanctions become potent there because a port can act through ordinary procedure rather than extraordinary confrontation. The ship does not need to be seized to feel the effect. It only needs to discover that the next berth, the next document check, or the next insurance query is no longer routine.

That leaves the harder question every port eventually faces. When a vessel's papers are formally present but substantively uneasy, and every institution involved can see enough to worry without seeing enough to conclude, what should count as responsible entry control: granting access unless a clear prohibition exists, or treating administrative incompleteness as the most defensible form of denial before the port becomes part of a larger problem?

Bills of lading, manifests, and origin claims

On 4 July 2019, when authorities in Gibraltar detained the tanker *Grace 1*, the argument did not turn only on where the ship was or who had boarded it. It turned on what the cargo was said to be doing, where it was said to be going, and whether the surrounding documentation could sustain those claims. The drama at sea drew cameras. The decisive struggle lay on paper. A voyage can survive rough weather more easily than it survives a document trail that no longer agrees with itself.

That is the first fact to hold steady. Cargo identity is not a natural property waiting quietly in the hold. It is constructed through records. A bill of lading describes goods for one commercial and legal purpose. A manifest frames them for another. A certificate of origin, customs declaration, invoice, inspection report, storage record, terminal note, and financing document each add a further layer. None of these documents is trivial. Taken together, they create the official story of what moved, who owned it, where it came from, where it is meant to go, and why the next institution should trust that account. The cargo exists physically. Commerce knows it through text.

Paper gives cargo a face.

This is why sanctions enforcement so often succeeds or fails at the level of documentary integrity rather than interdiction alone. Show the sequence in ordinary form. A shipment is loaded, sold, financed, and carried. The seller names the goods one way. The carrier describes them slightly differently. An intermediary trader adds another description designed to fit a contract template or local practice. A customs filing simplifies what the invoice had specified. A bank checks one set of documents; a port later sees another. No single variation proves deceit. Shipping produces small inconsistencies all the time. The concept is documentary construction. The implication is more uncomfortable: if institutions cannot compare those constructions effectively, cargo origin and destination become matters of administrative persuasion rather than stable fact.

Bills of lading sit at the centre of this problem because they perform more than one function at once. They acknowledge receipt, record shipment terms, and often operate as key documents in trade finance and cargo release. That multifunction role gives them unusual evidentiary weight. Yet a bill of lading rarely tells the whole truth of a cargo by itself. It reflects what the carrier or its agents were prepared to state at a given moment within a particular contractual framework. It can be accurate and still incomplete. It can be formally correct and still strategically vague. A broad commodity description may suit routine trade. Under sanctions pressure, the same breadth may become a shelter for ambiguity. The implication is practical. Enforcement agencies, banks, insurers, and ports do not ask whether a bill of lading exists. They ask whether its language survives comparison with the rest of the file.

Manifests complicate the picture because they are often treated as more administrative and therefore more trustworthy. They may indeed be useful. Yet they are also products of systems, intermediaries, and timing. A manifest can preserve cargo identity with care, or it can flatten detail into categories broad enough to ease logistics and customs processing while weakening origin analysis. Show the everyday problem. A cargo described precisely at loading is later carried through several layers of manifest language that gradually simplify, consolidate, or generalise the goods. What began as a narrowly traceable product can arrive as a looser commercial category. The concept is descriptive drift. The implication is that origin claims weaken not only through outright falsification, but through incremental loss of specificity across routine documentation.

This is where origin claims become so fragile. Origin is not merely a geographical fact. It is an institutional conclusion drawn from records, handling history, and accepted definitions. A cargo extracted in one place, stored in another, blended in a third, sold through a fourth, and loaded under documents issued in a fifth can arrive with several plausible narratives attached to it. Sanctions enforcement depends on knowing which narrative should govern. That task becomes difficult because different documents answer different questions. One may record where the cargo was loaded. Another where it was processed. Another who sold it. Another which terminal handled it last. The visible danger is obvious. A cargo can acquire the credibility of the most reputable step in its journey while leaving the most sensitive step half-buried in preceding paperwork.

A named example makes the point. In the years following intensified sanctions on Iranian and Venezuelan oil trades, public advisories and specialist reporting repeatedly warned that petroleum cargoes could be moved through ship-to-ship transfers, storage, or blending arrangements that obscured their true origin or diluted the relevance of any single source. The lesson was not that every blended cargo was suspicious. Blending has ordinary commercial uses. The sharper lesson was that once cargoes are mixed or relabelled through intermediate handling, the documentary burden rises sharply. A certificate of origin may no longer speak with the same authority if the physical product has passed through processes that change what "origin" means for commercial or regulatory purposes. The paper must now do more argumentative work than before.

Multiple intermediaries intensify this strain because each intermediary can add legal distance while subtracting evidentiary clarity. A cargo may pass from producer to trader, from trader to affiliate, from affiliate to reseller, from reseller to final buyer, with each step generating its own invoice, contract language, and preferred description. None of that is inherently improper. Commodity trades often involve several hands for ordinary reasons of finance, logistics, and market access. Yet every extra intermediary creates a further opportunity for language to soften, for liability to thin, and for the connection between physical origin and commercial identity to weaken. The concept is transactional diffusion. The implication is that enforcement attention often turns not to the cargo alone, but to whether the chain of intermediaries adds visible commercial function or merely administrative fog.

That distinction matters because complexity has lawful uses. A credible limitation must be admitted. Shipping and commodity trade are full of legitimate documentary inconsistencies caused by timing, translation, local practice, system limitations, or differing commercial conventions. One document may use a customs code, another a market shorthand, another a technical specification. A cargo can be lawfully blended, stored, resold, or relabelled for perfectly ordinary reasons. A sanctions analyst who treats every variance as evidence of deception will quickly generate false positives and undermine confidence in the enforcement process. The challenge is not to abolish ambiguity. It is to identify when ambiguity has ceased to be commercially innocent and started to become strategically useful.

This is why document integrity matters more than document abundance. A thick file can still be weak. Ten records that repeat the same softened description may tell us less than three records generated independently for different purposes that still point to the same underlying story. The question is not whether paperwork exists, but whether it coheres. Do the bill of lading, manifest, invoice, customs declaration, financing documents, and terminal records fit together without strain? Does each intermediary add a plausible commercial function? Does the origin claim remain stable as the cargo moves, or does it become conveniently less precise once scrutiny becomes more likely? Risk, here, becomes visible in behaviour: delayed payment, enhanced due diligence, port hesitation, insurer discomfort, or a demand for fresh certifications before discharge can continue.

A second named example lies in the scrutiny of grain shipments from the Black Sea after Russia's invasion of Ukraine in 2022. Disputes over whether particular consignments originated from occupied territories did not always turn on dramatic physical evidence. They often turned on documentary chains: where the grain had been loaded, how it had been described, which intermediaries had handled it, what certificates accompanied it, and whether the commercial paperwork supported the narrative being offered to ports and buyers. The broader lesson extends well beyond grain. Origin disputes in sanctions-sensitive trades rarely depend on one miraculous document. They depend on whether several imperfect documents can still support one defensible account.

This is also why banks and insurers care so much about cargo paper even though they rarely see the cargo itself. A letter of credit, a payment release, or cover confirmation often depends on documentary compliance. If the bill of lading says one thing, the invoice another, and the origin certificate something more elastic still, the institution faces a difficult choice. It can rely on formal sufficiency and hope the inconsistencies remain commercially tolerable, or it can treat those inconsistencies as signals that the trade may not survive later scrutiny. Efficiency, in this setting, is not speed alone. It is the ability to move goods without creating a future dispute that will expose the paper as thin. Good enforcement exploits that fear. Evasion depends on outrunning it.

This explains why cargo manipulation is so often subtle. A falsehood that is too obvious invites quick rejection. More effective manipulation often works by small documentary shifts: broader descriptions, intermediate resales, relabelled storage records, selective emphasis on loading point over extraction point, or reliance on a reputable hub's paperwork to quiet questions about earlier stages in the chain. The cargo does not need to become invisible. It only needs to become harder to classify with confidence under the rules that matter. The paper, not the commodity, does the hiding.

The quiet motif here is the stamp, because documentary integrity ultimately depends on institutions willing to stand behind what they have recorded. A stamped bill of lading, a stamped manifest, a stamped origin certificate, a stamped customs form - each invites the next institution to rely on it. That is the promise. The problem arises when the authority of the stamp exceeds the care with which the underlying facts were checked or preserved. A cargo that has passed through reputable terminals or free zones can inherit the authority of those stamps even while its earlier history has grown thinner. Enforcement works when the institutions seeing the stamp ask what exactly it certifies, and what it does not.

This is why ports, terminals, banks, and insurers do not merely read documents. They compare them. The bill of lading may be legally valid and still commercially troubling if its language drifts too far from other records. The manifest may be accurate in its own system and still insufficient to support the claimed origin. Multiple intermediaries may be lawful and still destructive of confidence if none appears to add real commercial function. Blended cargoes may be normal and still difficult to accept if the resulting origin story becomes too convenient to test. Document integrity therefore does not mean perfection. It means that the records remain strong enough to withstand cross-reading by institutions that do not share identical purposes but do share a fear of being misled.

The broader lesson is austere. Cargo identity is made, not merely found. That process of making can support enforcement when records preserve continuity, precision, and intelligible commercial purpose. It can undermine enforcement when descriptions drift, intermediaries multiply without clear function, and origin claims become more confident on paper even as the physical and transactional chain grows murkier. The struggle is rarely over whether documents exist. It is over whether they still deserve belief once compared against one another under pressure.

That leaves the harder question every sanctions-sensitive cargo eventually faces. When the paperwork is formally complete but the story it tells depends on softened descriptions, several intermediaries, and an origin claim that has grown cleaner as the cargo moved further from its source, should the next institution treat the file as adequate commerce - or as a sign that the paper has begun to do the very work the cargo itself can no longer honestly perform?

Storage, free zones, and transhipment terminals

In July 2022, the cargo vessel *Zhibek Zholy* reached the Turkish port of Karasu carrying grain that Ukraine alleged had been taken from occupied territory. The dispute did not turn only on what sat in the holds. It turned on where the grain had been loaded, how it had moved, which documents followed it, and whether intermediate handling had altered the confidence others were prepared to place in its stated origin. The physical cargo had not vanished. Its administrative identity had become harder to settle.

That difficulty sits at the centre of modern sanctions enforcement. Cargo rarely moves from producer to final buyer in a straight line. It pauses in tank farms, warehouses, silos, and bonded zones. It passes through free zones designed to speed commerce by reducing friction at the border. It is sorted, blended, repackaged, relabelled, consolidated, divided, and sold again while still in motion. These are not marginal practices. They are part of how global trade normally works. The warehouse changes the story.

That is why enforcement attention so often shifts away from the ship alone and towards terminals, logistics operators, and storage sites. A vessel may carry the cargo across water, but these onshore or near-shore handling points often determine what the cargo becomes on paper by the time it reaches the next jurisdiction. Show the sequence in ordinary terms. A shipment leaves one port with a particular identity and ownership profile. It enters storage at an intermediate hub. A trader resells it. A terminal handles it alongside other cargoes. A fresh set of documents is issued for onward movement. The concept is documentary transformation. The implication is crucial: by the time the shipment reaches the next port, the most consequential change may not be physical at all. It may be the administrative remaking of origin, ownership, or destination through the institutions that handled it between voyages.

Storage sites matter because they break the intuitive link between movement and meaning. In public imagination, a cargo's origin seems like a simple question: where did it come from? In commercial practice, that question becomes tangled as soon as goods enter storage and emerge later through new contracts and new paperwork. A tank farm can commingle products. A warehouse can consolidate consignments from several sellers. A grain terminal can blend stock across deliveries. A free zone can host transactions that change title without necessarily changing the cargo's physical condition. The concept here is layered provenance. The implication is that origin becomes less a natural fact than an institutional conclusion drawn from records that may have been generated for many different purposes and by many different actors.

That is why terminals and logistics operators occupy such an important place in sanctions enforcement. They are not merely passive handlers of goods. They create records, allocate storage, witness transfers, issue handling documents, confirm quantities, and often stand between the original shipment and its later commercial identity. Their systems can preserve continuity or dilute it. Trust, in this setting, is visible in whether a terminal's records align with shipping documents, whether stock movements can be reconciled cleanly, whether ownership changes are documented in ways outsiders can later verify, and whether the facility is willing to ask difficult questions before issuing the next layer of paperwork.

Once those records weaken, enforcement shifts from the cargo itself to the institutions that have made the cargo legible.

A named example from the oil trade clarifies the stakes. During the late 2010s and early 2020s, regulatory advisories and specialist reporting repeatedly highlighted how sanctioned-origin petroleum could be moved through storage, blending, or transhipment arrangements that complicated later claims about provenance. The important point was not that every transfer terminal or storage facility was acting improperly. It was that intermediate handling changed the evidentiary burden. Once cargo entered a reputable hub and emerged under fresh commercial documentation, the onward shipment could inherit some of the hub's credibility even if the underlying origin story had become less clear. The facility had not necessarily falsified anything. It had become the site where administrative respectability was renewed.

This is one reason free zones deserve careful attention. They are built to facilitate trade by reducing customs friction, allowing storage and re-export, and making logistics more efficient. Much of the time they do exactly that. Yet efficiency has an evidentiary cost when goods change hands, labels, or destination plans within a zone whose procedures are designed to favour speed. A consignment can sit in a bonded area, pass through several ownership structures, and leave with documentation that is formally complete while offering weaker insight into how the goods came to be there. The concept is buffered visibility. The implication is not that free zones are inherently suspect. It is that their very usefulness to lawful trade can also make them attractive to actors seeking administrative distance from earlier stages in the cargo's journey.

Transhipment terminals intensify this effect because they often sit at the seam between logistics and legal identity. A terminal receiving cargo for onward movement does not simply move boxes, liquids, or bulk commodities from one mode or vessel to another. It also helps create the next documentary life of the goods. A new manifest may be issued. Fresh handling records are generated. Cargoes may be consolidated or divided. An onward bill of lading may refer to the immediate terminal or load point more prominently than to the deeper chain behind it. The concept is jurisdictional resetting. The implication is that a reputable terminal can lend the next stage of the shipment a cleaner administrative starting point than the earlier voyage deserved on its own.

A brief, ordinary example makes the mechanism plain. A relabelled shipment stored and reissued from a major hub may inherit the quiet confidence that others place in the hub's systems, even if the relabelling itself did little to clarify the underlying source. The cargo now appears in a new stream of documents linked to a recognised facility, a new seller, and a fresh destination. A bank processing payment may feel more comfortable. A port seeing the inbound manifest may focus on the latest loading point. An insurer may read the recent records more readily than the deeper history. The hub has not magically erased origin. It has reframed what the next institution sees first.

This is why enforcement does not stop at the ship. A vessel can be tracked, inspected, and challenged, yet still leave the harder problem unresolved if the cargo later passes through storage or transhipment points that thin or reorder the evidentiary chain. Terminals and logistics operators therefore become significant not because they wield sovereign power, but because they control the records and physical custody events that often decide whether later scrutiny remains feasible. A warehouse receipt, a stock movement report, a handling certificate, or a transfer log may matter more than a political declaration once the goods have changed hands two or three times. The paper generated onshore begins to govern what the ship's movement at sea can later be made to mean.

A second named example lies in the broader scrutiny of grain, metals, and petroleum passing through major regional hubs after 2022, when sanctions, export controls, and contested origin claims placed greater pressure on intermediate logistics. Public disputes often centred on whether cargoes had acquired a misleadingly clean documentary profile after passing through storage or processing points outside the original zone of controversy. The lesson was structural. A well-run terminal can preserve traceability. It can also, without any overt misconduct, become the moment at which later actors stop asking about earlier stages because the most recent records look orderly enough to satisfy commercial appetite. Enforcement must therefore learn to read terminal orderliness with both respect and caution.

A credible limitation must be admitted. Storage, free zones, and transhipment are normal features of lawful commerce, not symptoms of evasion by default. Global supply chains would struggle badly without them. Goods are stored because timing matters, because buyers and sellers change, because shipping schedules misalign, because blending or sorting has legitimate commercial uses, and because ports and terminals are built precisely to absorb these frictions. An analyst who treats every free-zone movement or terminal transfer as presumptively suspect will misunderstand modern trade and generate false positives at damaging scale. Efficiency is not the enemy of enforcement. Often it is the condition that makes traceability possible at all.

That limitation does not weaken the main argument. It sharpens the distinction between useful intermediation and obscuring intermediation. The relevant question is not whether a cargo touched storage or a free zone, but what happened to its records and ownership claims while it was there. Did the documentation preserve continuity? Did title transfers make commercial sense? Did the terminal retain records detailed enough to reconstruct the chain later? Were multiple cargoes blended in ways that changed the meaning of origin? Did the onward shipment's description become broader, cleaner, or more detached from the earlier paperwork at the very moment scrutiny would have made the deeper story inconvenient? The answers lie in pattern, not in mere presence.

This is where document integrity and commercial reputation intersect. A reputable hub can improve trust by preserving strong records and disciplined procedures. It can also unintentionally provide cover because others rely on that reputation without re-opening the cargo's full history. Banks, insurers, ports, and buyers are not irrational to do this. Commerce would seize up if every terminal record required a full backward investigation. Yet that same practical reliance creates room for manipulation. Evasion does not always require false documents. Sometimes it requires only that the newest documents be treated as sufficient because they were issued within a respected logistical environment. The hub's credibility travels farther than the cargo's original truth.

The quiet motif here is the label. A label on a tank, a container, a warehouse lot, a stack in a bonded zone, or a new shipping document seems innocuous. Yet labels do more than identify goods for handling. They decide what the next institution thinks it is seeing. A relabelled cargo does not need to become physically different to become administratively easier to accept. The label inherits the authority of the place that issued or confirmed it. That is why storage and transhipment matter so much. They are the places where labels are refreshed, and with them the conditions of belief.

For maritime sanctions, the wider lesson is austere. Cargo handling sites complicate origin, ownership, and destination not because they are abnormal, but because they are central to how trade actually moves. Their records can sustain enforcement when they preserve continuity across transactions and physical handling. They can undermine enforcement when they allow administrative freshness to substitute for deeper traceability. The task is therefore not to romanticise original documents or demonise intermediary hubs. It is to understand where the cargo's identity is being remade, and whether that remaking preserves enough truth for the next institution to act responsibly.

That leaves the harder question hanging over every reputable terminal and free zone. When a shipment emerges from a trusted hub with formally complete new papers but a thinner and more comfortable origin story than the one with which it entered, should the next port, bank, or insurer treat the hub's credibility as enough - or as the very reason to ask what the cargo had to become on paper before that credibility could be borrowed?

Denial, delay, and negotiated compliance

In July 2022, the cargo vessel *Zhibek Zholy* reached the Turkish port of Karasu carrying grain that Ukraine said had been taken from occupied territory. The case did not turn on an immediate theatrical yes or no. It turned on hesitation: whether the ship would be held, what documentary basis existed, how long the port and Turkish authorities could justify delay, and what political cost would follow if the cargo proved innocent or illicit. The most revealing force in the episode was not outright refusal. It was time.

That is the first point worth holding. Ports do not need to ban a vessel dramatically in order to alter the fate of a voyage. A ship approaching berth lives on schedule, contract performance, financing windows, crew limits, cargo quality, onward connections, and the simple commercial fact that delay costs money long before anyone says the word "denied". A port that asks for one more certification, one clearer insurance confirmation, one more coherent cargo explanation, or a further ownership clarification has not necessarily refused the vessel. It has still changed the economics of the trade. A queue can punish.

This is why denial, delay, and negotiated compliance belong in the same analytical frame. They are not separate worlds. They are points along a continuum of port response through which uncertainty is converted into cost. Show the ordinary sequence. A vessel's documents appear formally complete, yet something in the file creates discomfort: cargo origin is not fully persuasive, ownership looks recently altered, insurance requires verification, a prior port call raises questions, or the manifest and bill of lading do not sit easily together. The port need not stage a confrontation.

It can defer berthing, require further confirmations, increase documentary checks, or request additional certificates before allowing normal operations to continue. The concept is calibrated friction. The implication is practical and severe: sanctions enforcement often works best not by stopping the ship outright, but by making continuation progressively more expensive and less predictable.

Ports favour this kind of calibrated friction for good reason. Formal refusal is legally and politically heavy. It can trigger diplomatic protest, commercial claims, retaliatory measures, or allegations that the port has exceeded its proper role. Standard procedures, by contrast, are easier to defend. A longer review of entry papers, a requirement for insurer confirmation from a recognised provider, a request for updated ownership details, or a pause pending customs clarification all fall within the ordinary grammar of port governance. The port can present itself as careful rather than confrontational. Yet the effect on the voyage can be almost as strong as refusal, especially when the ship is working within a narrow time window or a fragile commercial structure.

This is where delay becomes a sanction-like tool without needing to declare itself as one. A voyage's economics are rarely generous enough to absorb indefinite uncertainty. Charterers lose patience. Cargo buyers begin calculating replacement options or price concessions. Banks hold back settlement. Insurers reread the file. Agents and terminals start treating the vessel as awkward business. A delay of even a day or two may alter the viability of a time-sensitive or politically sensitive cargo. The concept is economic attrition. The implication is that ports can deter suspect trade simply by forcing it to bear the true administrative cost of its own ambiguity.

A named example from an earlier sanctions episode makes the point even more clearly. When Gibraltar detained *Grace 1* in July 2019, the visible event was seizure, but the wider operational lesson lay in how quickly a ship's legal and commercial life becomes hostage to documentary timing. The vessel's future did not turn only on the force used to stop it. It turned on the scrutiny that followed: destination claims, ownership narratives, sanctions interpretation, and the administrative basis on which further movement could or could not be permitted. Even in a high-profile case, the practical pressure came through delay, review, and the inability of the voyage to resume normal commercial status while the file remained contested. The ship had not simply been refused. It had been made to wait inside law.

This is why negotiated compliance so often emerges as the actual port outcome. Many difficult ships are neither simply admitted nor simply excluded. They are managed into a middle state. The port or terminal asks for extra comfort. The owner or charterer supplies new documents, amends declarations, changes agents, strengthens insurance evidence, or offers additional assurances. Sometimes the cargo proceeds after these adjustments. Sometimes it does not. The important point is that the negotiation itself is part of enforcement. The port is effectively saying: the voyage, as currently presented, is not acceptable enough to pass unaltered. Bring us a version of the file we can defend. The concept is conditional acceptance. The implication is that compliance is not always a pre-existing condition. It can become a bargain struck under pressure.

This bargain matters because it redistributes evidentiary burden. A direct refusal asks the port to justify a negative decision with confidence. Negotiated compliance asks the ship to repair its own credibility. That reversal is powerful. The port does not need omniscience. It needs enough unease to make the vessel or its counterparties produce more persuasive paper than they had originally intended to provide. Trust, here, becomes visible in what the ship is willing and able to furnish under pressure: fresh origin certificates, clearer insurer attestations, fuller ownership records, revised cargo descriptions, or more defensible agency arrangements. A file that cannot improve under scrutiny tells its own story.

That story becomes sharper when one considers innocent trade. A credible limitation must be faced directly. Delay does not only hurt bad actors. Ports that use friction as a screening tool will sometimes catch lawful cargoes in the same net. An origin certificate may be slow for mundane reasons. A vessel may have recently changed manager without any evasive purpose. Insurance confirmation may lag because of ordinary bureaucracy. Multiple intermediaries may reflect perfectly lawful commodity trading. If every uncertainty is treated as grounds for prolonged delay, the port risks damaging lawful commerce, inviting challenge, and undermining confidence in its own procedures. The diplomatic sensitivity is real because innocent trade caught in delay can quickly become a political grievance.

That limitation does not weaken the case for calibrated friction. It explains why procedure matters so much. A port that delays carelessly will create noise and resentment. A port that delays carefully, records its reasons, narrows its requests, and responds when the file improves can maintain both deterrent force and institutional legitimacy. The relevant question is not whether delay is blunt. It can be. The question is whether the delay is tethered to identifiable deficiencies or exposed risks rather than to vague unease alone. Good port governance turns discomfort into specific requests. Poor port governance turns discomfort into administrative fog.

This is also why delay can outperform denial in some cases. Refusal ends the immediate relationship but may also drive the ship towards a more permissive port without generating much additional information. Delay keeps the vessel within the administrative frame. While the ship waits, documents can be compared, insurers consulted, customs concerns clarified, ownership claims tested, and counterparties' willingness to remain involved measured in real time. A port can learn from the way the file responds. Does the owner answer quickly and coherently? Do new documents align or merely multiply? Do insurers stand firm or grow evasive? Does the buyer stay engaged? The queue becomes an investigative space.

A second named example lies in the repeated disputes over grain cargoes linked to contested Ukrainian origins after 2022. In such cases, ports and states often faced pressure from several directions at once: the risk of facilitating illicit trade, the need to avoid blocking legitimate food shipments, the sensitivity of regional diplomacy, and the limits of the available evidence. The practical response was often neither clean refusal nor blind admission, but some form of procedural slowing while documentation and claims were tested. The broader lesson is durable. Where evidence is incomplete and the stakes are high, ports often choose friction because friction preserves room to move later. It delays commitment while still imposing cost on the voyage now.

This cost matters because maritime commerce is built around predictability. A shipowner can price known fees and even known regulatory burdens. What degrades the trade is uncertainty about whether the port will accept the file in time, whether the berth slot will be kept open, whether the buyer will wait, whether the bank will release payment, whether the insurer will continue to support the call, and whether a further request for documents will arrive after the previous one has already been met. Delay turns a fixed cost into a variable one. That is why it deters so effectively. It attacks the confidence on which ordinary trade depends.

The quiet motif here is the queue. Every ship in port lives in some queue - for berthing, discharge, customs clearance, pilotage, bunkers, release, and onward movement. A suspect voyage suffers when its queue becomes longer, less predictable, and more conditional than the commercial model had assumed. The queue is not merely administrative time. It is a test of whether the ship's story can survive repeated asking. Some cargoes can. Others begin to fray as each request produces a new inconsistency, a slower answer, a weaker assurance. The port does not need to pronounce a moral verdict. It only needs to keep the queue honest.

This is why denial, delay, and negotiated compliance should be read as parts of one enforcement vocabulary rather than as separate categories. Denial is the most visible form. Delay is often the most useful. Negotiated compliance is the form that allows ports to extract better evidence, stronger assurances, or a more defensible file without claiming to resolve every geopolitical question on their own. Ports use these tools because they sit where movement becomes administration. They understand that a voyage can be stopped by cost, by time, or by the simple inability to satisfy ordinary procedures under non-ordinary scrutiny.

The unresolved question follows from that reality. When a ship's documents are troubling but not conclusively disqualifying, how long should a port be willing to make the voyage wait before delay itself becomes either an unjust punishment of innocent trade or the only honest way to force a doubtful cargo to reveal whether its paperwork can survive one more turn in the queue?

Chapter 9

Transhipment and Ship-to-Ship Transfers

How can a cargo change its story without changing its substance? That question sits at the centre of maritime sanctions more sharply than any image of a ship caught at sea. A cargo can leave one vessel, pass across hoses or cranes into another, acquire a fresh documentary life, and continue under a cleaner or at least more complicated narrative than the one with which it began. Nothing about that process is inherently illicit. Global shipping depends on transhipment every day. Yet the very normality of the practice is what gives it such power in evasive trade. The handover can hide.

That ambiguity matters because transhipment belongs to the ordinary grammar of maritime commerce. Cargoes are split for smaller ports, consolidated for long-haul efficiency, moved between ship types, routed around draught limits, and reorganised to suit terminal capacity, weather, schedules, and market demand. A vessel waiting offshore for a transfer does not immediately announce deception. Nor does a second vessel arriving to receive the load. The sea is full of legitimate interruptions in which cargo moves not towards concealment, but towards logistical sense. That is what makes the practice so difficult to police: the same choreography can serve efficiency or disguise.

The rendezvous changes everything.

That is the central tension of this chapter. Sanctions enforcement must distinguish between routine logistics and concealment without pretending that the distinction will always be obvious from a trackline or a suspicious-looking pause on a screen. A transfer at sea can be lawful, declared, and commercially sensible. It can also be used to dilute origin, alter destination, fragment accountability, or create just enough evidentiary distance that the next institution in line sees only the last leg of the journey. The problem is not merely that cargo moves. It is that information moves less cleanly than cargo does. Once the handover begins, the file often grows thinner at the very moment the physical chain grows more complex.

That matters because transhipment is one of the places where maritime sanctions become a struggle over narrative sequence rather than over prohibition alone. What moved, from which vessel to which vessel, under whose instruction, using which documents, at what point in the chain of sale or carriage, and with which declared destination afterwards? Each question sounds technical. Together, they decide whether a transfer remains ordinary commerce or becomes the administrative pivot through which a cargo loses its earlier identity. A transfer that cannot be reconstructed later may be commercially useful in the present precisely because it reduces the confidence with which ports, banks, insurers, and regulators can connect the cargo's first story to its final one.

The stakes rise because evidence in this field is often indirect. AIS gaps, unusual loitering, repeated rendezvous, nighttime operations, route deviations, and offshore waiting patterns all attract attention for obvious reasons. Yet none of them settles the matter. Harsh weather, congestion, safety practice, convoying needs, and commercial timing can produce signatures that look suspicious from a distance and ordinary up close. Enforcement therefore lives with a constant risk of over-reading. It must notice patterns without turning every pattern into proof. That discipline is harder than public rhetoric allows, and more important. A sanctions system that confuses signals with conclusions will soon lose the trust of the very institutions it asks to act.

The problem does not end with detection. Pressure applied in one corridor often drives activity elsewhere. If a transfer zone becomes too visible, cargoes are broken into smaller parcels, intermediaries multiply, routes shift, and more of the trade migrates into paperwork before it migrates physically at all. This is why sanctions must be understood as a moving contest rather than a static barrier. Networks adapt not only by changing ships or flags, but by changing where and how information fragments. A better-monitored anchorage may produce clearer evidence. It may also push the next transfer into remoter waters, a less familiar hub, or a chain of transactions in which no single actor feels responsible for the whole movement.

That adaptation matters because the sea does not erase institutional dependence. Even the most carefully arranged transfer must still meet the next port, the next insurer, the next bank, the next cargo buyer, and the next set of documents asked to explain what happened offshore. The argument ahead follows that sequence rather than trying to pin all meaning to the transfer itself. It begins with why transhipment is so useful to evasive trade while remaining legitimate in ordinary commerce, then turns to the practical conduct of ship-to-ship operations, the fragile signals by which outsiders try to infer what occurred, and the way networks mutate when one route becomes too costly to sustain. The point is not to solve ambiguity with slogans. It is to understand how ambiguity is produced, managed, and sometimes mistaken for innocence.

A deeper friction runs beneath all of this. Maritime commerce needs transhipment because global trade would seize up without it. Sanctions enforcement fears transhipment because the same flexibility that keeps commerce fluid can also make cargo identity more contestable at precisely the moments when origin and destination matter most. Ports, terminals, insurers, and regulators are left to decide whether a transfer record is detailed enough, whether a receiving vessel's papers still deserve confidence, and whether an offshore operation that looks odd is truly odd in the sense that law should care about. Innocent trade depends on those institutions not becoming paranoid. Effective enforcement depends on them not becoming credulous.

That leaves the harder question waiting offshore with the two vessels lying alongside one another. When a transfer can be explained as ordinary logistics and used as strategic concealment at the same time, what should count as enough evidence for the next institution to treat the cargo as continuous rather than newly plausible, and how much uncertainty can the sanctions system bear before the rendezvous has already done the one thing it needed to do - break the chain of confidence without ever needing to break the chain of movement?

Why transhipment is central to evasion

In May 2020, the United States Departments of State, Treasury, and Coast Guard issued a sanctions advisory warning that ship-to-ship transfers could be used to obscure the origin or destination of cargoes linked to sanctioned trade. The warning mattered not because it revealed a rare maritime trick, but because it named a practice already woven into ordinary commerce. Cargo moves between vessels every day for sensible reasons: to match ship size to port depth, to consolidate loads, to distribute parcels, to bridge logistics between terminal capacity and final delivery. The practice is normal enough to be useful. That is exactly why it is dangerous.

A cargo passing across open water can become administratively younger than it really is. The physical substance remains the same, but the commercial story surrounding it can change. One vessel leaves a sanctions-sensitive origin. Another continues from a more ambiguous midpoint. Bills of lading, manifests, certificates, and sales contracts can now be aligned around the later stage of the movement rather than the earlier one. The cargo has not vanished. Its paper trail has been rearranged. The handover writes a new beginning.

That is the first point to hold firmly. Transhipment is central to evasion because it exploits a feature of maritime commerce that is both lawful and useful. If ship-to-ship transfers were rare, exotic, or always suspect, they would be easier to police. They are none of those things. They are a standard logistical tool, and standard tools are the hardest to isolate when their use turns strategic. Show the ordinary logic. A vessel too large for a shallow port offloads part of its cargo offshore. A smaller vessel distributes it onward. A crude carrier consolidates parcels from different load points into a larger cargo. A product tanker receives fuel from a storage or shuttle arrangement before continuing to market. The concept is logistical normality. The implication is that enforcement cannot begin by treating every transfer as concealment without paralysing lawful trade.

That normality creates the operational advantage evasive networks need. A transfer at sea allows the trade to break the direct visual and documentary line between the first leg and the last. One ship may attract scrutiny because of origin, ownership, route, or insurer discomfort. Another ship, receiving the cargo later, may appear less exposed or may at least present a cleaner file to the next port, bank, or buyer. This is not magic. It is sequencing. The cargo is moved into a fresh commercial context before the institutions seeing it have had time or reason to reconstruct the full chain. The concept is evidentiary interruption. The implication is practical: transhipment does not need to falsify everything. It only needs to weaken continuity enough that the next gatekeeper sees a less troubling story first.

That weakening can occur through several ordinary mechanisms. A receiving vessel may carry a different flag, different management, different insurance, or a more acceptable trading profile. A new sale may be inserted between loading and discharge. The cargo description may broaden. The immediate load point may take on more prominence in the paperwork than the deeper source. A reputable transhipment or anchorage area may lend the operation a degree of routine credibility. None of this proves misconduct by itself. That is precisely the difficulty. The same steps that make commercial networks efficient can also make enforcement less certain. Risk, here, is visible in whether the cargo still looks continuous once documents, port calls, counterparties, and instructions are compared across both legs of the voyage.

A named example from the oil trade clarifies why this matters. During the late 2010s and early 2020s, regulatory advisories and specialist reporting repeatedly highlighted ship-to-ship transfers linked to Iranian and Venezuelan oil movements in waters near Fujairah, the eastern Mediterranean, and parts of East and Southeast Asia. The significance of these operations did not lie in the transfer alone. Ship-to-ship transfers occur lawfully in such waters for many reasons. What mattered was the pattern around them: AIS irregularities, shifting ownership structures, altered cargo narratives, fresh intermediaries, and a receiving vessel that could carry the cargo onward under a less politically visible profile. The transfer acted as a hinge. Before it, one story. After it, another.

This is why origin and destination are so vulnerable at the moment of handover. Origin, in sanctions practice, is not merely where a cargo first touched water. It is the commercial and legal claim institutions later accept about where the cargo meaningfully came from. Destination is not simply the port at the end of the route. It is the intended commercial endpoint recognised in contracts, payments, insurance, and customs treatment. A transhipment can complicate both. The first vessel may never approach the final buyer's jurisdiction. The second may never approach the original source. The cargo lives between them, and enforcement must decide which segment carries the more relevant truth. The concept is distributed narrative. The implication is that sanctions cases often turn less on movement itself than on which document set is treated as authoritative after the transfer.

This is also why multiple intermediaries often cluster around transhipment. A transfer at sea is easier to defend as ordinary logistics if the commercial chain has already been softened through traders, affiliates, or resellers who can explain the receiving vessel's role in conventional market terms. Again, the same structure can be lawful. Commodity trading often involves several hands. Yet every additional intermediary can dilute accountability while keeping the cargo moving. One company owns the first leg. Another arranges the transfer. A third sells onward. A fourth holds paper title for a period too brief to matter physically but long enough to alter the documentary frame. The concept is transactional cushioning. The implication is that evasion does not depend only on hidden ships.

It depends on enough plausible commercial layers that no single actor appears to own the difficult part of the story.

A credible limitation must be faced directly. Ship-to-ship transfer is not inherently suspicious, and treating it as such would be analytically lazy and commercially destructive. Offshore lightering, consolidation, and redistribution are routine in petroleum trade, bulk logistics, and port systems constrained by depth, congestion, or terminal design. Weather windows, scheduling pressures, and infrastructure limitations all make transfers sensible. A disciplined sanctions analysis therefore begins from context, not from reflex. A transfer near a known commercial anchorage in daylight, with coherent documents, stable AIS behaviour, ordinary counterparties, and commercially intelligible onward routing belongs to a different category from a transfer whose surrounding facts point elsewhere. The transfer itself is not the offence. The surrounding coherence is what matters.

That limitation, however, sharpens the deeper reason transhipment sits at the centre of evasion. The practice is powerful because it allows concealment to borrow the habits of legitimate trade. A network does not need to invent a bizarre route or implausible method. It can use a routine maritime operation and place it at the exact point where scrutiny is hardest to sustain across time. The ship receiving the cargo need not look spectacularly suspicious. It only needs to be different enough, new enough, or acceptably ordinary enough that the next institution in line does not immediately connect it to the earlier leg. The handover becomes a memory problem for enforcement.

This is where information chains become more important than vessel tracks alone. A transfer can be observed and still remain poorly understood. Two ships lie alongside. Time passes. One leaves fuller or emptier than before. That observation may be useful. It does not yet tell us what moved, under which contract, with what declared origin, for whose benefit, or whether the cargo's legal identity changed in ways that later paperwork will disguise. Enforcement therefore depends on stitching together operational evidence and documentary evidence without assuming that either one speaks clearly by itself. Trust, in this setting, is visible in whether insurers, ports, banks, and buyers are still willing to rely on the post-transfer file as though it were self-contained. Once they stop doing so, the value of transhipment as concealment begins to erode.

A second named example lies in the scrutiny of North Korean sanctions evasion, where ship-to-ship transfers received sustained international attention through United Nations reporting and partner-state enforcement efforts. The relevance of those cases is not that they offer a single model for every other sanctions regime. It is that they demonstrated, repeatedly, how hard it is to prove the full legal meaning of a transfer even when strong indicators exist. A receiving vessel, a timing pattern, a suspicious location, an identity change, or a payment anomaly may all suggest concealment. The evidentiary burden still remains demanding. This is why transhipment is so attractive to evasive networks. It reduces confidence faster than it reduces movement.

The quiet motif here is the handover. A handover is simple to picture and difficult to govern. It is the moment at which physical continuity and documentary continuity can part company. In ordinary trade, the handover keeps supply chains fluid. In evasive trade, it allows the cargo to leave one legal and political atmosphere and enter another without ever touching shore. The same motion serves both worlds. That is why sanctions enforcement must be more exacting than slogans. It must ask not merely whether a transfer occurred, but what the transfer was meant to accomplish in the life of the paper.

For maritime sanctions, the broader lesson is austere. Transhipment sits at the centre of evasion because it offers the most efficient form of administrative distance available in open water. It does not eliminate evidence. It redistributes it across two vessels, several documents, multiple counterparties, and a timing gap that the next port or insurer may never fully reconstruct. It thrives because global trade genuinely needs transfers, because many of those transfers are entirely lawful, and because the very ordinariness of the practice protects those who use it strategically from easy classification. The challenge is not to condemn the handover. It is to decide when the handover has become the place where the cargo's official story was deliberately broken and reassembled.

That leaves the harder question just offshore, where the receiving vessel prepares to sail. If a transfer can be explained as routine commerce and used as strategic concealment in the same movement, what exactly should the next institution demand before it treats the cargo as continuous rather than conveniently reborn?

Ship-to-ship transfer practices

In May 2020, the United States Departments of State, Treasury, and Coast Guard issued a sanctions advisory that drew pointed attention to ship-to-ship transfers as a deceptive shipping practice when used to obscure cargo origin or destination. The advisory did not condemn the practice in itself. It could not have done so honestly. Ship-to-ship transfer is embedded in lawful maritime commerce, from lightering operations near shallow ports to the redistribution of cargoes within ordinary tanker networks. The problem was not the transfer alone. It was the way a transfer could interrupt the chain of explanation.

That interruption is what makes ship-to-ship practices so difficult to govern. A transfer at sea can be professionally planned, safely executed, fully documented, and commercially sensible. It can also be arranged so that the physical movement of cargo remains real while the documentary continuity surrounding that movement becomes weaker, slower, or easier to contest. A receiving vessel can look like a fresh commercial beginning. It rarely is. The handover leaves traces.

This matters because a transfer is never merely a matter of hoses, fenders, mooring, and seamanship. It is a sequence of permissions. One party must nominate the ships. Another must assess compatibility. An operator or manager must approve the plan. Insurers may need notice. Agents, surveyors, superintendents, and in some cases coastal or port authorities may need to know where and when the operation will occur. Cargo figures must be recorded. Bills, manifests, logs, and internal instructions must line up well enough that the operation can later be explained. The concept is procedural density. The implication is clear: ship-to-ship transfer creates many opportunities for lawful control and, equally, many opportunities for strategic ambiguity if those control points are thinned or fragmented.

Show the ordinary mechanics. Two vessels are selected because one cannot enter the final port fully laden, because a larger cargo needs to be assembled, because terminal capacity is constrained, or because onward distribution makes commercial sense. The timing is chosen with weather, tide, traffic, available support, and commercial schedules in mind. Equipment is checked, quantities are measured, logs are kept, and transfer records are generated. None of this is suspicious. In fact, it is what makes legitimate transfer possible. The concept here is operational normality. The implication is that enforcement must begin from the uncomfortable truth that many features of a lawful transfer and a concealing transfer will look alike at first glance.

That truth sharpens the importance of location. Legitimate ship-to-ship transfers often occur in recognised lightering areas, established anchorages, or operational zones where local practice, support services, and documentary habits are known. Those locations matter because they provide a thicker institutional environment. Pilots, agents, surveyors, support craft, terminal interfaces, and administrative routines can all add to the evidentiary chain. A transfer conducted far from such settings may still be lawful. Harsh weather, congestion, route design, or specialised logistics can require unusual choices. Yet location affects what can later be proved. The concept is evidentiary terrain. The implication is that remote or less structured transfer locations are attractive not because remoteness proves concealment, but because remoteness reduces the number of independent records and witnesses that later reconstruction can rely upon.

Timing matters just as much. A transfer in ordinary daylight with stable traffic patterns and a coherent lead-up in vessel movements produces one kind of record. A transfer clustered around gaps in declared plans, rushed route changes, or awkward periods of low visibility produces another. Again, timing alone proves little. Maritime schedules are messy. Weather intrudes. Port congestion forces improvisation. Commercial windows close quickly. Still, timing shapes interpretability. A transfer that fits the commercial logic of both vessels is easier to defend than one that seems to exist mainly to create distance between the cargo's first leg and its next set of documents. The visible behaviour that matters is not only when the vessels met, but how well their meeting aligns with the rest of the voyage story.

A named example from the oil trade helps clarify the issue. During the late 2010s and early 2020s, public reporting and regulatory notices repeatedly identified ship-to-ship transfers linked to Iranian and Venezuelan oil movements in waters near Fujairah, the eastern Mediterranean, and parts of Asia. The transfer itself was not always the most revealing fact. Those waters host legitimate tanker operations. What mattered was the surrounding pattern: vessels arriving under one documentary profile, meeting offshore, then departing under altered commercial expectations about cargo origin, destination, or ownership. The transfer functioned as a hinge in the information chain. Before it, one set of claims was operative. After it, another could be presented more plausibly to the next institution.

This is why proving what moved between whom is harder than observers often assume. Physical transfer at sea can sometimes be inferred from draught change, vessel positioning, timing, or later cargo volumes. Yet proving the legal and commercial meaning of the transfer is another matter. Did the entire cargo move, or only part of it? Was the receiving vessel acting for the same beneficial interest or for a new buyer? Did the transfer alter title, destination, or merely the transport arrangement? Which instructions governed the operation: the owner's, the charterer's, the manager's, or an intermediary trader's? The concept is layered proof. The implication is austere: a transfer can be strongly suspected, and even physically evident, while still leaving the most important sanctions questions unresolved.

The documentary side of ship-to-ship practice is where this difficulty becomes most acute. Transfer plans, notices, cargo logs, ullage reports, survey records, statements of facts, bills of lading, manifests, and post-transfer invoices all contribute pieces of the story. In a well-run lawful operation, these pieces may still vary in form because they serve different functions. In a pressured or evasive operation, they may vary in ways that reveal more than those arranging the trade intended. One document may emphasise the transfer location, another the latest loading point, another the final buyer's needs, while the earlier origin quietly recedes into less visible parts of the file. The transfer itself does not need to erase history. It only needs to create enough documentary branching that later institutions can choose the branch most convenient to accept.

That is why the book's focus on information chains matters here more than anywhere else. A ship-to-ship transfer cannot be understood by watching tracks alone or by reading documents alone. One must connect vessel movement, timing, ownership, chartering, payment, and documentary sequence into a narrative strong enough to survive challenge. A vessel loiters. Another approaches. Both depart altered. This may be innocent logistics. It may also be a break in continuity designed to leave the next port, insurer, or bank with a narrower slice of the truth. Trust, in this setting, depends on whether enough records exist across enough institutions to reconnect the slices after the fact.

A second named example lies in the scrutiny of North Korean sanctions evasion, where United Nations reporting and partner-state investigations repeatedly returned to ship-to-ship transfers as a central operational method. These cases showed how difficult it can be to move from observable patterns to legally durable conclusions. A rendezvous at sea, suspicious timing, altered cargo declarations, or related counterparties may point in a strong direction. Yet each element still requires interpretation. The deeper lesson extends beyond any one regime. Enforcement succeeds when it can rebuild the information chain across the transfer. It struggles when the transfer leaves only fragments and the fragments can be narrated more than one way.

A credible limitation should be stated plainly. Not every unusual transfer practice is evasive. Commercial shipping is too adaptive, too weather-exposed, and too operationally constrained for such easy judgement. Smaller parcels may reflect buyer needs. Offshore transfer may reflect draft limits. A late change in timing may reflect safety or congestion rather than concealment. A receiving vessel's different flag or manager may be ordinary market structure rather than deliberate distancing. Analysts, insurers, and ports who over-read every irregularity will soon produce false positives and lose confidence in their own filters. The discipline required here is not suspicion alone. It is comparison.

That comparison is what differentiates routine logistics from concealment. Routine transfers tend to produce a commercially intelligible chain. The locations make sense. The timing fits the trade. The counterparties have plausible roles. The documentation may not be elegant, but it remains coherent across systems and purposes. Concealing transfers tend to accumulate strain. The rendezvous location adds opacity without adding clear logistical value. Timing becomes awkward in ways the commercial story does not quite explain. The receiving vessel's onward narrative is cleaner than the first vessel's history should comfortably allow. Intermediaries multiply. Documents do not quite agree about what changed and when. None of these signs alone proves intent. Together they define the pattern enforcement must learn to read.

The quiet motif here is the handover. In legitimate commerce, a handover solves a transport problem. In evasive trade, a handover solves an evidentiary problem. The physical motion may be identical. What changes is the purpose the transfer serves in the life of the paperwork. A transfer arranged to fit port depth or cargo assembly still leaves a trail designed to be relied upon. A transfer arranged to thin that trail still leaves records, but records that work harder to separate the receiving vessel from the inconvenient part of the cargo's past. The challenge is not to moralise the handover. It is to ask what the handover was really for.

For maritime sanctions, the wider lesson is austere. Ship-to-ship transfer practices become central not because the operation itself is inherently dark, but because it sits at the exact point where cargo, vessels, documents, and instructions can all be rearranged without ever touching shore. That gives the practice great lawful value and great evasive potential. Enforcement attention therefore shifts from the physical transfer alone to the chain of information around it: who planned it, how it was documented, where it occurred, what changed in the paperwork afterwards, and whether the next institution in line can still connect the cargo to its earlier life without having to guess.

That leaves the harder question waiting after every offshore handover. When enough evidence exists to suspect a transfer, but not yet enough to prove what cargo moved, under whose authority, or with what legal consequence, how should the next port, insurer, or bank decide whether it is looking at routine maritime logistics - or at the precise moment a voyage's official story was deliberately broken and rebuilt?

Detection signals and their limits

In May 2020, the United States Departments of State, Treasury, and Coast Guard issued a sanctions advisory that gave unusual prominence to a set of maritime behaviours many operators already knew well: AIS gaps, suspicious loitering, and ship-to-ship transfers in places where the commercial explanation was not immediately obvious. The advisory did not claim that such signals proved wrongdoing. It could not have done so honestly. The signals mattered because they pointed attention, not because they settled the case.

That distinction is the beginning of seriousness in sanctions analysis. Modern shipping produces an immense amount of movement data, and movement data tempts observers into certainty. A vessel stops transmitting. Two ships drift near one another. A tanker lingers offshore without entering port. A route bends in an odd way. On a screen, these patterns can look almost confessional. At sea, they are often less obliging. A gap may reflect equipment failure, poor reception, or deliberate concealment. Loitering may signal a covert transfer, weather avoidance, congestion, pilot delay, or a commercial pause waiting for instructions. The screen shows behaviour. It does not explain it.

That is why detection signals must be treated as prompts rather than verdicts. Show the ordinary sequence. An analyst reviewing a vessel history notices a period without AIS transmission near a known transfer area. Later, another ship with a compatible cargo profile appears on a route that would make commercial sense if a transfer had occurred. The pattern is interesting. It may even be troubling. The concept is indicator logic. The implication is that the case has only just begun. One must still ask what else is known about the ships, the timing, the weather, the surrounding traffic, the documentary chain, the commercial actors, and the legal context in which the movement occurred. Signals narrow the field of attention. They do not end the inquiry.

AIS gaps are the most famous example because they offer a clean visual drama: the ship was visible, then it was not. That apparent simplicity is deceptive. AIS was not designed as a sanctions detection system. It was designed for navigational awareness and traffic management. That means its failures are not always sinister. Equipment can malfunction. Human operators can mis-enter data. Transmission may degrade in remote areas, harsh weather, or congested environments. Commercial tracking services may display incomplete coverage even where transmission existed. And yes, crews or managers may also switch systems off, manipulate settings, or otherwise use the system in ways that create intentional darkness. The point is not that AIS gaps are meaningless. The point is that they are multivalent. An institution that treats every silence as concealment will quickly lose analytical discipline.

A named example shows both the value and the weakness of such signals. During the late 2010s and early 2020s, public reporting on Iranian and Venezuelan oil movements repeatedly highlighted AIS interruptions combined with offshore rendezvous near waters around Fujairah, the eastern Mediterranean, and parts of East and Southeast Asia. In some cases, those signals formed part of a broader pattern later supported by regulatory action, insurance scrutiny, or documentary inconsistencies. The lesson was not that AIS darkness alone exposed the scheme. It was that AIS darkness became meaningful when joined to other facts: repeated counterparties, unusual route changes, ship-to-ship transfer indications, and cargo stories that weakened under comparison. The gap was a clue. The rest of the file did the heavier work.

Unusual loitering presents a different challenge because it can look suspicious even when it is perfectly ordinary. Ships wait. They wait for berths, cargo readiness, pilots, weather windows, bunkers, instructions from charterers, and decisions from ports or insurers. In crowded or politically sensitive waters, waiting can also be part of a vessel's attempt to preserve optionality while counterparties negotiate behind the scenes. The concept here is ambiguous delay. The implication is that loitering becomes analytically useful only when the waiting departs from the commercial logic one would otherwise expect. A tanker drifting in a recognised anchorage may tell us very little. A vessel repeatedly loitering in remote areas with compatible counterparties nearby may tell us more. The pattern matters, but so does the setting in which it appears.

Repeated rendezvous patterns are more suggestive because they imply relationship rather than mere anomaly. If the same vessels, or vessels linked through ownership, management, or trade pattern, keep approaching one another in operationally unusual places, the case for closer scrutiny grows. Here the signal lies not in a single event but in recurrence. Show how that works. One meeting offshore might be weather-driven or commercially innocent. Several meetings across months, especially if followed by altered route logic or documentary uncertainty, begin to look like coordination. The concept is patterned association. The implication is still one of caution. Repetition strengthens suspicion; it does not relieve the investigator of the burden to ask what moved, under whose instruction, and how the surrounding records changed after the meeting.

This is where harsh conditions complicate interpretation further. Northern and remote waters punish lazy inference. A vessel may reduce speed, alter course, or pause in ways that look strange to a distant analyst but entirely sensible to a master facing ice, visibility loss, traffic constraints, or weather systems. A reception gap in higher latitudes or adverse conditions may reflect environmental difficulty rather than intention. Even rendezvous can be more ambiguous in remote routes where support, convoying, or cargo redistribution follows different operational rhythms from dense southern trade lanes. The sea can imitate concealment. That is why analysts must resist the seduction of the dramatic trackline. The harsh environment adds noise precisely where scrutiny is already hungry for signal.

A second named example lies in the broader international scrutiny of North Korean ship-to-ship transfers, where United Nations reporting repeatedly identified suspicious meetings, AIS anomalies, and transfer patterns. Those cases were valuable not because they turned indicators into proof automatically, but because they revealed how much work is required to move from observable behaviour to defensible conclusion. Location, timing, vessel characteristics, cargo compatibility, sanctions designations, and documentary follow-through all had to be compared. The key lesson extends beyond that regime. Good enforcement does not confuse recurring signals with final answers. It uses them to organise further checking, not to skip it.

A credible limitation must be stated plainly. Signals can mislead in both directions. False positives occur when ordinary maritime behaviour is read too darkly. False negatives occur when analysts discount suspicious patterns because each individual anomaly can be explained away on its own. A vessel may genuinely have suffered transmission problems and still be part of an evasive trade. Another may have loitered awkwardly for entirely innocent commercial reasons. The difficulty is not only technical. It is epistemic. Maritime enforcement lives in a world where partial visibility is normal, and the temptation to overcompensate for that normality is constant.

That limitation does not mean signals are weak. It means their proper strength lies in combination. AIS gaps become more probative when they align with route discontinuity, counterparty opacity, or post-gap cargo narratives that do not cohere. Loitering becomes more important when it occurs outside commercially obvious waiting zones and coincides with a second vessel whose later voyage raises similar questions. Repeated rendezvous gain weight when the ships involved show linked ownership features, recurring document anomalies, or altered destinations inconsistent with the pre-transfer story. The disciplined approach is cumulative. One asks not whether one sign proves the case, but whether several signs, generated independently, begin to point in the same direction strongly enough to justify action or deeper inquiry.

This is where information chains matter more than spectacle. A strong sanctions case rarely depends on a single dramatic visual event. It depends on the ability to connect behavioural signals with documentary and commercial records. Did the AIS gap coincide with a later change in cargo description? Did the loitering precede a ship-to-ship transfer later reflected in survey records, payment flows, or altered manifests? Did the repeated rendezvous correspond to a network of managers, insurers, or traders that already sat under scrutiny? Trust, in this setting, becomes visible in whether the post-signal paperwork still holds. If the documents remain coherent, suspicion may recede. If they do not, the signal becomes harder to dismiss as noise.

The quiet motif here is the screen. On the screen, a ship appears, vanishes, slows, turns, meets another, and departs. The screen is useful. It is also dangerous because it rewards confidence before understanding. A disciplined analyst learns to ask what the screen cannot show: cargo title, instructions, ownership, weather judgment, insurance caution, chartering pressure, and the quality of the records created before and after the movement. The screen gives shape to a question. The answer lives elsewhere.

This is why the most serious enforcement work treats detection as probabilistic rather than theatrical. Signals increase or decrease confidence. They do not absolve institutions of the need to compare evidence across systems. Ports, insurers, banks, and regulators need a working method that respects both urgency and uncertainty: urgent enough to notice patterns before trade has moved too far, uncertain enough not to turn every operational irregularity into a sanctions conclusion. That balance is difficult, but the alternative is worse. Either one becomes credulous and misses the pattern, or one becomes overconfident and punishes shadows.

The broader lesson is austere. Detection signals matter because maritime concealment often leaves behavioural traces before it leaves documentary admissions. Their value lies in helping institutions decide where to look harder. Their danger lies in making those institutions think they have already found what they are actually only beginning to suspect. A sanctions regime that forgets this will either seize on spectacle or drown in ambiguity. Neither failure serves enforcement well.

The unresolved question follows every time a troubling trackline appears. When the signals are strong enough to disturb but not strong enough to conclude, how much uncertainty should the next institution tolerate before acting, and how much of its own credibility is it willing to risk if the screen has shown only the outline of a pattern that harsher conditions, weaker data, or a shrewd network knew perfectly well how to imitate?

When enforcement tightens, networks shift

In May 2020, when the United States Departments of State, Treasury, and Coast Guard warned maritime actors about deceptive shipping practices, the warning carried an implication broader than any one route or cargo. Pressure does not simply stop trade. It moves it. Once a corridor becomes too visible, too administratively costly, or too saturated with insurers, ports, banks, and service providers asking sharper questions, the trade seeks relief elsewhere. The cargo still wants water under it. The network still wants distance from scrutiny.

That is why sanctions at sea rarely behave like a wall. They behave more like weather. A shipping pattern exposed in one region can disperse, reform, and reappear under altered shapes in another. The ships may change. The parcel sizes may shrink. The intermediaries may multiply. More of the transaction may move into paper before it moves physically. The route itself may grow less direct not because commercial logic has failed, but because commercial logic has adapted to pressure. The map does not stay still.

Routes learn fast.

This is the first fact that matters if sanctions are to be understood as a moving contest rather than a one-time act of interdiction. Show the ordinary sequence. A transfer zone or trade corridor attracts scrutiny because repeated ship-to-ship transfers, suspicious routing, or unstable documentation have made the pattern too easy to notice. Insurers grow wary. Banks ask harder questions. Ports and service providers require more. The cost of continuing there rises. The network responds by redistributing the same commercial objective across more steps. A cargo once moved in one leg may now move in three. A cargo once carried by one large tanker may now be divided into smaller parcels. A direct buyer may give way to several intermediaries. The concept is displacement under pressure. The implication is that enforcement success is often partial and geographic. It closes one window while opening the incentive to find another.

This is why smaller parcels become attractive. A large cargo moved in one conspicuous block invites concentrated attention. It requires a bigger ship, clearer financing, fuller documentation, more visible service support, and often fewer chances to hide administrative strain. Break the same cargo into smaller movements and the profile changes. Each leg may look less dramatic. Each receiving counterparty may see only a fragment. The operational burden spreads outward rather than upward. This does not make the trade simple. It makes it harder to reconstruct as a single event. Risk, here, is visible in the number of handoffs required and in how much documentary coherence the network is willing to sacrifice in exchange for lower immediate visibility.

Intermediaries multiply for the same reason. One trader, one vessel, and one destination create a sharper story than three traders, two holding companies, a storage interval, and a final buyer who can truthfully say it encountered the cargo only at the end of the chain. This is not a peculiarity of illicit trade. Commodity commerce often uses intermediaries lawfully. The difficulty is that sanctions pressure makes the commercial value of intermediation rise precisely when evidentiary continuity matters most. A new company can receive title briefly. Another can handle financing. A third can manage the onward sale. Each step may be formally valid. Taken together, they cushion the point at which the original source or intended destination would otherwise have appeared too clearly. The concept is transactional insulation. The implication is that enforcement must follow not only ships, but the reasons why a trade suddenly needs more paperwork and more people than its physical movement seems to require.

A named example from the oil trade makes this plain. In the later phases of sanctions pressure on Iranian petroleum movements, public reporting and regulatory advisories repeatedly described how activity shifted between areas of attention as one zone became too exposed. A transfer pattern visible near one recognised anchorage or shipping lane would be followed by altered routing, different receiving vessels, or more fragmented commercial structures elsewhere. The lesson was not that scrutiny failed. It was that scrutiny produced adaptation. Once a route began to cost too much in documentation, insurance friction, or reputational risk, the network did not abandon the cargo. It redesigned the path by which the cargo could become administratively tolerable to the next set of institutions.

Remote waters become attractive in this context for reasons that are both obvious and dangerous. Fewer ports mean fewer routine checks. Fewer observers mean fewer incidental witnesses. Harsh conditions can make unusual movement patterns easier to explain away as operational prudence. Sparse infrastructure can reduce the number of institutions generating records. Yet remoteness is not a magical shelter. It also imposes cost. Fuel becomes harder to arrange. Repairs become more consequential. Weather and distance punish error. Insurance and service providers may become more selective precisely because contingency options are thinner. The concept is costly concealment. The implication is that networks moving outward are not escaping discipline entirely. They are trading one form of exposure for another.

This is especially important in northern or peripheral routes, where geography can simultaneously aid evasion and strengthen enforcement. A corridor with fewer eyes may produce weaker real-time detection. It may also depend on fewer acceptable ports, specialised support, and narrower weather windows. That means a network shifting into remote waters may buy evidentiary ambiguity while losing commercial resilience. A delay that might be manageable elsewhere becomes decisive. A missing document matters more. A service refusal travels further. This is why sanctions analysis should avoid romanticising displacement as either total failure or total success. Movement into remote waters often signals adaptation under constraint, not freedom from it.

A second named example lies in the broader response to Russian shipping after 2022. As mainstream insurers, registries, ports, service providers, and financial institutions tightened their treatment of certain vessels and cargoes, the market did not simply stop. Trade structures adjusted. Some shipments moved under different flags, through different traders, on different routes, or with different supporting services. Some activity became more reliant on paper transactions that distributed title and responsibility across several entities before the cargo reached its next obvious checkpoint. Again, the lesson is structural. Enforcement did not end movement. It made movement more administratively elaborate, more commercially fragile, and often more expensive to explain.

That reliance on paper transactions deserves special attention because it reveals how maritime adaptation is increasingly documentary before it is nautical. When one corridor tightens physically, networks do not only change route. They change the legal and commercial form in which the cargo appears. A sale may be inserted where none existed before. A cargo may be relabelled through storage or blending. A new intermediary may briefly own it. A financing arrangement may be restructured so that no single bank or trader sees the entire chain. The ship still sails, but the real adaptation may already have happened in contracts, invoices, and title papers before the hull altered course. The concept is pre-emptive dilution. The implication is that enforcement attentive only to vessel movement will miss half the contest.

A credible limitation must be faced. Not every route change, smaller parcel, or additional intermediary signals evasive adaptation. Shipping responds to freight rates, weather, port congestion, storage availability, insurance appetite, draft limits, and ordinary commercial opportunity. Markets fragment for reasons unrelated to sanctions. Cargoes are split because buyers differ. Remote routes may be chosen for seasonality or efficiency. A sanctions system that treats every sign of adaptation as proof of bad faith will quickly lose the discipline it needs to distinguish ordinary commercial flexibility from strategic concealment. False positives are not a side issue. They distort trade and weaken confidence in enforcement.

That limitation does not weaken the central argument. It clarifies what should be compared. The relevant question is not whether a network has changed, but why the change occurred and what else changed with it. Did the route shift coincide with thinner insurance, altered ownership presentation, or greater documentary complexity? Did smaller parcels appear alongside more intermediaries and weaker cargo descriptions? Did remote waters become attractive at the same moment that mainstream ports, service providers, or transfer zones grew less permissive? Does the paper now do more work than the route? The answers lie in pattern, timing, and the relationship between physical movement and administrative reinvention.

This is why sanctions should be seen as a moving contest rather than a binary test of blockage. Pressure produces learning. Networks measure which parts of the maritime system are tightening and which still offer enough room to continue, even at reduced efficiency. They adapt by redistributing risk: from ship to paper, from one corridor to another, from one large parcel to many small ones, from one visible counterparty to several less visible ones. Enforcement, in turn, must decide whether it can follow that redistribution without overextending itself or mistaking normal market motion for evasive intelligence. The contest is less about stopping the next voyage completely than about shaping the cost and coherence of the routes that remain.

The quiet motif here is the detour. A detour does not always mean the road is blocked. Sometimes it means the driver has learned where the cameras are. Maritime sanctions work in much the same way. A cargo forced off one route may reach its destination by a longer, weaker, or more administratively layered path. The detour itself becomes evidence of pressure and adaptation at once. It tells us that enforcement is biting. It also tells us that the network is still capable of redesign.

That leaves the harder question where any serious sanctions regime must eventually face it. When a corridor tightens and the trade responds by scattering into smaller parcels, more remote waters, denser paperwork, and more intermediaries, should that be read as proof that enforcement is working - or as a warning that the next phase of the contest will be harder to detect precisely because the pressure has taught the network to fragment before it can be found?

Chapter 10

Financial Messaging and Trade Finance

How can a ship complete its voyage and still fail to trade? That question unsettles the romance of maritime power because it shifts attention away from hulls, flags, and ports towards something less visible and often more decisive: the payment. Cargo can be loaded, carried, and discharged. None of that guarantees that the trade has succeeded. Until money moves through institutions willing to recognise the transaction as acceptable, the voyage remains commercially unfinished. The sea may carry the goods. The bank decides whether the story holds.

That is why financial messaging and trade finance matter so profoundly to sanctions enforcement. Maritime trade depends on distance being made routine through documents, assurances, and timing. A buyer far from the loading port relies on paper. A seller relies on payment promises. A shipowner relies on freight. A bank relies on the proposition that the documents before it correspond closely enough to the cargo, counterparties, and route it is being asked to finance or settle. Once that proposition weakens, the whole trade begins to slow. The transfer of value becomes the point where doubt stops being theoretical and starts becoming expensive.

The message can stop movement.

This is the central tension of the chapter. Financial systems were built to reduce uncertainty in commerce, yet sanctions force them to become instruments for producing friction whenever uncertainty grows too difficult to price or explain. A payment processor does not need to board a ship in order to change the voyage's fate. A bank does not need to know everything about the cargo in order to withhold settlement. It needs only enough concern about the parties, the paperwork, or the pattern of the transaction to conclude that ordinary processing is no longer defensible. When that happens, financial infrastructure stops looking like neutral plumbing and starts looking like jurisdiction expressed through caution.

That shift matters because maritime trade runs on predictability even when the voyage itself takes place far from immediate oversight. The ship may disappear beyond the horizon, but the transaction cannot disappear from the systems that clear funds, confirm letters of credit, handle collections, and monitor counterparties. This is one reason sanctions often bite hardest in finance. Payment rails are repetitive, rule-bound, and intolerant of unresolved ambiguity. A cargo that can survive a murky route or a delayed port call may still fail when its documents hit a bank that sees one mismatch too many or a compliance team unwilling to inherit a doubtful file. Enforcement, in this sense, does not chase the ship. It waits for the paper to ask for money.

The stakes rise because financial verification and cargo verification are not separate worlds. They lean on one another. A bank reviewing a trade finance package is not usually confirming the cargo by direct physical inspection. It is comparing documents that claim to represent the cargo, the seller, the buyer, the vessel, and the terms of the deal. If a bill of lading, invoice, certificate, freight instruction, or origin statement does not sit comfortably with the rest, the problem does not remain administrative for long. It becomes institutional. Someone must decide whether the inconsistency reflects ordinary commercial untidiness or a deeper attempt to move value under cover of plausible paperwork. That judgement can delay, reshape, or kill a transaction without any public declaration.

Price introduces a further difficulty because commerce often reveals what documents conceal. A transaction can look formally complete while its economics feel wrong. Freight terms may be unusually generous. Opaque fees may cluster around intermediaries whose practical role is thin. A cargo may appear to move on terms that make little commercial sense unless someone is absorbing risk off the books or compensating for the stigma attached to the voyage. None of this proves a sanctions breach. It does, however, show why price should be treated as a clue rather than a conclusion. Markets tell stories too, and one of the chapter's deeper concerns is how to read those stories without mistaking strangeness for guilt or neatness for innocence.

That concern becomes sharper inside firms, where compliance is not an abstract virtue but an organised process of triage, escalation, and institutional self-protection. A transaction may begin as routine business on one desk and become a problem on another. Operations want speed. Clients want certainty. Relationship managers want continuity. Compliance teams want defensible decisions under incomplete information. The conflict is structural, not personal. Private governance grows powerful here because firms often refuse more than the law expressly forbids, not out of grand principle, but because ambiguity itself becomes too costly to carry. The result is one of the book's recurring truths in another setting: the line between public enforcement and private caution is neither clean nor stable.

The path ahead follows that instability where it becomes operational. It begins with payments themselves, where screening and de-risking turn financial messaging into a practical control surface. It then moves into letters of credit, collections, and the documentary architecture through which maritime trade asks to be believed. From there it turns to the revealing distortions of price, freight, and fee structure, before settling inside the institutions that must decide, under time pressure, whether to move the money or stop the message. The order matters because each stage asks the same question in a different register: when does a plausible trade become too uncertain to process as ordinary commerce?

The deeper friction is not simply between law and evasion. It is between the speed demanded by trade and the slower discipline required by verification. Maritime commerce wants documents to function quickly, almost automatically, so that goods can move, credit can clear, and contracts can perform across distance. Sanctions insist that some documents should no longer pass so easily. Banks, processors, and compliance teams are left to arbitrate between those pressures while knowing that a wrong decision can trigger regulatory, financial, and reputational consequences out of all proportion to the immediate transaction. Their caution can therefore exceed formal law, and once it does, private refusal becomes one of the most effective sanctions tools available.

That leaves a harder question than the language of screening and de-risking usually admits. When the ship is at sea, the cargo is moving, and the documents are just coherent enough to ask for payment, what should matter more to the institution holding the message in its hands: the formal sufficiency of the paper, or the colder judgement that the transaction only looks complete because no one has yet forced its story to stand still long enough to be fully compared?

Payments as a control surface

In September 2019, when the United States designated COSCO Shipping Tanker (Dalian) entities under its Iran programme, the most revealing effect was not a naval one. Ships did not suddenly lose the ability to float or crews the ability to navigate. What changed, with unnerving speed, was the willingness of banks, charterers, insurers, and counterparties to let money move through ordinary channels attached to those voyages. A legal act issued in Washington reached into desks in London, Singapore, Athens, and elsewhere because maritime trade cannot live on cargo movement alone. The payment is part of the voyage.

That fact is easy to miss because the sea flatters physical imagination. We picture ships, straits, terminals, and cargoes. Yet every maritime transaction depends on an invisible choreography of invoices, freight payments, letters of credit, disbursements, premiums, wage transfers, agency fees, bunker settlements, and claims reserves. A vessel can move far from oversight in one sense and remain deeply dependent on institutions that are not remote at all. Banks do not need to see the ship from the shore. They only need to decide whether the trade passing through their systems still looks acceptable enough to process. The message stops the ship.

This is why payments should be treated as a control surface rather than as a mere after-effect of trade. Show the ordinary sequence. A cargo is fixed. A vessel is nominated. Freight terms are agreed. Supporting services are arranged. None of this becomes economically real until payments start flowing through institutions that can settle obligations predictably. A bank must honour instructions. A processor must pass the message. A correspondent relationship must remain open. The concept is financial dependence. The implication is severe: a transaction can fail commercially while the ship is still performing physically, simply because the payment architecture supporting the voyage has begun to reject ambiguity.

That architecture matters because maritime trade is built on timing as much as distance. Sellers need assurance that shipment will lead to payment. Buyers need confidence that documents will release value only when contractual conditions are met. Owners need freight. Managers need to pay wages and suppliers. Ports and agents need disbursements cleared. This entire chain depends on the expectation that funds can move through ordinary rails without forcing every institution involved into a fresh political or legal argument. The moment that expectation weakens, the trade becomes less a commercial routine and more a compliance event. Trust, in this setting, is visible in whether the payment is processed without escalation, whether the bank seeks further explanation, whether the transaction is delayed, and whether the parties begin looking for more awkward routes to settle what should have been ordinary business.

Banks and payment processors become decisive enforcers for exactly this reason. They are not maritime authorities, yet they sit at the point where uncertainty becomes costly. A vessel owner or trader may be willing to accept route risk, reputational discomfort, or a difficult port. A bank is usually less sentimental. It must ask whether the names, documents, counterparties, and commercial logic attached to the payment are strong enough to survive later scrutiny. If the answer becomes doubtful, the institution need not prove a sanctions breach to act decisively. It can freeze, escalate, decline, or quietly step back. The concept is defensive refusal. The implication is that enforcement can bite hardest where the ship is absent and the paperwork is asking for money.

This is one reason de-risking has become such a consequential force in maritime sanctions. The term is overused and often poorly understood, but the underlying behaviour is plain enough. A bank or processor confronted by a class of transactions that now carries disproportionate regulatory, legal, or reputational uncertainty may decide that the profit or client relationship is no longer worth the burden. It exits not because every payment is prohibited in black-letter terms, but because the cost of distinguishing safe from unsafe has become too high. The visible behaviour is familiar: broader client reviews, narrower correspondent access, more aggressive screening, longer delays, rising documentary demands, and eventual refusal where earlier the file would have passed routinely. The ship need not be touched. The trade has still been altered.

A named example from the Russian shipping environment after February 2022 makes the mechanism plain. As sanctions widened and financial institutions reassessed exposure to Russian-linked trade, the practical question for many voyages was not simply whether cargo could still be loaded or discharged. It was whether freight, premiums, agency disbursements, bunker payments, and sale proceeds could still pass through trusted channels without triggering blocks, queries, or reputational alarms. Some trades continued. But they often did so under heavier administrative strain, with narrower banking options and greater dependence on institutions willing to tolerate uncertainty that mainstream providers no longer wished to carry. The legal rules mattered. The greater commercial force often came from the way financial systems internalised them.

This is also why payment processing should not be mistaken for a neutral technical service. Messaging systems, correspondent arrangements, sanctions screening tools, and compliance teams all shape what counts as executable commerce. A payment instruction may be accurate in every formal field and still be treated as too exposed because the wider pattern around it - recent ownership change, unusual routing, opaque intermediary, difficult cargo narrative - makes later defence unattractive. The bank sees the transaction not as the parties see it, as a single trade that deserves its own explanation, but as one file inside a wider supervisory and institutional risk environment. The transaction is judged by pattern as much as by individual merit. That is what gives banks such disproportionate influence over maritime sanctions: they are not paying only for this payment if they get it wrong.

A second named example comes from the Iranian oil trade during the later 2010s and early 2020s, when public advisories repeatedly warned financial institutions that deceptive shipping practices could make documentary sufficiency misleading. The lesson was not simply that banks should be suspicious. It was that maritime trade could remain outwardly coherent while the underlying payment request had become uncomfortably detached from the full voyage story. A vessel might change flag, manager, or route. Cargo descriptions might soften. Intermediaries might multiply. The physical shipment could still look plausible. The payment, however, forced the whole structure back into a single institutional frame. Someone had to decide whether the story was still good enough to honour with money.

That does not mean financial control is absolute. A credible limitation must be faced. Payment networks can adapt. Alternative banks, different currencies, offset arrangements, state-backed institutions, barter-like structures, or more opaque settlement pathways can emerge when mainstream rails narrow. Some trades continue precisely because actors are willing to accept slower, less transparent, or less efficient methods of payment. Sanctions analysis becomes lazy when it assumes that a blocked mainstream payment equals the death of the trade. Often it means the trade will survive under degraded financial conditions rather than disappear altogether. Still, degradation matters. Money moved through less trusted channels carries higher cost, lower speed, and greater fragility. The trade becomes harder to sustain at scale and harder to normalise in the eyes of the next institution asked to engage.

That limitation sharpens the central point rather than weakening it. The value of payment controls lies not only in stopping transactions outright, but in altering the quality of commerce around them. A seller kept waiting for funds behaves differently. A ship manager unsure whether payroll or suppliers will clear behaves differently. A charterer facing uncertain freight settlement behaves differently. Delayed or uncertain payment turns operational confidence into hesitation. It may force prepayment, shorten credit, increase documentary demands, or drive counterparties away from otherwise possible fixtures. The maritime trade still moves, perhaps, but with more strain in every link. That strain is itself a form of enforcement.

This is why banks and processors often become more consequential than public rhetoric allows. They do not simply react to law. They organise risk through internal thresholds that can exceed law. A transaction may be technically permissible yet still fail because the institution asked to process it no longer believes the documentation, counterparties, or route can be defended comfortably to regulators, auditors, or correspondent partners later. Private governance thereby extends formal sanctions through ordinary caution. The legal boundary remains one thing. The practical boundary becomes whatever the institution is willing to explain after the fact. That difference is one of the hardest realities for maritime actors to absorb, because it means the decisive refusal may come not from a prohibition but from an appetite.

The quiet motif here is the message itself. A payment message looks modest - a string of names, accounts, banks, references, amounts, and instructions. Yet it carries the whole voyage in compressed form. If the message is clean enough, money moves and the trade becomes commercially complete. If it is not, the voyage remains suspended between physical performance and economic recognition. The ship may have delivered. The transaction has not yet arrived.

For maritime sanctions, the deeper lesson is austere. Payment systems matter because they force distant trades back into zones of institutional judgement where ambiguity is costly and routine cannot survive without explanation. Banks and processors become decisive enforcers not by patrolling the sea, but by deciding whether the documentary and commercial story attached to a voyage is still stable enough to carry value. The refusal may look administrative. Its consequences are strategic. A ship that can still sail may already have lost the one permission that made the voyage worth undertaking.

That leaves the harder question where sanctions often do their quietest work. When a maritime transaction remains just plausible enough on paper to request payment, but not quite persuasive enough to reassure the institution reading it, what should matter more: the formal possibility that the trade is lawful, or the colder institutional judgement that lawful trades do not usually need this much explanation merely to move money?

Letters of credit, collections, and documentation

In September 2001, banks and trade lawyers were reminded with unusual force that commerce can be impeccably documented and still dangerously misunderstood. The point did not belong only to the world of fraud or sanctions. It belonged to trade itself. Letters of credit and documentary collections were built on a disciplined fiction: that if the right papers appear in the right form at the right moment, distant parties can trust a transaction they cannot physically supervise. That fiction works remarkably well. It also creates the precise surface on which manipulation becomes possible.

The bank does not see cargo.

That blunt fact governs the whole field. A vessel may be half a world away. The goods may have changed hands, entered storage, been relabelled, blended, or routed through several intermediaries. Yet when the documents arrive for payment or collection, the financial institution is not being asked to inspect the steel, the hold, or the terminal tank. It is being asked to decide whether the paper before it is good enough to stand in for the trade behind it. The transaction moves because documents claim to describe reality. Enforcement follows because those claims can fracture under pressure.

This is why letters of credit and documentary collections matter so deeply to maritime sanctions. They do not merely facilitate trade; they formalise trust through sequences of paper that must appear coherent to institutions that cannot directly verify the cargo. Show the sequence in ordinary terms. A buyer wants assurance that payment will not be released before shipment. A seller wants assurance that shipment will lead to payment if the required documents are presented. A bank or banks stand between them, not as all-knowing arbiters of fact, but as disciplined readers of documentary compliance. Bills of lading, invoices, origin certificates, inspection reports, packing lists, manifests, insurance papers, and ancillary declarations begin to do legal work far beyond their physical modesty. The concept is documentary substitution. The implication is sharp: where the documents become unreliable, the financial instrument stops being a bridge and starts becoming a trigger for inquiry.

That inquiry matters because documentary trade finance is designed to be both rigorous and limited. Banks engaged in letters of credit famously deal in documents, not goods. Collections are somewhat different in structure and risk allocation, yet they too depend on the proposition that paper can move value across distance without requiring every participant to witness the cargo first-hand. This creates a peculiar vulnerability. The system is highly formal, yet formality itself can be exploited. A forged certificate may imitate compliance. A laundered bill of lading may preserve a lawful shape while weakening the truth it is meant to carry. An origin claim may be clean on the page because the dirtier part of the story has already been pushed behind a storage interval, an intermediary sale, or a relabelled shipment. The implication is not that documentary finance is naive. It is that the very discipline of the system gives evasion a precise target.

A named example from the sanctions environment around Iranian trade makes the point. During the later 2010s and early 2020s, public advisories and enforcement materials repeatedly warned that trade documents linked to certain maritime shipments could be manipulated through altered cargo descriptions, opaque intermediary structures, and misleading origin narratives. The significance was not merely that some documents were false. It was that the payment architecture depended on those documents being sufficiently trustworthy to support the release of funds. Once doubts emerged about whether a bill of lading, invoice, or certificate described the cargo's real origin or destination, the financial transaction ceased to be routine. The paper had become a scene of contest.

This is where financial verification and cargo verification begin to collapse into one another. A mismatch in trade finance is rarely just a banking problem. If the invoice says one thing, the bill of lading another, the origin certificate something cleaner still, and the vessel history points in a fourth direction, the institution processing the documents is being asked to decide whether the inconsistency is clerical untidiness or evidence that the underlying cargo story has been rearranged for strategic reasons. The concept is documentary strain. The implication is that enforcement can begin with a bank's discomfort even when no ship has yet been stopped, no cargo seized, and no formal accusation issued. A file under financial review can become the first real investigation the voyage has faced.

That review is often triggered by exactly the sort of mismatches trade practitioners know too well. Dates do not align neatly. Quantities vary within explainable but uncomfortable margins. A loading port appears inconsistent with the stated origin. An intermediary suddenly appears in a role too thin to explain its share of the transaction. The named vessel changes after earlier drafts of the paperwork suggested another. A certificate arrives in the right form but from a source the bank or confirming institution no longer regards as easy to trust. None of these discrepancies proves sanctions evasion by itself. Shipping and commodity trade are administratively untidy by nature. Yet the pattern matters because documentary finance depends on coherence. The stronger the payment instrument, the less tolerance it often has for unexplained documentary drift.

A second named example lies in the wider reordering of Russian-linked maritime trade after 2022. As sanctions widened and market participants reassessed exposure, banks and trade finance teams were forced to test not only counterparties and vessel links but the documentary logic of cargo movements that had become more circuitous, more intermediated, and more politically loaded. Again, the decisive issue was rarely one dramatic forgery. It was the gradual weakening of documentary continuity. A cargo could still move. The payment file could still fail, not because every paper was facially false, but because together they no longer formed a story a cautious institution was willing to honour with money. That is what gives documentary mismatches their power: they turn commercial unease into a defensible reason to stop the transaction.

This is also why forged documents and laundered documents should not be confused. Forgery is the cruder problem and, in some ways, the simpler one. A forged certificate or falsified bill may eventually be exposed by direct inconsistency or external checking. Laundering is more subtle. A laundered document may be formally real, issued by a legitimate actor, and still function as a device for shifting attention away from the more difficult parts of the trade. A cargo stored, blended, relabelled, or resold through a reputable hub may emerge with documents that are authentic in the narrow sense while telling a more comfortable truth than the full chain deserves. The concept here is documentary cleansing. The implication is that enforcement must ask not only whether a document is genuine, but what portion of the cargo's history it has been allowed to represent.

A credible limitation must be faced directly. Documentary mismatches do not arise only from bad faith. Maritime trade crosses languages, legal cultures, customs systems, terminal practices, and banking routines that were not designed to produce perfect textual harmony. A vessel may be described one way for customs purposes, another for commercial shorthand, and another for technical accuracy. Dates may shift because documents are issued at different moments in the loading and financing sequence. Intermediaries may be commercially genuine even when their role appears thin to an outsider. A sanctions system that treats every discrepancy as evidence of concealment will soon become analytically crude and commercially damaging. False positives are not a side concern here. They are a structural risk of document-based enforcement.

That limitation, however, does not weaken the central point. It clarifies what kind of discipline is required. The issue is not whether the papers are identical; they rarely are. The issue is whether they remain reconcilable. Can the differences be explained by the normal grammar of trade, or do they accumulate in ways that suggest the documents are no longer describing one stable transaction? Do the changes serve intelligible commercial purposes, or do they consistently soften origin, complicate ownership, and diffuse responsibility at the precise points where sanctions exposure would otherwise sharpen? The answer emerges not from a single mismatch, but from whether the file still holds together after comparison.

This is why investigative triggers often look modest at first. A confirming bank asks for one more certificate. A collections team pauses release because the consignee details have shifted. A compliance officer notices that the cargo description in the invoice is cleaner than the vessel history suggests it should be. The friction begins not with accusation but with doubt. That doubt is operationally important because time matters. Trade finance instruments rely on speed. Sellers want prompt payment. Buyers want prompt control of documents. Banks want files to move, not to become miniature inquiries. Once a mismatch forces escalation, the transaction has already entered a different world. The pace slows. More desks become involved. More records are compared. The paper trail thickens because it has started to resist itself.

The quiet motif here is the stamp. A stamped bill of lading, a stamped certificate, a stamped collection instruction, a stamped bank presentation: each mark invites the next institution to proceed. Yet the stamp does not certify the whole truth of the cargo. It certifies that someone, somewhere, has accepted responsibility for a fragment of that truth. Documentary finance works when those fragments still align. It falters when the stamps remain individually persuasive but collectively unstable. The paper can look official and still fail the deeper test of continuity.

That is why the larger theme of the book returns so forcefully here. Enforcement follows paper because paper is where distance becomes governable. A ship at sea can evade sight. A cargo can be blended. An intermediary can disappear after a brief role in title transfer. The documents must still ask to be believed by someone holding the money.

Banks and processors become consequential not because they know the sea better than maritime actors do, but because they are asked to convert documentary coherence into released value. Once coherence breaks, the payment instrument becomes an investigative instrument.

The unresolved question comes at the moment of presentation, when the documents are formally complete, commercially plausible, and just misaligned enough to trouble an experienced eye. Should the institution processing them treat the mismatch as the ordinary untidiness of global trade, or as the point at which the cargo's official story has become too carefully repaired to deserve the money it is asking to unlock?

Pricing, freight, and hidden subsidies

In April 2020, oil futures briefly traded at prices so distorted that outside observers were reminded of an old commercial truth: price can cease to describe value cleanly when storage, urgency, and constraint overwhelm ordinary market logic. Maritime sanctions generate a quieter version of the same disturbance. A cargo may still move under a contract that looks commercially recognisable, yet the price, freight structure, or surrounding fees begin to carry meanings not visible in the cargo description alone. The arithmetic grows nervous.

That is where this subject begins. Price does not confess. It hints. A freight rate may be unusually generous because risk has genuinely risen. A discount may reflect quality, timing, distance, or a desperate seller. An opaque service fee may hide nothing more sinister than poor contractual drafting. And yet price is often the first place where a sanctions-sensitive trade stops looking like routine commerce and starts looking like a negotiation over danger. Money bends before paper breaks.

This is why pricing should be treated as a clue rather than a conclusion. Show the ordinary sequence. A buyer agrees to take a cargo that carries more uncertainty than comparable trades. The ship may face greater insurance friction, more difficult port calls, slower banking, thinner service options, or a narrower circle of willing counterparties. Someone must absorb that burden. The concept is risk compensation. The implication is that the price of the cargo or the freight terms around it may begin to carry costs not fully explained by distance, quality, or market conditions alone. A discount may be the visible price of administrative discomfort.

That discomfort can express itself in several ways without ever becoming an open confession. The headline cargo price may appear low, but ancillary fees rise. Freight may look unusually favourable to one side of the transaction because commercial risk is being shifted elsewhere in the file. A charterer may accept terms that make little sense unless the voyage carries hidden compensations for difficulty or stigma. Service charges may appear in forms too vague to test easily: handling fees, agency uplifts, security supplements, consultancy margins, facilitation costs, storage adjustments, or other line items broad enough to gather several motives at once. The concept is compensatory opacity. The implication is that sanctions-sensitive trade often becomes economically legible not through one shocking number, but through the relationship between the visible price and the supporting charges required to keep the deal alive.

This matters because maritime trade rarely runs on cargo price alone. Freight, insurance, port costs, demurrage exposure, credit terms, payment timing, and the cost of documentary and compliance labour all sit inside the real economic shape of a voyage. A transaction can therefore look superficially normal if one reads only the invoice price while missing the way risk has been redistributed across the surrounding contract architecture. A seller may offer a discount while a shipping affiliate recovers value through generous freight. A trader may accept a narrow margin on paper while a related service company invoices the rest elsewhere. A cargo may seem underpriced only because the true subsidy lies in state-backed insurance, favourable credit, or tolerated payment delay. The question is not simply what the goods cost. It is where the rest of the cost has gone.

That is why non-market pricing deserves careful treatment. The phrase sounds accusatory, but it is better understood as an analytical warning. A price becomes non-market in a useful sanctions sense not merely when it departs from a benchmark, but when the departure appears connected to pressures the ordinary commercial file cannot explain persuasively. If a shipment repeatedly moves under terms that look unusually forgiving given route complexity, service friction, insurance uncertainty, and reputational exposure, the analyst is entitled to ask who is absorbing the difference and why. The visible behaviour that matters is practical: who keeps accepting thin margins, who keeps providing transport on terms others avoid, who keeps financing the delays, and which related parties seem consistently willing to carry costs the open market would usually price more harshly.

Freight is especially revealing because it sits at the seam between the cargo's commercial value and the ship's operational exposure. A freight rate that appears detached from route difficulty, service constraints, or evident compliance burden may suggest that something else is subsidising the movement. That does not prove sanctions evasion. Freight markets are volatile, personal relationships matter, and strategic shippers often accept unusual terms for reasons outsiders do not fully see. Still, freight is one of the places where hidden subsidy can become visible by distortion. A voyage that looks too easy to carry may not be easy at all; it may simply be paid for elsewhere in the structure. The concept is displaced cost. The implication is that analysts should read freight not as an isolated market signal but as one part of a wider compensation pattern.

The same is true of opaque fees. Opaque fees are attractive to high-risk trades because they are capacious. They can gather together extra insurance cost, compliance friction, agent discomfort, political risk premia, delay compensation, or less defensible transfers of value under labels broad enough to resist neat challenge. Some such fees are perfectly ordinary. Shipping is full of imperfectly described charges. Yet opacity becomes analytically significant when it clusters around already difficult trades and when the actors involved seem unable or unwilling to explain the commercial purpose of the fee with precision. Trust, in this setting, is visible in whether a counterparty can break down the economics into recognisable parts. A file that grows blurrier as one approaches the money is telling its own story.

A credible limitation should be stated plainly. Pricing anomalies are among the easiest things to over-read. Markets move. Cargo quality differs. Timing matters. Political events affect appetite. Longstanding commercial relationships can produce terms that look odd to outsiders but make sense within a broader portfolio or strategic arrangement. Some trades are deliberately priced to secure market share, clear storage, or preserve customer ties under stressed conditions. A sanctions analyst who treats every discount or every vague charge as hidden subsidy will soon confuse commercial messiness with concealment. Price is noisy evidence. It earns attention, not belief.

That limitation does not weaken the value of price analysis. It refines the method. Price becomes more informative when compared with other parts of the file. Does the unusual freight term appear alongside ownership opacity, altered routing, thinner insurance, or difficult payment channels? Do vague fees cluster around shipments whose documentation is already strained? Do commercial terms remain oddly favourable across repeated deals where risk should have made counterparties more cautious? The relevant question is not whether one number looks wrong. It is whether the economic structure of the deal is too generous, too vague, or too stable under stress to be explained by ordinary market behaviour alone.

This is where hidden subsidy becomes a useful, if delicate, idea. A hidden subsidy is not only direct state support. It can also take the form of tolerated losses, affiliated service providers carrying uncommercial terms, extended credit no ordinary lender would grant, or a network willing to absorb recurring friction in one place because it recovers value somewhere harder to see. In sanctions-sensitive trade, such support can keep cargo moving when the open market would otherwise demand either sharper discounts or outright refusal. The trade survives not because the risk disappeared, but because someone decided to socialise it quietly. The analyst's burden is not to denounce every unexplained comfort as corruption. It is to ask whether the comfort has a coherent commercial source.

This becomes especially important inside firms asked to process the transaction. Banks, insurers, charterers, and compliance teams may not know the whole economics of the deal, but they can often sense when the visible numbers no longer match the visible risks. A payment team notices recurring side charges. An insurer sees freight terms that feel detached from the route's operational strain. A charterer wonders why a service provider remains willing when others have stepped away. These institutions do not need to resolve the full political story before acting. They need only conclude that the commercial story has become too peculiar to treat as routine. Price, in that sense, becomes a trigger for further inquiry rather than a verdict on its own.

The quiet motif here is the margin. In ordinary trade, margins may be thin or generous, but they still answer roughly to the burdens the transaction carries. In pressured trade, the margin can become a place where risk leaves fingerprints. A margin kept artificially calm in the face of mounting friction suggests that value is entering or leaving through another door. The transaction may still look complete on the main invoice. The missing logic often sits at the edge of the deal, where the margin should have widened but did not.

That is why the most disciplined reading of price is comparative rather than dramatic. One asks how the freight aligns with route difficulty, how the fees align with the services actually described, how the payment terms align with the counterparties' apparent risk, and whether the commercial architecture looks increasingly designed to hide who is paying for the trade's awkwardness. None of this proves evasion. It does, however, reveal where the formal file may be too tidy for the economics underneath it. Enforcement follows paper, but price often tells us which paper deserves a colder second look.

The unresolved question is the one every cautious institution eventually faces. When a maritime trade looks administratively plausible but commercially too forgiving for the risks it plainly carries, should the analyst treat the distorted pricing as ordinary market adaptation - or as the point at which the economics themselves begin to admit what the documents are still trying not to say?

Compliance teams as institutional actors

In September 2019, when sanctions pressure struck COSCO Shipping Tanker (Dalian) entities, one of the most consequential maritime decisions was made far from any bridge or berth. It was made on compliance desks inside banks, insurers, brokers, and shipping firms that suddenly had to decide whether apparently ordinary transactions still fell within an acceptable range of institutional risk. The law named certain actors. The compliance function translated that naming into slowed payments, withdrawn comfort, escalated files, and transactions that no longer moved at the pace commerce expected. The voyage met the inbox.

That is the starting truth. Compliance teams are not peripheral to sanctions enforcement; they are among its most practical institutional actors. A firm may own no ships, command no port, and issue no public prohibition. If its compliance staff decide that a payment, insurance confirmation, charter fixture, or service contract can no longer be justified, the commercial effect can rival formal state action. The officer reading the file does not need sovereign power. The file itself carries enough consequence. Caution can travel faster than law.

This matters because compliance inside firms is not simply a matter of checking names against lists. Show the ordinary sequence. A transaction begins on the business side: a client asks for payment processing, a vessel nomination, an insurance extension, a freight approval, or a trade finance document release. Something in the file triggers discomfort. The case moves from routine handling to enhanced review. More documents are requested. Sanctions screening is rerun. Vessel history, ownership, route, cargo description, bank details, and service providers are compared. If uncertainty remains, the file climbs another internal rung to managers, specialist reviewers, legal advisers, or committees empowered to make harder calls. The concept is escalation architecture. The implication is that enforcement often happens inside a firm before the state ever acts directly on the voyage itself.

That architecture gives compliance teams disproportionate influence because they sit between commercial appetite and institutional memory. Front-line staff are usually paid to move business. Compliance staff are paid, more or less, to ask whether moving this particular business will later look indefensible. Those are different missions, and the difference matters. A trader may see a profitable cargo. A relationship manager may see an important client. An operations team may see a transaction that looks formally complete. Compliance sees a future explanation that may have to be given to regulators, correspondent banks, auditors, or a board after something has gone wrong. The concept is anticipatory accountability. The implication is severe: a file can fail not because it is plainly prohibited, but because nobody inside the institution wants to own its future.

This is where risk appetite becomes more than a phrase. Risk appetite is visible in decisions. Which files can be cleared by junior staff and which must escalate. How much documentary mismatch is tolerated before a transaction is paused. Whether the institution accepts certain flags, insurers, counterparties, or transfer patterns at all. Whether uncertainty is treated as a manageable condition of trade or as a reason to refuse. Two firms reading the same facts may therefore behave differently not because one understands the law and the other does not, but because they have drawn different lines around what kind of ambiguity they are willing to carry. Private governance begins there.

A named example from the Russian trade environment after February 2022 makes this plain. As sanctions expanded and commercial relationships came under renewed scrutiny, many transactions did not collapse because a single statutory sentence made them impossible. They stalled because compliance teams inside banks, insurers, brokers, and shipping service firms concluded that the burden of understanding the file now exceeded the institution's appetite. Payments were escalated. Cover confirmations slowed. Certain counterparties became functionally untouchable even where legal analysis remained more qualified. The law mattered. Internal governance often mattered sooner.

This is why private governance can exceed formal law. A statute or regulation may define a prohibited zone with some precision. A firm's compliance system often defines a wider zone of discomfort around it. The reason is not mysterious. Legal exposure is only one cost. Reputational harm, supervisory attention, litigation risk, and the potential loss of correspondent or market access all encourage institutions to step back from files that are technically arguable but institutionally unpleasant. The visible behaviour is familiar: broad client exits, refusal to touch certain corridors, rejection of payment structures that may be lawful in principle, and reliance on internal policy language stricter than the minimum legal text. The implication is profound. Sanctions operate not only through what states ban, but through what firms no longer find worth defending.

That widening of caution creates real power. A vessel may still be insurable somewhere, financeable somewhere, payable somewhere. If enough mainstream institutions decide the file belongs outside their appetite, the voyage is pushed towards thinner, slower, less trusted channels. Compliance teams do not need to coordinate perfectly for this effect to emerge. They only need to react to similar pressures with similar caution. An individual bank's refusal becomes a market signal. An insurer's hesitation informs a broker's judgement. A payment processor's query changes the confidence of a charterer or trader. The queue lengthens.

Yet this power comes with a structural weakness. Compliance teams work under uncertainty, and uncertainty is not distributed evenly across files. Some transactions arrive with dense records, stable counterparties, and coherent commercial logic. Others arrive with recent ownership changes, vague cargo descriptions, unusual routes, multiple intermediaries, and time pressure from clients already impatient for performance. The team must decide how much uncertainty is tolerable before speed itself becomes a threat. That is the deepest tension in this field: commerce wants velocity, while compliance requires comparison, escalation, and sometimes waiting for records that do not arrive quickly enough to satisfy either side.

That tension becomes acute because maritime trade is unforgiving of delay. A cargo can miss a window. A vessel can lose a berth. A seller can lose financing confidence. A buyer can turn elsewhere. A manager can fail to clear wages or service invoices on time. Every extra hour spent inside compliance review therefore imposes cost even before any refusal is issued. The institution knows this. So does the client. The file begins to carry not only legal ambiguity but internal organisational strain. Operations wants movement. Compliance wants an explanation. Senior management wants both, but not at the cost of inheriting a scandal later. This is why escalation paths matter so much. They are the channels through which institutions convert discomfort into either permission or stoppage without pretending the choice is easy.

A second named example can be drawn from the repeated advisories issued in relation to Iranian and deceptive shipping practices during the late 2010s and early 2020s. Those advisories did more than warn about specific conduct. They shifted internal thresholds. Once firms were told that particular combinations of AIS behaviour, ownership opacity, document inconsistency, and transfer practice deserved heightened attention, compliance teams had stronger institutional reasons to escalate files that might previously have passed. The significance lay not only in the content of the warning, but in the fact that it reorganised internal behaviour. A new advisory can change a market before a new prosecution ever appears.

A credible limitation must be admitted. Compliance teams are not wise tribunals sitting above commerce. They can overreact. They can rely too heavily on weak indicators. They can generate false positives, delay lawful trade, and treat ordinary maritime untidiness as though it were evidence of wrongdoing. They can also be inconsistent across offices, products, and regions, especially when guidance is thin and political pressure high. A cautious refusal may protect the institution while imposing costs on innocent actors who simply happen to resemble riskier files in superficial ways. This is not a side effect. It is one of the central moral and operational problems of modern sanctions practice.

That limitation does not weaken the argument. It sharpens it. The question is not whether compliance teams wield power. They plainly do. The question is how that power is structured and what kinds of evidence it rewards or punishes. Good compliance does not confuse uncertainty with guilt, but it does insist that the burden of ambiguity cannot always be shifted onto the institution processing the deal. It asks whether the commercial story remains coherent when ownership, route, cargo, price, service providers, and payment instructions are compared. If the answer weakens under comparison, refusal becomes less an act of moral certainty than an act of organisational self-preservation.

This is why compliance should be seen as institutional action rather than technical administration. Teams do not merely apply rules; they interpret thresholds, distribute delay, and decide which files deserve further life inside the firm's systems. Their decisions shape markets. They teach clients what kinds of ambiguity are still tolerated and what kinds will now attract friction. They create shadow boundaries around formal law. They can close a corridor without any minister announcing it. The quiet motif here is the queue again, because compliance power often appears not as a slammed door but as a file moved from one desk to another until the trade can no longer bear the time required to prove itself harmless.

The broader lesson is austere. Sanctions enforcement does not end where legal texts stop. It continues inside firms that must decide how much uncertainty they can absorb while still calling themselves prudent. Compliance teams become institutional actors because they sit at the point where formal law, commercial pressure, internal process, and fear of future scrutiny converge. Their caution can exceed law, their delay can outmatch denial, and their internal procedures can become one of the most effective mechanisms by which states influence trade without physically interfering with a ship.

The unresolved question is the one every serious firm eventually faces. When a file is not clearly prohibited but not cleanly explainable either, who should bear the burden of uncertainty - the market that wants speed, the client that wants payment, or the compliance team that knows a cautious refusal may exceed the law yet still seems easier to defend than a hurried yes?

Chapter 11

Compliance Investigations and Evidence Building

What does it mean to know what happened at sea? Not to suspect it, not to sense it, not to watch a vessel track bend in an odd direction and feel the shape of a story forming, but to know it in a way an institution can act upon and later defend. That question hardens quickly in sanctions work. A ship may have moved under a changed flag, a cargo may have passed through several hands, a payment may have cleared through an unexpected route, and a denial or designation may still rest on evidence too thin to survive serious challenge. Information is abundant. Proof is not.

That gap between abundance and proof is where investigations live. Modern maritime enforcement generates records constantly: vessel signals, registry extracts, insurance notes, customs filings, satellite imagery, port records, payment messages, news reports, corporate searches, and the internal correspondence of firms trying to decide whether a transaction still belongs inside their risk appetite. Yet none of these materials arrives with a guarantee of reliability or relevance. A fact that looks decisive in isolation may turn out to be a mistranslation, a stale filing, a recycled media claim, or a pattern with several innocent explanations. The file grows thick. The centre can remain uncertain.

The folder never closes easily.

That is the central tension of this chapter. An investigation must be broad enough to reconstruct a moving commercial reality and disciplined enough not to mistake volume for certainty. It must decide what needs to be proved, which sources can speak to which parts of the story, how institutions share or withhold what they know, and what happens when an initial judgement later turns out to be wrong, incomplete, or unfair. Maritime sanctions are often described as a matter of political will. At the investigative level they look more like a contest over epistemic restraint:

who knows enough, who only thinks they do, and who is willing to act before the answer is fully comfortable.

That matters because the difference between suspicion and evidence determines whether enforcement remains credible. A weak investigation can still produce a temporary denial, a frozen payment, or a delayed voyage. It may even appear effective for a time. But if the underlying case cannot survive scrutiny, correction, or contest, the apparent success carries its own cost. Legitimate trade grows wary. Private actors become erratic. Allies hesitate to rely on shared findings. Firms start treating enforcement not as disciplined governance but as a field of arbitrary institutional nerves. Once that impression spreads, even strong cases become harder to carry because confidence in the process has thinned.

The stakes are therefore practical as well as moral. An investigation that asks the wrong question gathers the wrong evidence. An investigation that relies too heavily on open-source fragments without understanding their failure modes will either miss what matters or overread what does not. An investigation that depends on information sharing may discover that banks, ports, insurers, and registries do not cooperate symmetrically, and often have good reasons not to. An investigation that cannot correct itself when challenged will eventually produce the kind of error that chills lawful commerce and gives evasive actors a ready argument about overreach. Resilience in this field does not mean stubbornness. It means building cases strong enough to withstand revision without collapsing into paralysis.

This is why information quality becomes the real bottleneck. The public imagination still likes the idea that more data automatically means more truth. Maritime sanctions practice teaches the opposite lesson. More data can widen the search and deepen the confusion at the same time. A satellite image may suggest a transfer and misidentify its meaning. A corporate registry may reveal a company and conceal who actually directs it. A media report may surface a lead and quietly recycle another report's untested claim. Even direct institutional records can mislead when they preserve one phase of a transaction and miss the rest. The investigator's task is not merely to gather. It is to sort, compare, downgrade, and sometimes discard.

The path ahead follows the life of a case rather than the life of a voyage. It begins by asking what an investigation is really trying to prove when it says it is examining a ship, a cargo, a payment, or a network. It then moves into the seductive and treacherous world of open-source material, before turning to the uneven channels through which institutions share what they know and what they prefer not to reveal. From there it reaches the point at which cases are contested, corrected, or reversed, where the strength of an enforcement system is measured less by its initial confidence than by the quality of its self-correction.

A deeper friction runs through all of this. States and firms want investigations to move quickly enough to matter before the cargo is discharged, the money is gone, or the ship has changed its identity again. Good investigations, however, often move more slowly than decision-makers would like because each key proposition requires different kinds of proof. Identity is not the same as control. Origin is not the same as loading point. Destination is not the same as declared consignee. Service provision is not the same as beneficial ownership. To collapse these distinctions is to speed up at the cost of reliability. To honour them fully is to risk arriving too late for the first decision. The folder returns here because every investigation is, in part, an argument about what can be known fast enough to act on.

That leaves a harder question than the politics of sanctions usually admits. When an institution believes it has enough to intervene but not enough to silence future challenge, what exactly should count as a strong case: the quantity of material assembled, the coherence of the story it tells, or the confidence that the case can survive the moment an affected party opens the folder and begins, line by line, to argue back?

What an investigation needs to prove

In July 2019, when the tanker *Grace 1* was detained in Gibraltar, the public argument sounded simpler than the investigative one. To the casual observer, the question seemed to be whether a single ship carrying a single cargo had breached a single sanctions rule. The actual problem was more demanding. Which ship, exactly, in its changing legal and commercial identities? Controlled by whom? Carrying what cargo from where, bound for which destination, and serviced by which institutions along the way? The visible event was one detention. The underlying case was several investigations folded into one.

That is the first truth worth fixing in place. A compliance investigation rarely asks one question. It asks a chain of them, and each link requires a different kind of proof. Identity is not proved in the same way as control. Origin is not proved in the same way as destination. Service provision is not proved in the same way as ownership. Trouble begins when institutions slide too quickly from one category to another, as though a suspicious vessel track automatically resolved beneficial ownership, or a troubling payment route automatically settled cargo origin. A strong case separates the questions before it tries to connect them.

The file must be sorted.

This is where investigative scope becomes more important than investigative volume. Show the ordinary scene. A vessel appears on a screening system because its route looks odd, its ownership changed recently, or a counterparty has been flagged by another institution. The pressure to "build the case" begins immediately. Yet a serious investigator does not begin by gathering everything indiscriminately. The serious investigator begins by deciding what exactly must be proved for the decision at hand. If the issue is whether to deny a service, the evidentiary burden may differ from the burden required for a formal designation, a payment block, or a public accusation. The concept is scoped proof. The implication is practical: a file that contains too much undifferentiated material may still fail because it never clarified which proposition each item was supposed to support.

Identity usually comes first because without it the rest of the inquiry floats. A ship may change name, flag, manager, or registered owner with surprising speed. A company may appear under variant spellings across registries, invoices, insurance papers, and media reports. A human subject may be obscured by transliteration, nominee structures, or common surnames. To prove identity is not merely to find a similar name. It is to establish that the vessel, company, or person in one part of the file is the same one appearing elsewhere despite administrative drift. The evidence required here tends to be structural: IMO numbers, historical registry records, corporate filings, consistent addresses when meaningful, repeated identifiers, and documentary continuity that survives superficial change. The implication is austere. If identity remains unstable, every later conclusion risks attaching itself to the wrong object.

Control is harder because it does not sit obediently on the surface of legal ownership. A registered owner may hold title and still direct very little. A manager may appear secondary and still make the operational decisions that matter. A trader, financier, state entity, or beneficial owner may sit behind layers of formal distance while continuing to decide the trade's real direction. To prove control, investigators need evidence of instruction, influence, and benefit rather than title alone. Payment authority matters. Management contracts matter. Repeated operational contacts matter. So do who appoints whom, who absorbs risk, who receives value, and who can alter the ship's behaviour without needing to appear publicly at all. The concept is effective command. The implication is that ownership records may open the inquiry while leaving the decisive relationship still hidden one layer deeper.

Origin poses a different challenge because cargoes do not preserve their administrative meaning as faithfully as investigators might wish. A commodity can be loaded in one place, stored in another, blended in a third, sold through a fourth, and documented in a fifth. The question "where did this come from?" sounds simple until the cargo has moved through enough commercial stages that source, load point, and legally relevant origin no longer coincide. To prove origin, investigators often need to compare documents created for different purposes: bills of lading, manifests, terminal records, invoices, certificates, trade correspondence, storage logs, and sometimes imagery or shipping histories that place the cargo in context. The implication is sobering. Origin is not always disproved by one bad document, nor proved by one good one. It is built through consistency across records that were not originally designed to tell one unified story.

A named example from the Black Sea grain disputes after 2022 clarifies the point. Arguments over whether particular shipments originated from occupied Ukrainian territory did not hinge on one miraculous piece of evidence. They turned on whether several kinds of evidence - loading information, port movements, commercial paperwork, ownership claims, and state positions - could be made to support the same account strongly enough for a port or buyer to act. The lesson is broader than grain. Origin investigations live or die not by moral confidence but by evidentiary alignment across institutions that do not all record the cargo for the same reasons.

Destination, meanwhile, is often misunderstood because it is treated as a simple endpoint rather than a contested intention. A ship may physically head one way and commercially be meant for another market after storage, transhipment, or onward sale. A declared consignee may be real yet not final. A discharge port may not resolve where the cargo is ultimately intended to go in legally relevant terms. To prove destination, investigators often need evidence of planning and expectation: charter terms, sales contracts, payment structures, insurance arrangements, instructions to masters or agents, terminal bookings, and later commercial behaviour that makes sense only if a different endpoint had been in view all along. The concept is intended destination. The implication is that route alone is often too crude. A vessel can tell the truth about its next stop while still hiding the transaction's real destination farther down the chain.

Service provision asks a different question again: who enabled the trade, and in what way? This matters because sanctions frequently reach beyond ship and cargo to the supporting web of management, insurance, finance, classification, bunkering, crewing, broking, and logistics. To prove service provision, one usually needs traces of institutional involvement rather than cargo facts alone. Payment instructions, cover confirmations, management correspondence, port agency records, invoices, procurement trails, and contractual links become important here. The point is not merely to identify who touched the file. It is to establish what kind of support was actually given, under what knowledge conditions, and how central that support was to the voyage's continuation. The implication is that the same transaction can be well evidenced on cargo and poorly evidenced on services, or the reverse. Each claim requires its own proof.

A second named example lies in the repeated advisories concerning Iranian and deceptive shipping practices during the later 2010s and early 2020s. These advisories mattered not because they solved cases on their own, but because they implicitly separated the questions investigators needed to answer. Vessel identity, beneficial ownership, cargo origin, destination masking, and support by insurers or managers were related but not identical propositions. A disciplined investigation could not simply prove one and assume the rest. That structural lesson remains one of the most important in maritime compliance work.

A credible limitation should be admitted plainly. Real cases rarely arrive sorted by category. Evidence overlaps, and some forms of proof do double duty. A payment trail may illuminate both control and service provision. A vessel track may support identity continuity while also raising questions about origin or destination. A media report may point towards a useful lead even if it proves almost nothing by itself. The danger lies not in overlap, but in laziness: treating a clue gathered for one purpose as though it automatically satisfied another. Investigators under time pressure are especially prone to this error because the file feels fuller than it really is. Fullness is not proof.

That limitation does not weaken the structured approach. It justifies it. The relevant discipline is to ask, for every important claim, what kind of evidence would actually move confidence in that category. Does this document help prove identity, or only association? Does this registry record help prove ownership, or only one legal shell? Does this cargo paper help prove origin, or merely the latest stage of handling? Does this invoice prove service provision, or only proposed service that may never have been rendered? These questions are not bureaucratic fussiness. They are the difference between an investigation that can withstand challenge and one that collapses when someone finally asks what, exactly, each piece of the file was doing there.

The quiet motif here is the folder tab. Each tab names a different problem: identity, control, origin, destination, service. In weak investigations, the papers slide between them until the whole folder feels persuasive without becoming precise. In stronger investigations, the tabs force a kind of honesty. One sees which parts of the case are well supported, which remain inferential, and where the gaps still lie. That honesty is not an indulgence. It is what allows institutions to act proportionately rather than theatrically.

For maritime sanctions, the deeper lesson is austere. An investigation succeeds not because it gathers the most material, but because it proves the right things with the right kinds of evidence for the decision it is trying to support. That is the only way to resist the seduction of narrative momentum, where suspicion about one part of the trade quietly begins doing evidentiary work for all the rest. Enforcement follows paper, but paper must still be sorted by the question it is answering.

That leaves the harder question facing every investigator once the file begins to grow. When several parts of the story look troubling, but only one or two can actually be proved to the standard needed for action, should the institution act on the strongest fragment of the case - or hold back until identity, control, origin, destination, and service provision all stand firmly enough together to survive the moment someone opens the folder and starts pulling the tabs apart?

Open-source data and its pitfalls

In May 2020, the United States Departments of State, Treasury, and Coast Guard issued a sanctions advisory that reflected a striking reality of modern maritime enforcement: some of the most useful clues about a voyage now come from publicly accessible or commercially available information streams that no investigator fully controls. Vessel tracks, registry extracts, satellite imagery reports, sanctions databases, archived media coverage, leaked documents, and company profiles can all help reconstruct a trade that was designed to pass quickly and leave little behind. Yet the same abundance creates a trap. The file can look richer than it is.

That is because open-source data does not arrive as evidence. It arrives as material. A vessel track may suggest a rendezvous. A corporate registry may show a new owner. A satellite image may appear to capture two ships alongside. A media article may connect a cargo to a contested destination. Each of these can be valuable. None speaks with sovereign authority merely because it exists. Publicly visible information is often fragmentary, delayed, mistranslated, duplicated, or strategically seeded. The screenshot is not the case.

This is where the subject becomes harder than it first appears. Open-source information is attractive because it is accessible, fast, and often cross-border in a way official records are not. Show the ordinary sequence. A compliance analyst receives a troubling payment file or an insurer is asked to support a voyage whose documentary story feels thin. The first response is often to search outward: vessel tracking platforms, corporate databases, mapping tools, specialist reporting, archived port calls, and public sanctions materials. The concept is distributed visibility. The implication is that investigators now build cases from information gathered across systems never designed to produce one coherent truth. That can be an extraordinary strength. It can also be the point where error begins.

Vessel tracking is the most familiar example because it flatters the eye. Ships appear to move in clean lines across a screen, and those lines seem to promise objective narrative. A route changes. A signal disappears. A vessel slows offshore. Two ships linger near one another. The temptation is obvious: the track looks like behaviour without mediation. In reality, vessel tracking is already an interpretation built on transmissions, reception, coverage, formatting, and platform display. AIS entries can be inaccurate, absent, delayed, or confusing for reasons ranging from weather and equipment problems to deliberate manipulation. A track can be highly suggestive and still incomplete. The implication is not that tracking data are weak. It is that they become strong only when joined to other evidence that explains what the movement actually meant.

Corporate registries create a different illusion. They look official, and often they are. Yet official is not the same as current, complete, or practically meaningful. A registry may show legal ownership while saying little about control. It may update too slowly to reflect a recent transfer that matters. It may preserve a shell company name without revealing the interests that sit behind it. It may also encode ambiguity through local filing rules, nominee practices, varying disclosure thresholds, or language conventions unfamiliar to the user. The concept here is formal visibility. The implication is that registry data can stabilise identity while still failing to resolve the more difficult questions of beneficial ownership, instruction, or economic benefit.

A named example helps anchor the point. During the later 2010s and early 2020s, public reporting on sanctions-sensitive oil movements repeatedly relied on combinations of AIS analysis, registry research, and shipping database comparisons to identify suspicious transfers and ownership changes. Sometimes those reconstructions proved highly persuasive because independent strands aligned: the same vessel history, the same counterparties, the same route patterns, the same insurer discomfort, the same documentary inconsistencies. The lesson was not that open-source material was self-sufficient. The lesson was that its value rose sharply when it stopped operating alone.

Satellite imagery reports are powerful for a different reason. They seem to restore physical reality to a trade otherwise mediated through paper and signals. A vessel appears at an anchorage. Storage tanks seem fuller or emptier. Two hulls can be seen in close proximity. That visual force is real. It is also vulnerable to overconfidence. Imagery may be misdated, misread, cropped without context, or interpreted by analysts who know enough to be useful but not enough to be definitive. Weather, angle, resolution, wake patterns, shadows, and normal operational configurations can all complicate what the image is actually showing. A satellite image can confirm presence more readily than purpose. The implication is that imagery should often be treated as corroboration or contradiction, not as a complete story in itself.

Media accounts introduce another set of complications because they are both indispensable and unstable. Journalists often surface leads before regulators, ports, or firms are ready to speak publicly. Specialist trade reporting can provide context, naming patterns, and commercial logic that raw data cannot. Yet media accounts also recycle claims, compress uncertainty, and sometimes inherit earlier reporting errors so thoroughly that repetition begins to look like independent verification. Show the ordinary problem. A report names a vessel, cites anonymous officials, links the ship to a sanctions-sensitive cargo, and is repeated across several outlets. The file now looks populated. But if every later article rests on the same initial claim, the apparent consensus is thinner than it seems. The concept is citation echo. The implication is that investigators must distinguish between multiple sources and multiple retellings of one source.

This is where translation errors become especially dangerous. Maritime trade crosses alphabets, naming conventions, legal forms, and local commercial idioms that do not travel cleanly into English or across databases. A company name may be transliterated several ways. A port or anchorage may appear under local and international names. A cargo description may shift subtly between technical and commercial terms. A person's name may be entered with or without patronymics, middle names, or variant ordering. These are not minor nuisances. They can create false matches, obscure real continuity, or make one entity look like three. Information quality suffers not only from concealment but from language friction. The file can mislead simply because it was translated too quickly.

Deliberate deception makes all this worse because it exploits the known habits of investigators. If open-source researchers rely heavily on names, identifiers, declared routes, or searchable company data, those are precisely the surfaces an evasive network will learn to manipulate. A ship may adopt a fresh manager. A company may file a timely but strategically thin update. AIS data may be altered or interrupted. A press release, corporate website, or intermediary document may be crafted not to withstand full judicial scrutiny but to survive the first round of open-source checking. The implication is sobering. Deception need not defeat the most sophisticated investigation. It only needs to misdirect the initial one long enough for the cargo, payment, or service provision to move on.

A second named example lies in the repeated scrutiny of North Korean ship-to-ship transfers, where public-facing evidence often combined imagery, tracking data, registry records, and official reporting. Those cases illustrated both the promise and the fragility of open-source reconstruction. Strong findings emerged when many strands converged. Weakness entered when one type of source was asked to bear more interpretive weight than it could carry. The broader lesson extends beyond any one sanctions regime. Open-source material is often indispensable because official cooperation is slow, partial, or absent. It is also dangerous when investigators confuse availability with reliability.

A credible limitation must be admitted plainly. Open-source data can do things official systems cannot. It can reveal patterns across jurisdictions. It can preserve older records that firms or registries later overwrite. It can provide early warning when institutions are still silent. It can democratise scrutiny, allowing analysts outside the state to detect behaviour that might otherwise pass unnoticed. A system that dismissed open-source information because it is imperfect would blind itself needlessly. The problem is not openness. The problem is the temptation to act as though open-source visibility resolves the deeper issues of provenance, control, and meaning.

That limitation brings the central argument into focus. Information quality is the bottleneck because the key investigative problem is rarely simple absence of data. More often it is the unevenness of what exists. One source is fresh but narrow. Another is broad but stale. One is visual but ambiguous. Another is official but incomplete. One is translated but possibly distorted. Another is commercially insightful but hearsay-heavy. The disciplined investigator does not ask which source looks most authoritative in isolation. The disciplined investigator asks which source can be checked against another, which proposition it really supports, and how much uncertainty remains after the comparison. Good investigations advance by narrowing ambiguity, not by accumulating screenshots.

The quiet motif here is the magnifying glass. It helps one see more. It also magnifies dust. Open-source work often feels powerful because it brings hidden details into view: old company links, missed port calls, altered ship names, image traces, archived statements, inconsistent narratives. But the magnifying glass does not sort signal from noise on its own. The more intensely one looks, the more material appears that must itself be assessed. That is why the strongest investigators are not merely curious. They are sceptical of their own excitement.

For maritime sanctions, the broader lesson is austere. Open-source data have transformed the visibility of trade, but they have not abolished the old investigative burdens of verification, context, and restraint. Vessel tracking, registries, imagery, and media reporting can illuminate a case or contaminate it, depending on how they are used. The real shortage is not information. It is confidence in which information deserves to carry the next decision. Enforcement follows paper, but paper now includes public fragments whose authority must be earned, not assumed.

The unresolved question is therefore not whether open-source material is useful. It plainly is. The harder question is what an institution should do when the public evidence is strong enough to disturb, rich enough to tempt action, and still fragile enough that one translation error, one stale registry extract, or one misread image could turn a compelling narrative into a very expensive mistake.

Information sharing across institutions

In July 2019, when the tanker *Grace 1* was detained in Gibraltar, the public saw a ship, a cargo, and a legal dispute. The investigative reality was less singular. A port authority held one part of the story, insurers another, shipping databases something else, banks and service providers still more. None of these actors possessed the whole file, and not all of them could or would share what they knew on the same terms. The case exposed a stubborn truth about maritime sanctions: information rarely sits in one place long enough to become convenient.

That truth matters because modern trade is governed through distributed knowledge. A bank may know the payment route but not the cargo's physical handling. A port may know who requested entry but not who truly benefits from the voyage. An insurer may understand liabilities and service relationships better than customs authorities do. A flag registry may hold formal ownership and certification records while knowing much less about the commercial life of the ship than a manager or charterer. Each institution sees a slice. None sees the sea entire.

The file travels badly.

This is why information sharing across institutions is so uneven and so important. Sanctions enforcement depends not only on what any one actor knows, but on whether different actors can connect their partial views before the cargo is discharged, the payment is settled, or the ship disappears into another jurisdictional and administrative identity. Show the ordinary sequence. A vessel appears questionable to a bank because the payment chain feels strained. A port notices documentary inconsistencies. An insurer becomes uneasy about ownership changes. A registry has records that might stabilise identity. The concept is fragmented visibility. The implication is severe: unless these fragments can be exchanged, aligned, and trusted, each institution may act cautiously in isolation or not act at all. Enforcement strength becomes a function of relationships as much as of law.

Legal constraints explain part of this unevenness. Information does not circulate freely simply because sharing it would be useful. Banks face confidentiality duties, data protection rules, and legal risks if they disclose client information too broadly or too casually. Insurers must consider contractual obligations, claims sensitivity, and the possibility that sharing too much could prejudice later disputes. Ports and customs authorities operate under public-law mandates that may empower some disclosures and forbid others. Registries vary in what they can reveal, how quickly they can reveal it, and to whom. The concept is lawful withholding. The implication is that non-cooperation is not always a sign of bad faith or institutional laziness. Sometimes the law itself makes the file hard to assemble.

Commercial confidentiality adds a second layer of resistance, and often a more practical one. Maritime trade is full of information that firms treat as commercially sensitive even when it is not formally secret in the intelligence sense. Chartering patterns, freight terms, client identities, routing choices, management structures, and service relationships can all carry market value. A broker, bank, insurer, or manager may fear that disclosing too much will not only expose a questionable trade but also weaken client trust, damage competitive advantage, or invite litigation from counterparties who believe their information was shared too readily. The visible result is familiar: a cautious willingness to cooperate in principle, combined with a narrow interpretation of what can safely be released in practice.

Reputational risk complicates the picture further because institutions do not merely ask, "Can we share?" They also ask, "What happens if the shared information proves incomplete, inaccurate, or embarrassing?" A bank may hesitate to speak because doing so would reveal that it processed earlier transactions it now regrets. An insurer may worry that open disclosure will make its own due diligence look thinner than it wants others to know. A registry may fear becoming publicly associated with a vessel it is trying to distance from quietly. A port authority may want to avoid politicising what it would prefer to frame as ordinary administration. The concept here is defensive silence. The implication is that reputational self-protection can weaken cooperation even where law would permit more candour.

A named example from the Russian maritime environment after February 2022 makes this structure plain. As sanctions widened and scrutiny intensified, many cases turned not only on what any one actor knew, but on whether ports, insurers, banks, service providers, and registries could align their concerns quickly enough to matter. Some institutions withdrew or delayed on the basis of their own files. Others lacked enough confidence to act because the missing parts sat elsewhere. The broader lesson was not that information sharing had failed absolutely. It was that uneven cooperation changed the quality of enforcement. A network could survive longer when no single institution could bridge the gaps between route, cargo, beneficial ownership, insurance, and payment.

This is why protocols matter so much. Protocols sound drab, but they are the working architecture of trust between institutions that do not naturally speak to one another with equal ease. A port may know how to ask an insurer the right narrow question without demanding the impossible. A bank may have established channels for escalating concerns to authorities or trusted counterparties without breaching every boundary around client confidentiality. A registry may share more readily where the requesting institution can demonstrate a recognised basis and a disciplined use of the information received. The concept is structured cooperation. The implication is that enforcement often works best not when institutions suddenly become radically transparent, but when they develop repeatable ways of sharing enough, soon enough, with the right degree of precision.

A second named example lies in the repeated international scrutiny of North Korean ship-to-ship transfer networks, where reporting and enforcement depended heavily on connecting data held by different institutions and states. The significance of those efforts was not merely that information existed. It was that progress came when vessel tracking, imagery, registry data, port records, and official findings could be brought into conversation rather than left in separate silos. The lesson extends beyond any one sanctions regime. When institutions lack protocols or trusted channels, even strong clues can remain inert. When they possess them, weak clues can sometimes be turned into defensible patterns.

Still, a credible limitation must be faced directly. More sharing is not always better. Institutions can spread error as efficiently as they spread truth. A mistranslated registry extract, a misread satellite image, a weak media allegation, or an overconfident compliance note can travel quickly once passed through trusted channels. Cooperation can therefore amplify mistakes as well as strengths. This matters because the same relational networks that make enforcement stronger can also make correction harder if institutions become too eager to trust one another's suspicions without preserving their own independent standards. Information sharing does not remove the need for evidence discipline. It raises the stakes of it.

That limitation sharpens the point rather than weakening it. The relevant question is not whether institutions share, but how. Do they pass raw suspicion or scoped requests? Do they distinguish between confirmed fact, operational concern, and preliminary inference? Do they preserve enough context that the receiving institution can judge the weight of the material instead of inheriting someone else's certainty? Good protocols do not simply increase flow. They sort it. They tell the next actor what kind of thing they are being handed: a lead, a contradiction, a formal record, a commercial concern, a legal basis, or a still-unresolved problem. Without that sorting, the file becomes louder without becoming clearer.

This is also why relationships matter in ways formal process alone cannot fully replace. Institutions share more effectively when they know that the other side understands the difference between actionable evidence and reputational gossip, between confidential commercial data and information that can safely be acted upon, between urgency and panic. Familiarity does not solve legal barriers, but it can reduce hesitation about how a carefully framed disclosure will be handled. A port official may answer a narrower, better-aimed question. An insurer may confirm or deny a specific point more readily than it would respond to a broad fishing exercise. A bank may escalate internally faster when it trusts that the concern originated from a disciplined source. The human dimension is not sentimental. It is operational.

The quiet motif here is the handoff. One institution passes something to another: a warning, a query, a partial record, a concern, a confirmed fact. The quality of the handoff often determines whether the next actor can do anything useful with it. A poor handoff produces delay, duplication, defensiveness, or error. A good handoff preserves the uncertainty honestly while still making the issue legible enough to act upon. Sanctions enforcement is full of such handoffs, and many of its failures begin not with lack of information but with badly shaped transfer between institutions that were never designed to think as one.

For maritime sanctions, the broader lesson is austere. Ports, banks, insurers, and flag registries share information unevenly because they are governed by different laws, incentives, liabilities, and fears. That unevenness is not incidental. It is one of the main reasons some cases move swiftly while others remain frustratingly incomplete. Enforcement strength therefore depends less on fantasies of seamless transparency than on protocols, trust, and disciplined exchange capable of turning fragmented visibility into coordinated judgement without destroying the confidentiality and legal restraint on which ordinary trade also depends.

That leaves the harder question where every serious case eventually arrives. When several institutions each know enough to worry but none can reveal everything it knows, what kind of relationship or protocol is strong enough to let them act together before the trade moves on - and careful enough to prevent shared suspicion from hardening into shared error?

Due process, contestation, and reversals

In September 2019, when sanctions pressure hit COSCO Shipping Tanker (Dalian) entities, markets reacted with a speed that far exceeded the pace of legal clarification. Shipowners, charterers, banks, insurers, and traders did not wait for a seminar on doctrinal nuance. They withdrew, delayed, escalated, and re-priced. Later, when the designation landscape shifted and some of the immediate panic was corrected, the deeper lesson remained. A sanctions decision can be revised on paper more quickly than trust returns in practice.

That is why due process matters in maritime enforcement even to readers who care less about legal philosophy than about whether ships move and trade survives scrutiny. Designations and denials are not self-validating merely because they are forceful. They must remain open to challenge, correction, and sometimes reversal because maritime sanctions depend on the confidence of institutions that do not like being conscripted into opaque or error-prone systems. If a case cannot survive contest, it may still hurt the target for a time. It also damages the credibility of the whole enforcement architecture that asked others to rely on it. The correction comes late.

This matters because sanctions at sea operate through distributed obedience. Ports, insurers, banks, registries, managers, and service providers act not only because a state has spoken, but because they believe the underlying judgement is sufficiently disciplined to justify their own exposure. Show the ordinary sequence. A vessel is designated or denied service. Commercial actors retreat at once because the cost of waiting for perfect clarity is too high. The affected party contests the decision, offers documents, challenges the evidence, or exploits mistakes in identity, ownership, origin, or destination. Investigators or authorities then revisit the file. The concept is revisable coercion. The implication is that a strong sanctions system must be able to change its mind without appearing to confess institutional weakness. If it cannot, every early error becomes a wider market lesson in why caution should eventually harden into distrust.

That distrust has commercial consequences long after a formal reversal. A delisted ship or corrected counterparty does not instantly recover mainstream insurance, easy payments, ordinary chartering, or untroubled port access. Compliance systems remember pain more vividly than they remember nuance. Front-line staff who once watched a file become radioactive will often keep treating similar files as dangerous even after the formal legal basis has shifted. The visible behaviour is familiar: slower onboarding, deeper escalation, internal caveats, narrower appetite, and the quiet phrase that does so much hidden work in commerce - "we would rather not." This is why due process is not a ceremonial luxury. It is one of the few mechanisms capable of keeping private overreaction from becoming the permanent shadow law of the market.

A named example from the European courts makes the point with unusual sharpness. The *Kadi* litigation, beginning with the Court of Justice of the European Union's 2008 judgment, became famous not because it weakened sanctions as such, but because it insisted that even security measures carrying international political weight must remain vulnerable to meaningful review. The lesson for maritime enforcement is broader than the case itself. When institutions know that designations and restrictions may later be tested for evidentiary sufficiency and fairness, the quality of initial case-building tends to improve. The implication is practical. Review is not merely protective of the targeted party; it disciplines the system that targets them.

This is also why contestation should not be mistaken for obstruction. A challenge can be self-serving, evasive, and still useful to the integrity of enforcement. It forces the case to declare what exactly it is alleging and on what basis. Was the wrong entity linked through a weak name match? Was legal ownership confused with control? Was a cargo's origin inferred too confidently from route rather than documents? Was a denial built on a service relationship that never truly existed? These are not technical embarrassments. They are the difference between a resilient enforcement action and one that depends on institutions never looking too closely at their own assumptions. The concept is adversarial clarification. The implication is that the capacity to endure challenge is part of what makes sanctions credible rather than merely coercive.

A second named example lies in the wider pattern of delisting and adjustment across sanctions regimes involving shipping, trade, and politically exposed commercial actors over the last two decades. The specific files differ too much to flatten into one script, but the structural lesson is stable. Some designations were narrowed, some corrected, some allowed to lapse, and some effectively softened through licensing, guidance, or refined interpretation as evidence improved or alliances shifted. That should not be read as proof of failure. It should be read as evidence that maritime sanctions live in a world of moving facts, contested records, and institutional recalibration. A system incapable of revision would not be strong. It would be brittle.

Still, a credible limitation must be faced squarely. Due process does not guarantee justice in any simple sense, and reversals do not always repair the damage done by an initial error. A lawful trader caught in the first blast radius of a mistaken designation or an overbroad denial may lose clients, financing, insurance continuity, and market reputation in ways no later clarification fully restores. Allied governments and private firms notice these episodes closely. If they begin to believe that the evidentiary threshold for coercive action is low while the threshold for repair is high, their willingness to follow later designations may weaken. This matters because sanctions gain power from coalition discipline. Errors can chill not only legitimate trade but allied enthusiasm for future cooperation.

That chilling effect is especially dangerous in maritime contexts because the industry is already built around layers of caution. A shipowner, bank, or insurer does not need to be convinced that a target is certainly culpable in order to step away. It needs only to believe that the file has become institutionally unpleasant. If reversals are too rare, too slow, or too opaque, the market learns the wrong lesson: not merely that the state may be mistaken, but that correction arrives too late to justify any meaningful commercial re-engagement. Private governance then outruns public law even more aggressively. Compliance teams, already inclined towards caution, begin to treat contestation as noise rather than as part of a system designed to test itself. The result is a harsher and less accountable sanctions environment than the formal rules alone would seem to support.

This is why institutional resilience matters more than punitive confidence. A resilient system can absorb correction without losing authority because it treats reversibility as evidence of discipline rather than embarrassment. It records why a designation or denial was made, what evidence supported it, how the affected party can contest it, and what sort of material could change the decision later. The visible behaviour here is not rhetorical humility but procedural competence: reasoned files, review mechanisms, clear communication with allied institutions, and the willingness to distinguish between a lead, a provisional judgement, and a settled case. Such habits matter because the market watches not only who is designated, but how authorities behave when the file is tested.

The quiet motif here is the ledger. A designation enters one side of the institutional ledger as action. A challenge enters the other as scrutiny.

A reversal or correction does not wipe the first entry away; it alters the balance and forces a more honest accounting of what the system knew, what it merely inferred, and what it should have checked before moving. Weak systems fear this because they confuse balance with hesitation. Stronger systems understand that the ledger must be examinable if others are to rely on it. Maritime sanctions need that examinability because so much of their force is exercised by private actors who are constantly asking whether the official risk they are being asked to carry has been built on something sturdy enough to survive later audit.

This is also why allied support depends on more than shared political preference. Allied states and commercial institutions may agree on strategic aims and still diverge over evidentiary comfort. One government may accept a certain threshold for designation; another may require more documentary stability before expecting its ports, firms, or courts to fall into line. Reversals and corrected denials matter in this setting because they signal whether the system values precision enough to remain interoperable across jurisdictions. A coalition can withstand differences in legal culture more easily than it can withstand a reputation for careless listing or opaque non-correction. The broader implication is not legalistic but strategic: credibility is part of enforcement capacity.

The deeper lesson is austere. Designations and denials must be contestable because maritime sanctions do not operate in a closed sovereign chamber. They operate through markets, alliances, service networks, and institutions that need to know not only how to comply, but whether the cases they are being asked to honour are robust enough to merit the disruption they cause. Errors are inevitable in a field shaped by changing ownership, imperfect data, and fast-moving trade. The true test of the system is not whether it avoids all mistakes. It is whether it can correct them without teaching the market that caution is safer than justice forever.

That leaves the harder question where all serious enforcement systems eventually arrive. When an early restriction appears justified enough to prevent immediate harm but later turns out to rest on weaker evidence than first believed, what should matter more to institutional credibility - the willingness to act quickly in uncertainty, or the willingness to unwind that action clearly and publicly before the market decides that every future correction will come too late to trust?

Chapter 12

Evasion Adaptation and Counter-Adaptation

What happens when enforcement succeeds just enough to be felt, but not enough to end the trade? That is the question at the centre of maritime sanctions once one stops treating evasion as a static body of tricks and starts seeing it as a learning process. Pressure closes one route, and behaviour changes. A paperwork demand becomes standard, and a workaround appears. A registry grows less available, and ownership begins to move faster. The system does not freeze. It answers back.

That answer is rarely theatrical. It comes through experiment, attrition, and observation. A network tries a method, watches which part of the chain reacts first, notes where the delay occurred, which payment failed, which insurer hesitated, which port demanded more, which service provider still said yes. Then it adjusts. The next transaction is not wholly new. It is a revision built from the previous one. The voyage becomes a draft.

This is why evasion should be understood less as a secret art than as a cycle of trial and response. Static rules invite dynamic avoidance because every rule teaches the market something about where the real pressure lies. If a cargo can still move but no longer be financed in the same way, finance becomes the site of adaptation. If a ship can no longer keep its old flag, the ownership chain begins to absorb the strain. If documentation is questioned more aggressively, the paper trail becomes denser, cleaner in places, and thinner in others. The underlying contest is not between law and lawlessness in the abstract. It is between institutions trying to stabilise meaning and networks trying to redistribute uncertainty.

That tension matters because enforcement never falls only on the intended target. Once a sector learns that one kind of ambiguity attracts costly attention, caution spreads far beyond the file that caused the alarm. More questions are asked. More documents are requested. More approvals are routed upward. Screening becomes broader, files heavier, timings slower. This can deter evasive trade effectively. It can also impose real burdens on compliant actors who now have to prove their ordinariness in a system growing less willing to presume it. The ratchet turns once, and routine commerce must adjust to the new weight.

The stakes are therefore larger than tactical success. A sanctions regime that forces adaptation may degrade the target's operating environment while also teaching the wider market how to live with thicker compliance and higher friction. Some firms absorb that pressure and stay inside mainstream channels. Others retreat. Still others discover commercial opportunities in the newly widened gap between what lawful institutions will still do and what the trade still needs done. That is where the chapter's harder argument begins. Pressure does not only suppress. It can also rearrange incentives in ways that reward a different class of provider, a different form of ownership, and a different tolerance for opacity.

This is why continuity matters more than appearance. A vessel may cycle through paper owners, new managers, fresh intermediaries, and short-lived companies while its practical network remains recognisably stable underneath. The names change. The commercial habits do not. A ship can acquire a new legal shell faster than it can acquire a wholly new ecosystem of financiers, service firms, routes, and counterparties. Enforcement that follows only the newest paper will always feel one step late. Enforcement that follows continuity of control may still struggle, but it at least asks the right question about what has actually endured.

The argument ahead moves through that endurance in sequence. It begins with the way evasion networks learn from the reactions they provoke, then turns to the compliance ratchet that spreads caution beyond the immediate target. From there it follows the fragmentation of ownership and the use of disposable entities that complicate attribution while leaving deeper commercial patterns intact. It ends where pressure often leads if it lasts long enough: not to silence, but to the growth of parallel markets in finance, insurance, and service provision that exist because mainstream actors have stepped back.

A deeper friction runs beneath all of this. Enforcement wants to raise the cost of concealment until the trade becomes unattractive or unsustainable. Yet every increase in cost creates a commercial question: who is now willing to earn a premium for carrying the new risk, the new secrecy, or the new inconvenience? That is why counter-adaptation is not merely a side effect. It is part of the enforcement environment itself. A rule changes the market. The market studies the rule. Over time, the most capable evasive actors may become not less organised but more professional, because sustained pressure rewards those able to industrialise ambiguity rather than merely improvise it.

That leaves the harder question waiting behind every fresh compliance demand and every newly cautious refusal. When a sanctions system becomes strong enough to force repeated adaptation, is it steadily exhausting evasion capacity, or is it also helping to build a more disciplined shadow trade whose operators have learned exactly where formal pressure bites and where the next opening is likely to appear?

Learning cycles in evasion networks

In May 2020, when the United States Departments of State, Treasury, and Coast Guard issued a maritime sanctions advisory warning about deceptive shipping practices, the most important effect was not simply that certain behaviours were named. It was that the naming itself taught the market something. Once a tactic is identified publicly, everyone watching learns from the disclosure - regulators, insurers, banks, ports, ship managers, and the networks trying to keep trade moving despite pressure. Enforcement does not speak into silence. It speaks into an audience that is already studying the reaction.

That is why evasion should not be imagined as a fixed repertoire of tricks. It behaves more like an iterative craft. A network tests a method, watches which institution notices first, measures where cost or delay enters the chain, and then adjusts. A payment gets blocked, so the next transaction changes its intermediary. A flag becomes too exposed, so the following vessel moves under a different registry. A transfer zone attracts too much scrutiny, so the operation shifts in timing or geography. The move is made, the response is observed, and the lesson is carried forward. The route learns.

This is the first principle worth stating plainly. Static rules invite dynamic avoidance because rules do more than prohibit. They reveal priorities. Show the process in ordinary terms. A sanctions measure tightens around a certain set of counterparties, routes, services, or documentary requirements. Actors under pressure do not need to know every detail of the legal architecture to adapt. They need only notice where the transaction actually failed. Was the friction in payment? Insurance? Port access? Registry acceptance? Service provision? The concept is reactive learning. The implication is that evasion networks often become smarter not by mastering the law in the abstract, but by treating each blocked voyage, delayed payment, or refused service as a field report on the enforcement system's real choke points.

This matters because maritime trade provides unusually rich feedback. A failed sanctions-evasion attempt rarely disappears without leaving information behind. The cargo stalls. The bank asks for more. The insurer hesitates. The port delays entry. A service provider refuses the file. A vessel is tracked more closely after a suspicious transfer. These reactions reveal which parts of the trade remain pliable and which are hardening. The network studies the pattern. It may not need perfect insight into why one institution acted as it did. It only needs to identify where compliance pressure manifested in practice. The visible behaviour becomes the lesson plan.

A named example from the Iranian oil trade illustrates the pattern. During the later 2010s and early 2020s, public advisories and enforcement actions repeatedly identified ship-to-ship transfers, AIS irregularities, shifting vessel identities, and layered ownership structures as relevant to sanctions evasion. The significance of these repeated notices was not simply that they exposed misconduct. They also changed the learning environment. Once particular transfer zones, documentation weaknesses, and ownership arrangements became too conspicuous, networks had reason to revise them. The lesson was not "stop moving". It was "move differently". A tactic that draws too much attention ceases to be useful, and the trade evolves towards methods that preserve uncertainty longer or displace it onto a different institution.

This is why one should think in cycles rather than tricks. A trick implies a stable device that can be catalogued and neutralised. A cycle implies a relationship between pressure and response. The network tries something because it seems viable. Institutions react, sometimes predictably, sometimes unevenly. The network interprets that reaction and tests a modified version. That version succeeds for a while, then begins to produce recognisable patterns of its own. Compliance systems update. Advisories are issued. Service providers become more cautious. The process repeats. The concept here is adaptive sequencing. The implication is that enforcement gains little from memorising yesterday's visible methods if it cannot anticipate the learning logic that will produce tomorrow's subtler ones.

The learning process is not always elegant. It often looks messy because it occurs through commercial trial rather than formal doctrine. A vessel changes manager and finds that insurance becomes harder to maintain.

A cargo is split into smaller parcels and attracts less attention at one stage but more at another. An intermediary company proves useful until banks start treating its corporate profile as too thin. The next version of the trade retains what worked and discards what did not. This is organisational learning without a boardroom presentation. It happens through invoices, refusals, route changes, delayed clearances, and the slow accumulation of market memory.

A second named example can be seen in the broader maritime adjustments that followed sanctions pressure on Russian trade after February 2022. As insurers, banks, registries, ports, and service providers altered their treatment of Russian-linked activity, the market did not respond in one uniform way. Some actors withdrew. Others narrowed. Some trades reorganised around new corporate vehicles, different service providers, altered routes, or more fragmented commercial chains. The important point is not that every change amounted to evasion. The point is that sustained pressure produced a learning environment in which legal, commercial, and logistical actors were constantly testing what remained possible. One side tightened. The other side adapted. That reciprocal movement is the real subject.

A credible limitation should be faced directly. Not every adjustment under sanctions pressure reflects cunning evasion. Commercial actors often change behaviour for ordinary reasons: shifting freight markets, insurance appetite, weather exposure, political uncertainty, port congestion, or simple trial and error unrelated to concealment. A route change may be prudent rather than strategic. A new intermediary may reflect financing convenience rather than deliberate opacity. An analyst who reads every commercial adjustment as an intelligent counter-move will overstate the coherence of the network and risk mistaking disorder for design. Some evasive systems are more opportunistic than masterful.

That limitation does not weaken the strategic model. It refines it. Learning cycles do not require perfect central coordination. They can emerge from distributed observation. One shipowner hears that a certain transfer area has become too exposed. One manager learns that a certain insurer now asks different questions. One broker notices that a payment structure which passed six months earlier now triggers escalation. These fragments circulate through markets, personal relationships, service networks, and public advisories. No mastermind is needed. The maritime sector itself becomes a medium through which tactics are tested and lessons spread.

The implication is crucial: adaptation can be systemic even when no single actor understands the whole system.

This is why enforcement must pay attention to reaction time as much as to rule content. A regulation may look impressive on paper and still fail strategically if the affected networks can identify and route around its practical effect faster than institutions can update their own habits. Conversely, a modest intervention may matter greatly if it changes the cost structure of adaptation - if it makes each workaround more expensive, slower, or more dependent on fragile intermediaries. The serious question is not merely whether a rule exists. It is how quickly the surrounding ecosystem learns what the rule actually bites and how quickly enforcement learns from the evasive answer. Speed matters twice.

The quiet motif here is the draft. Each evasive attempt is a draft, not a finished manuscript. A voyage is tried, the response is read, the next version is edited. Some lines are cut: a visible service provider, a familiar transfer point, a too-obvious payment route. Some lines are added: another intermediary, a different registry, a fresh cargo description, a more patient bank. The trade becomes a text revised under pressure. Enforcement often loses when it attacks the published sentence and ignores the editing process that produced it.

This makes the wider stakes harder than they first appear. If evasion networks learn from compliance reactions, then enforcement itself becomes part of the adversary's educational environment. Every advisory, refusal, seizure, or tightened screening pattern carries information. That does not mean authorities should remain silent or inactive. It means each action should be judged not only by the immediate disruption it causes but by the adaptive lesson it teaches. A sanctions regime that repeatedly announces the same vulnerabilities without changing its own mode of observation risks professionalising the very conduct it seeks to suppress.

The unresolved question follows naturally. When a network fails, what has really been achieved if the failure also reveals exactly which part of the trade was still too visible, too centralised, or too dependent on mainstream tolerance - and how quickly will the next voyage appear having learned that lesson better than the institutions that first forced it to fail?

The compliance ratchet effect

In May 2020, the United States Departments of State, Treasury, and Coast Guard issued a maritime advisory that did more than warn about deceptive shipping practices. It changed behaviour far beyond the actors most directly implicated. Banks asked for more. Insurers hesitated sooner. Ports read files more closely. Managers escalated routine decisions that, a year earlier, might have passed with a few signatures and a little commercial confidence. One advisory became many internal rules. The burden spread.

That spread is what makes the compliance ratchet such an important part of sanctions enforcement. A ratchet does not merely tighten. It tends not to slip back easily. Once a sector learns that a certain kind of ambiguity can lead to enforcement risk, reputational damage, blocked payments, or embarrassing review, the response rarely remains confined to the original case. Paperwork multiplies. Screening widens. Tolerance narrows. A new baseline of caution settles into ordinary trade. The extra question remains.

This is the first point worth fixing clearly. The compliance ratchet effect is not simply more regulation in the abstract. It is the cumulative tightening that occurs when institutions internalise past shocks and redesign their ordinary processes to avoid being caught unprepared again. Show the sequence in practical terms. A sanctions-evasion case exposes a weakness in documentation, screening, or service provision. Firms respond by adding checks, revising onboarding, broadening restricted categories, or requiring stronger evidence before they process payments, insure voyages, extend services, or confirm counterparties. The concept is institutional memory. The implication is that one enforcement episode can reshape the working habits of an entire sector, including actors who were never part of the original case.

This matters because maritime trade depends on velocity. Ships wait for no theory. Cargoes age. Financing windows close. Berths are lost. Crew and service arrangements depend on rhythm as much as legality. The ratchet alters that rhythm by inserting more verification into more stages of the trade. A bank wants fuller ownership detail. An insurer asks for clearer route logic. A port agent requests extra certificates. A manager seeks stronger assurances before paying suppliers or arranging bunkers. None of these demands is necessarily unreasonable. Together they slow the commercial bloodstream. The visible behaviour is plain: longer processing times, more escalations, more refusals based on uncertainty rather than prohibition, and a sharper divide between trades that remain easy to explain and those that now carry a permanent administrative weight.

That weight can deter evasion effectively because evasive trade often relies on speed, ambiguity, and the hope that no one institution will stop the transaction long enough to compare the whole file. The ratchet frustrates that hope. A voyage that once moved through several permissive or inattentive gates now meets a thicker sequence of questions. Screening catches patterns earlier. Documentation gaps become costlier. Service providers step back sooner. The concept here is distributed hardening. The implication is that the compliance ratchet extends enforcement beyond the original legal text by making more of the market behave as though the risky edge of trade deserves broader suspicion.

A named example from the post-2022 Russian shipping environment makes the mechanism especially clear. As sanctions widened and commercial exposure deepened, institutions did not merely apply the new rules to the named targets and stop there. They revised their surrounding processes. Trades involving similar cargoes, routes, counterparties, or service patterns often attracted heavier scrutiny even where the formal legal position remained more nuanced. The lesson was not that compliance had become irrational. It was that firms learned from the cost of being wrong, and then redesigned ordinary business to reduce their future exposure. The result was a wider field of caution than the legal text alone might have suggested.

That wider field has real costs for compliant actors, and this must be stated without euphemism. A lawful trader with a complicated route, an unfamiliar but innocent intermediary, or a cargo whose documentation reflects ordinary commercial messiness may still be caught in the tighter mesh. A shipowner may be asked for repeated explanations of ownership continuity. A neutral service provider may lose time and money satisfying new verification demands. A bank may delay payments because the transaction resembles, in structure rather than substance, the sort of file that previously caused trouble. The ratchet therefore does not only target the evasive. It redistributes compliance costs across the whole sector. Some firms can absorb that redistribution more easily than others.

This is why the effect is politically and commercially important beyond the immediate question of sanctions success. When compliant actors begin to experience ordinary trade as administratively heavier, they do not always respond by praising the discipline of the system. They may experience it as friction imposed by someone else's misconduct. Neutral carriers, smaller traders, regional banks, and service firms with limited compliance budgets can feel this pressure particularly sharply. The concept is collateral procedural burden. The implication is that sanctions enforcement can strain allied and neutral tolerance not only through headline disputes, but through the quieter accumulation of work required to prove innocence under thicker sector-wide caution.

A second named example can be drawn from the Iranian shipping and energy trade under sustained sanctions pressure during the later 2010s and early 2020s. Public advisories warning of deceptive practices did not simply inform a narrow circle of investigators. They altered market expectations around vessel ownership opacity, ship-to-ship transfer patterns, cargo documentation, and payment structures. Firms that had no desire to participate in evasion still had to respond to the new atmosphere by increasing their own documentary demands and review procedures. That is what makes the ratchet an institutional phenomenon rather than a legal one. Enforcement teaches the market to ask more from everyone.

A credible limitation should be admitted. Caution is not the same as wisdom. Institutions can over-learn from striking cases and begin treating low-quality signals as though they justified broad procedural tightening. That produces false positives, wasted labour, and sectoral fatigue. It can also generate a kind of compliance theatre in which firms collect more documents without becoming meaningfully better at identifying real risk. More paper does not always produce more clarity. Sometimes it merely creates thicker files and slower trade. A ratchet can stiffen into bureaucracy if it loses sight of what the added controls are actually meant to prove.

That limitation does not weaken the central argument. It sharpens it. The relevant question is not whether the compliance ratchet exists, but whether the additional burden it creates remains tied to real learning about where evasion succeeds. Good tightening follows observed weaknesses: unstable ownership continuity, weak documentation chains, implausible pricing, difficult service structures, or payment arrangements that no longer withstand comparison. Poor tightening follows anxiety alone. It asks more from everyone because the institution has forgotten how to separate discomfort from evidence. The difference matters because a sector can carry only so much inherited caution before normal commerce starts searching for its own workarounds.

This is also why the ratchet tends to favour larger institutions and more established actors. Bigger firms can build compliance teams, absorb delay, and standardise documentation demands across clients and regions. Smaller firms, or firms operating in neutral jurisdictions with thinner administrative capacity, may find the cumulative burden much harder to sustain. That asymmetry matters for enforcement because it can reshape who remains in mainstream trade and who drifts towards more marginal spaces where scrutiny is weaker but risk is higher. The ratchet is therefore not only a defensive tool. It is a market-shaping force. It can push traffic towards actors with stronger compliance muscle, or towards actors willing to profit from everyone else's reluctance.

The quiet motif here is the form. One more form, one more declaration, one more ownership chart, one more insurer confirmation, one more internal escalation note. Each form is individually defensible. Together they reveal the ratchet's logic. The form does not simply collect information. It records that the institution no longer trusts the old level of reassurance. Once forms accumulate, they are hard to remove, because taking one away feels riskier than keeping it. That is how temporary alarm becomes permanent process.

For maritime sanctions, the deeper lesson is austere. The compliance ratchet effect helps explain why enforcement can become stronger without more dramatic legal action. It diffuses caution across the entire commercial field, making evasive trade harder to hide inside ordinary routines. Yet it also explains why compliant actors increasingly speak of cost, delay, and procedural drag rather than only of law. A sanctions system that relies on sector-wide hardening must eventually confront the burden it has taught the whole market to carry.

That leaves the harder question where any mature enforcement regime must eventually face itself. When tighter compliance begins to deter risky trade by making all trade heavier, how much of that sector-wide friction counts as a necessary price of discipline - and at what point does the ratchet start teaching compliant, allied, and neutral actors that the burden of proving normality has become almost as consequential as the burden of being suspected?

Fragmented ownership and disposable entities

In May 2020, the United States Departments of State, Treasury, and Coast Guard issued a sanctions advisory that placed unusual emphasis on deceptive ownership and management practices in maritime trade. That emphasis was telling. Cargoes move through ships, but accountability moves through paper, and paper can be rearranged far more quickly than steel. A vessel may appear under one owner this season, another the next, a new manager after that, and a different commercial intermediary by the time the cargo reaches discharge. To the inattentive eye, the trail looks broken. To the more careful one, the pattern often looks preserved beneath the break.

That is why fragmented ownership matters so much to sanctions enforcement. The problem is not merely that ships can be hidden. It is that responsibility can be diluted by multiplying legal persons faster than investigators, banks, ports, and insurers can stabilise the underlying commercial network. A company is incorporated, holds title briefly, then disappears. A manager is replaced. A beneficial owner retreats another layer behind service firms and nominees. The registry changes. The operational habits remain. The paper sheds skin.

This is the first fact that should be stated without euphemism. Disposable entities are useful because they absorb scrutiny. Show the ordinary sequence. A vessel engaged in risky or politically sensitive trade begins to attract attention. Rather than keep the same legal owner and face accumulating consequences, the trade is reconfigured. Title shifts to a new one-ship company. Management is transferred. A fresh set of directors appears. The old entity may be wound down, left dormant, or preserved only long enough to receive the burden of the previous scrutiny. The concept is accountability dilution. The implication is practical and severe: if enforcement follows only the most recent legal shell, it will spend its energy chasing surfaces while the commercial logic of the vessel continues with surprisingly little interruption.

This is why formal ownership is never enough. In shipping, title has always been less revealing than outsiders imagine. Special-purpose companies, one-ship entities, management outsourcing, and jurisdictional layering all have ordinary commercial uses. That is what makes this terrain difficult. Fragmentation is not suspicious merely because it exists. It becomes analytically important when changes in ownership, management, and service provision occur in patterns that seem designed less to improve commercial function than to redistribute scrutiny. The concept here is strategic re-papering. The implication is that investigators must separate the lawful flexibility of maritime corporate form from the tactical use of that flexibility to preserve a risky trade under a procession of expendable names.

A named example from the Iranian shipping environment helps clarify the structure. During the later 2010s and early 2020s, public advisories repeatedly described how front companies, altered ownership records, and management changes could be used to shield sanctioned trade from straightforward identification. The lesson was not that every one-ship company or ownership transfer was a sham. The sharper point was that continuity of commercial behaviour often outlived continuity of legal identity. A vessel's registered owner might change. The same counterparties, routes, service providers, payment habits, or managerial instructions could remain close enough to suggest that the underlying centre of control had not really moved very far at all.

This is where continuity of control becomes the decisive investigative idea. To prove continuity of control is not to deny that paper changes have occurred. It is to ask whether those changes have meaningfully altered who directs, benefits from, pays for, and sustains the vessel's trade. Who appoints the manager? Who handles the freight? Who chooses the cargoes and routes? Who pays crew wages and suppliers? Which insurer, bank, broker, or service network remains in place despite the latest transfer? The concept is commercial persistence. The implication is that enforcement gains strength only when it can follow these durable relationships through the revolving door of paper owners.

A brief, ordinary example shows why this matters. A vessel changes registered owner twice within a short period. On paper, the transformation looks substantial. But the new companies share related addresses, use the same management office, retain the same crewing arrangements, continue similar routing patterns, and rely on familiar service intermediaries. No single fact proves that the changes were cosmetic. Taken together, however, they suggest that the ship's commercial network has persisted through multiple formal owners. The legal shell changed. The operating skeleton did not. This is exactly the sort of pattern static ownership screening misses.

Frequent management changes intensify the problem because they can preserve operational continuity while muddying attribution. A new manager may be genuine and commercially sensible. It may also function as a buffer, giving the vessel a refreshed administrative face without severing deeper connections to the same beneficial interests, service providers, or trading strategy. A bank or insurer reviewing the file may see a new manager and infer meaningful change. A more careful investigation asks whether the practical relationships around the ship have materially altered or merely been redressed. The visible behaviour that matters is not just the filing. It is whether the ship's money flows, service chains, insurance habits, and trade pattern now look genuinely different.

This is where asset transfers become especially attractive under pressure. A vessel is a movable revenue-generating asset that can be placed into a new corporate wrapper faster than most institutions can update their internal confidence. If an owner or manager anticipates greater scrutiny, transferring the ship into a fresher entity can buy time, create uncertainty, and complicate efforts to attach prior concerns to the new paper structure. The concept is temporal arbitrage. The implication is that disposable entities do not need to be durable to be useful. They only need to survive long enough to carry the vessel through the next voyage, the next payment cycle, or the next compliance review.

A second named example lies in the broader maritime adjustments that followed sanctions pressure on Russian trade after February 2022. As insurers, registries, banks, and service firms tightened their treatment of certain vessels and counterparties, public reporting increasingly described ships moving through altered ownership structures, changed managers, and newly formed entities. Again, the point is not that every such change concealed sanctioned control. Many reflected real commercial adaptation under difficult conditions. Yet the investigative burden grew because the more frequently ownership shifted, the more institutions had to decide whether they were looking at a genuinely new commercial actor or a disposable paper vehicle carrying forward much the same underlying network.

A credible limitation needs to be stated plainly. Shipping has long used fragmented ownership for legitimate reasons. One-ship companies, sale-and-leaseback arrangements, management transfers, and jurisdictional layering can all reflect sensible decisions about tax, liability, finance, or operational specialisation. A sanctions analyst who treats fragmentation itself as proof of evasion will generate false positives at dangerous scale. Lawful owners will be burdened. Ordinary corporate restructuring will be recast as concealment. The discipline required here lies in distinguishing commercially intelligible complexity from strategically convenient instability. Not every fresh entity is a disposable one. Not every ownership change is evasive.

That limitation does not weaken the central argument. It refines the test. The real question is not whether paper changed, but whether the trade changed with it. Did the transfer produce a new financing pattern, a new service network, a new operational logic, a new set of counterparties, or a new risk profile? Or did it produce mainly a new certificate, a new company name, and a short breathing space before scrutiny had to start again from the beginning? The answer emerges from convergence across evidence types. Registry records matter. So do insurance contacts, freight arrangements, payment routes, management practices, crewing continuity, and repeated commercial associations that survive each formal rearrangement.

This is why enforcement must learn to think in chains rather than snapshots. A snapshot catches the current legal owner and perhaps the current manager. A chain shows what persisted across the last three owners, the last two managers, the repeated service providers, and the counterparties that keep reappearing even as the formal structure mutates. The quiet motif here is the relay baton. Ownership passes from hand to hand, but the race may still be run by the same team. The baton attracts attention because it is visible. The team matters because it determines where the vessel actually goes.

For maritime sanctions, the deeper lesson is austere. Fragmented ownership and disposable entities do not defeat enforcement because they make ships invisible. They complicate enforcement because they force institutions to decide whether they are judging legal form or commercial continuity, and those two things do not always point to the same answer. A system that honours only the latest filing will always be vulnerable to rapid re-papering. A system that follows continuity of control stands a better chance, though it pays for that seriousness with slower, harder investigation.

That leaves the harder question waiting behind every fresh registry extract and every newly incorporated holding company. When a vessel's paper owners keep changing but its routes, services, counterparties, and financial habits continue to rhyme, what should count as the real identity of the trade - the latest name on the certificate, or the network that has quietly survived each legal death and come back wearing another suit?

When pressure creates new markets

In September 2019, when sanctions pressure struck COSCO Shipping Tanker (Dalian) entities, the most important consequence was not only that mainstream firms stepped back. It was that the withdrawal itself altered demand. If ordinary insurers hesitate, someone else is invited to price the risk. If banks refuse the payment, someone else is asked to move the money. If ports, managers, and service providers narrow their appetite, the trade does not merely vanish. It begins searching for those willing to earn from what others now find too difficult to touch.

That is the paradox sanctions create at their most effective edge. The stronger the exclusion from mainstream systems, the more valuable become the actors prepared to operate beyond them. A market closing in one place can open in another. The cargo still needs finance, cover, certification, management, crewing, bunkers, and someone willing to say yes where reputable institutions have begun saying no. Pressure therefore does not act only as prohibition. It also acts as selection. The vacancy becomes profitable.

This is the first principle that must be grasped if sanctions are to be understood structurally rather than morally. When enforcement raises the cost of a trade, it does not abolish the incentives inside that trade. It redistributes them. Show the ordinary sequence. A bank refuses a payment route because the file has become too exposed. A mainstream insurer narrows or withdraws cover. A service firm decides the ownership structure or cargo path is no longer worth defending. The transaction does not automatically die. Instead, the parties look for a thinner bank, a more opaque financial intermediary, a lesser-known insurer, or a specialist operator willing to handle the file for a premium or under conditions the mainstream market would reject. The concept is induced substitution. The implication is that enforcement can weaken one set of channels while simultaneously strengthening the commercial case for parallel ones.

This matters because markets are disciplined by scarcity, and sanctions manufacture scarcity deliberately. Once ordinary financial rails are narrowed, opaque finance becomes more valuable not because it is inherently efficient, but because it is one of the few remaining routes through which the transaction can still pass. Once widely trusted insurers retreat, high-risk or politically protected cover becomes more marketable. Once reputable service providers refuse difficult vessels, marginal operators can charge for their tolerance as much as for the service itself. The visible behaviour is familiar: thinner disclosures, slower payments, more bespoke structures, wider use of intermediaries, and fees that appear to compensate not only for commercial labour but for the willingness to absorb legal and reputational discomfort.

Opaque finance is especially revealing in this respect. A payment system that moves funds through less transparent or more weakly supervised channels may be slower, costlier, and more fragile than the mainstream alternative. That does not stop it from becoming attractive when mainstream institutions close. The point is not to romanticise shadow finance as clever. It is often clumsy and expensive. But sanctions pressure can make clumsy systems commercially viable by reducing the supply of cleaner ones. The concept is scarcity pricing. The implication is that enforcement can unintentionally nourish providers whose business model depends on the exclusion produced by enforcement itself.

High-risk insurance follows the same logic. A vessel excluded from widely trusted cover does not cease to require insurance in any practical sense. Ports, counterparties, cargo interests, and service providers still want to know who stands behind the liabilities, even if the answer now inspires less confidence. This creates a market for insurers or quasi-insurers prepared to offer cover where mainstream providers no longer will. That cover may be narrower, less credible, more opaque, or more politically dependent. It may satisfy some formal needs while falling short of the broader confidence the old market supplied. Yet it remains commercially meaningful because it enables at least some continuation of trade. Risk itself becomes a product.

A named example from the Russian maritime environment after February 2022 makes the structure plain. As mainstream Western insurers, banks, service providers, and some registries tightened their treatment of Russian-linked trade, alternative arrangements did not appear because the market suddenly discovered a new taste for opacity. They appeared because exclusion changed the opportunity set. New or less established providers found room to operate where old ones had stepped back. The lesson is not confined to Russia, nor does it require claims about every new actor's legitimacy. The important point is structural: sustained pressure can produce niches in which firms willing to accept higher uncertainty, weaker transparency, or stronger political entanglement now find a paying clientele.

This is one reason marginal services matter so much. The market for difficult voyages does not only require money and insurance. It requires ship managers willing to handle unstable ownership structures, brokers willing to place awkward business, crewing agencies willing to staff vessels others distrust, bunker suppliers willing to work with unusual counterparties, and technical or documentary intermediaries prepared to inhabit the gaps left by mainstream withdrawal. None of these actors needs to be a criminal specialist. They may simply be firms whose cost tolerance, jurisdictional exposure, or reputational horizon differs from that of more established competitors. Still, the cumulative effect is the same. A more professional ecosystem begins to gather around the very uncertainty enforcement has intensified.

That is why sanctions can unintentionally professionalise evasion capacity. Improvised workarounds are one thing. Repeated demand is another. Once a sufficient volume of difficult trade starts seeking alternative finance, insurance, management, and logistics, the providers servicing it gain experience, contacts, routines, and commercial confidence. What began as ad hoc accommodation can harden into expertise. The concept here is market learning under pressure. The implication is troubling: the more often the same kinds of files are refused by mainstream institutions, the more opportunities arise for peripheral institutions to specialise in understanding, pricing, and sustaining those files better.

A credible limitation must be stated plainly. Not every alternative market created by sanctions is inherently illicit or destabilising. Some parallel arrangements may emerge because lawful trade still needs mechanisms to continue under altered political conditions. Not every less familiar insurer is unserious. Not every non-mainstream financier is a covert enabler. Not every marginal service provider is part of an organised evasion system. Markets adapt in lawful as well as unlawful ways. A serious analysis therefore cannot assume that unfamiliarity equals misconduct. To do so would confuse the sociology of exclusion with proof of wrongdoing.

That limitation does not weaken the main argument. It refines the point of inquiry. The relevant question is not whether a new market is mainstream, but what incentives brought it into being and what standards govern it. Does it exist because mainstream institutions overreached, leaving a lawful trade underserved? Or does it thrive because opacity, thin verification, and reduced reputational sensitivity have themselves become saleable assets? Does the provider price real risk in intelligible ways, or does it rely on ambiguity as part of the service? Does it preserve continuity of records and responsibility, or does it profit by helping clients remain harder to reconstruct later? The answers matter because they distinguish adaptive commerce from the institutional maturation of evasion.

This is where structural incentives do more explanatory work than moral categories. A provider entering a pressure-created market does not need to share the political aims of the cargo owner or the sanctioned network. It needs only to see that others have exited and that a premium now exists for handling a transaction under weaker transparency and higher uncertainty. The law may still matter greatly. So do business model and risk appetite. This is why enforcement should avoid the comforting fiction that marginal markets are driven only by ideological solidarity or criminal intent. Often they are driven by the same commercial instinct that animates lawful trade, merely redirected towards a field made unusually profitable by exclusion.

The quiet motif here is the vacancy. A bank exits and leaves a vacancy. An insurer withdraws and leaves a vacancy. A service provider refuses and leaves a vacancy. Vacancies do not remain empty for long if cargo, freight, and payment are still seeking passage. The market studies the gap and asks who can occupy it profitably. That question is one of sanctions' least discussed consequences. The vacancy is not just absence. It is an invitation.

This is why enforcement must be judged not only by the transactions it blocks, but by the ecosystems it helps create around the blocked trade. A sanctions regime can be genuinely effective and still alter the commercial landscape in ways that reward thinner disclosure, weaker accountability, and providers newly skilled at operating where mainstream systems no longer tread. That does not mean sanctions are self-defeating. It means their success changes the market's composition. Some actors retreat. Others specialise. Over time, those specialists may become more disciplined, not less, because repeated demand trains them.

The unresolved question follows from that uncomfortable logic. When exclusion from mainstream finance, insurance, and services becomes strong enough to make alternative providers commercially indispensable, is the sanctions system steadily constraining the trade - or is it also helping to build a more experienced shadow infrastructure whose comparative advantage lies precisely in handling the uncertainty that enforcement has made so profitable?

Chapter 13

Allies, Neutral Carriers, and Economic Costs

How much strain can a coalition bear before it begins to confuse shared purpose with unequal sacrifice? That question sits beneath every maritime sanctions regime once the first wave of legal design gives way to ordinary commercial life. A rule agreed in one capital does not land evenly across fleets, ports, insurers, traders, and coastal states. Some actors encounter it as a principle. Others encounter it as rerouted voyages, delayed payments, harder insurance, longer compliance queues, and the daily irritation of being asked to carry a burden they did not design.

The unevenness is not accidental. Maritime trade is geographically lopsided, commercially specialised, and institutionally layered. A state with a strategic port, a large neutral fleet, a strong insurance market, or a shipping-dependent economy will feel pressure differently from a state whose role in the trade is thinner or more protected. The same is true of firms. One carrier inherits reputational exposure because of where it sails. Another inherits compliance cost because of who it services. A third inherits political scrutiny simply because it sits in the middle of a transaction nobody wants to own outright. The bill arrives unevenly.

That inequality matters because coalition discipline depends not only on legal agreement but on the tolerability of the burdens created by enforcement. If some states and firms repeatedly absorb more friction than others, they begin to ask harder questions about fairness, compensation, and strategic patience. The question is rarely framed in grand moral language. It appears in more practical forms. Why must this port bear the inspection delay? Why must this insurer lose the business? Why must this neutral carrier explain itself again when the political decision was made elsewhere? The ledger starts to matter.

This is the chapter's central tension. Sanctions at sea claim legitimacy by presenting themselves as instruments of collective discipline, yet they often operate through highly unequal exposure distributed across geography, fleet structure, and market role. That inequality is not merely a political inconvenience. It shapes whether allies stay aligned, whether neutrals remain cooperative, and whether private actors continue treating enforcement as a system worth obeying rather than a cost worth escaping. Maritime sanctions do not fail only when they are openly defied. They also weaken when the actors asked to carry them begin to feel that the arrangement is no longer proportionate.

The stakes rise because neutral carriers sit in the most uncomfortable part of this arrangement. They may be engaged in lawful trade, operating under ordinary commercial logic, and still find themselves drawn into geopolitical enforcement through insurance pressure, payment friction, service denials, or reputational suspicion. Neutrality on paper does not guarantee neutrality in practice if the surrounding private governance system has decided that certain routes, cargoes, or counterparties now belong to a zone of discomfort. The result is a grey market of legitimacy in which the carrier may be legally entitled to proceed and commercially punished for trying. That tension between open commerce and coercive policy is not a side issue. It is one of the places where the credibility of sanctions is most severely tested.

The costs do not stop with profit and politics. Delays, rerouting, and service denial can create safety and welfare risks that are easy to underestimate from shore, especially in harsher waters where options are fewer and mistakes travel further. A compliance hold that looks administrative in an office may look very different to a crew facing narrowing weather windows, thinner service support, or greater distance from safe alternatives. A denial that seems prudent in legal terms may still produce practical consequences that policymakers and firms cannot honestly treat as invisible. Legitimacy begins to erode when a sanctions system speaks fluently about pressure and awkwardly about the externalities that pressure creates.

That is why ordinary contracting starts to change. Firms do not wait passively for the next dispute. They revise clauses, seek fallback ports, add verification steps, and redesign responsibility around the expectation that compliance friction is no longer exceptional but built into the voyage. Maritime trade learns to bargain with sanctions the way it bargains with weather, congestion, and political risk: by reshaping ordinary commercial practice. The adaptation is not always evasive. Often it is the behaviour of lawful actors trying to preserve predictability in a world where rules now travel through private caution as much as public law.

The path ahead follows that reshaping where it bites hardest. It begins with the uneven distribution of compliance cost and political exposure, then moves into the awkward position of neutral carriers whose legality may remain intact while their legitimacy becomes contested. From there it turns to the externalities that gather around delay, rerouting, and denial in difficult operating conditions, before arriving at the contractual and institutional fallback mechanisms through which firms try to keep trade governable without pretending the old assumptions still hold. The argument is not that sanctions create disorder everywhere. It is that they reorganise order unevenly, and the unevenness has strategic consequences.

The deeper friction lies here: a sanctions coalition needs breadth to be effective, but the broader the system becomes, the more it depends on actors who are not equally committed, equally protected, or equally compensated. A port state with exposure to disruption, a neutral carrier with lawful cargo, an insurer with reputational downside, and a coastal service provider operating in a harsh environment do not experience "coalition discipline" as the same thing. They experience different versions of the same rule, and those differences accumulate. The harder question, then, is not whether sanctions can impose cost. It is how much unequal cost a maritime system can absorb before allied patience thins, neutral cooperation hardens into resentment, and lawful actors begin treating compliance not as a shared obligation but as someone else's strategy written onto their balance sheet.

Burden sharing and uneven exposure

In June 2022, when the European Union adopted its sixth sanctions package in Brussels, the political act was collective but the commercial exposure was not. The legal text travelled outward through very different maritime worlds. For some member states, the measure was chiefly a matter of diplomatic alignment and administrative adjustment. For others, especially those with powerful shipping sectors, insurance linkages, port services, and long experience in tanker trade, the decision landed inside a far denser web of contracts, client relationships, and operational dependencies. The coalition spoke with one voice. The invoice did not.

That disparity is easy to overlook because sanctions are often narrated at the level of governments and principles. Maritime enforcement, however, works through fleets, insurers, registries, banks, ports, brokers, managers, and coastal service providers whose exposure is shaped by geography and market position long before politics enters the room. A state with a strategic chokepoint, a large commercial fleet, or a major maritime services cluster will feel the same restriction differently from a state whose economy touches the trade only at a distance. A firm's burden is likewise uneven. One insurer may inherit immediate reputational risk. One carrier may lose access to cargoes it once treated as routine. Another may see only a change in screening procedure. The flag is shared. The cost is not.

This is the central fact that any serious analysis of burden sharing must hold in view. Sanctions coalitions do not distribute pain according to legal elegance. They distribute it according to existing patterns of maritime dependence. Show the ordinary mechanism. A rule prohibits or narrows a category of trade. The immediate consequences fall heaviest on actors already closest to that trade: owners whose vessels served the route, ports positioned on the corridor, insurers whose books carried the risk, service providers whose business depended on continuity, and states whose geography made abstention more expensive than solidarity sounded in principle. The concept is uneven exposure. The implication is that coalition discipline is never tested only by political conviction. It is tested by whether those carrying the heaviest burdens continue to judge the collective strategy worth the unequal cost.

Geography matters first because maritime sanctions are never abstractly global in their effects. A northern port, a canal state, an island registry economy, or a country whose coastline sits beside a sensitive trade artery enters the sanctions question from a different place than an inland or lightly exposed partner. A government whose firms must answer daily for delayed voyages, diverted traffic, more intrusive inspections, and rising compliance demands will experience "burden sharing" not as an ethical slogan but as a recurring managerial problem. The concept is geographic concentration. The implication is that sanctions may be legally multilateral while remaining operationally local in the places where ships actually seek services, shelter, finance, and legitimacy.

Fleet composition sharpens that concentration. A state or firm specialised in tankers, bulk carriers, or support services linked to the affected commodity faces a different burden from one with a more diversified or less directly exposed maritime profile. This does not require any heroic theory. It is visible in ordinary decisions: which ships lose business, which managers must answer more questions, which insurers and brokers see their client base become politically difficult, which compliance desks are suddenly flooded with escalations that used to pass as routine. Risk, in this setting, is visible in idle tonnage, narrower counterparties, more fragile payment expectations, and the quiet rearrangement of business lines away from trades now deemed too troublesome. A sanction aimed at one state can therefore function as a restructuring event for an allied maritime sector.

A named example shows the pattern clearly. When the European Union's sixth sanctions package took effect in 2022, member states with large shipping interests and maritime services exposure faced a distinct practical challenge: they were not only helping design the enforcement architecture, they were also among those most likely to lose business, absorb legal complexity, and manage downstream commercial disruption. The burden was not merely ideological. It had to be carried through chartering decisions, insurance relationships, payment controls, port administration, and the reputational management of firms suddenly operating inside a more politicised market. The lesson was not that solidarity failed. The lesson was that solidarity required actors with heavier maritime exposure to bear more than others, and to do so repeatedly.

Market role matters just as much as geography or fleet type because some firms are simply more central to maritime legitimacy than others. A bank that clears payments, an insurer whose cover opens ports, a classification society whose certificates sustain confidence, or a major neutral carrier whose vessels connect politically awkward trades all encounter sanctions at a deeper level than a peripheral contractor does. Their burden is not just the loss of revenue from one route. It is the need to become part-time governors of the policy. Once that happens, they begin absorbing costs in staff time, compliance escalation, reputational management, client triage, and strategic hesitation. The concept here is institutional centrality. The implication is that sanctions coalitions often rely most heavily on actors whose business model was built for commercial neutrality, not geopolitical service.

This is where coalition discipline can begin to fray, not always through open dissent but through accumulated reluctance. A state or firm that repeatedly bears higher compliance cost will start asking harder questions about proportionality, reciprocity, and duration. How long should it carry the commercial downside? Which partners are exposed to similar sacrifice, and which are largely shielded by their structure or location? Are the strategic gains real enough to justify the asymmetry? These are not signs of disloyalty. They are signs that political sustainability has entered the ledger. Once that ledger feels persistently unbalanced, public solidarity may remain intact while private commitment begins to thin.

A second named example helps illuminate the wider principle. The G7 price-cap arrangements introduced in late 2022 depended heavily on service providers, insurers, and maritime intermediaries located in allied jurisdictions. That structure gave the policy force precisely because those actors sat near the transaction's practical centre. It also meant that some allied markets carried more of the implementation burden than others. Firms in those markets had to verify documents, interpret guidance, decide how much uncertainty to tolerate, and manage the risk of getting a politically sensitive file wrong. Again, the point is not that the policy was unsound. The point is that effective enforcement often rests on an unequal allocation of administrative labour and commercial exposure, and that inequality becomes part of the politics of endurance.

A credible limitation must be stated plainly. Uneven exposure does not automatically destroy coalition discipline. States and firms often accept unequal burdens when they regard the strategic objective as important enough, the burden as temporary enough, or the compensating political benefits as real enough. Maritime actors are not passive victims of policy. Some adapt well. Some gain from the displacement of competitors. Some use stronger compliance capacity as a commercial advantage. It would therefore be simplistic to treat unevenness as synonymous with failure. Coalitions are rarely balanced in any perfect sense, and still they sometimes hold.

That limitation does not weaken the argument. It sharpens the evaluative lens. The important question is not whether burdens are perfectly equal; they never are. The important question is whether the unequal burdens remain politically and commercially intelligible to those asked to bear them. Do the most exposed states and firms believe the strategy has coherent goals, credible adjustment mechanisms, and some recognition of the asymmetry involved? Or do they begin to feel that "shared enforcement" has become a polite name for concentrated sacrifice? The answer matters because coalitions can withstand hardship more easily than they can withstand the sense that hardship is being normalised without acknowledgement.

This is why burden sharing should be read as a test of political sustainability, not merely a moral aspiration. A sanctions regime may look formidable on paper and still weaken in practice if it repeatedly leans on the same maritime sectors, the same ports, the same insurers, the same neutral service providers, and the same coastal states to absorb disruption while others offer mainly rhetorical support. Compliance then becomes a geography of patience. Some places and firms can endure longer. Others start building quiet exceptions into their commercial behaviour or pressing for softer interpretation, slower tightening, or more room to protect domestic actors from the sharpest consequences. The coalition does not necessarily break. It begins to negotiate itself from within.

The quiet motif here is the ledger. Not because states and firms reduce principle to bookkeeping, but because principle without accounting rarely survives long in maritime commerce. One side of the ledger records strategic intention, alliance value, reputational alignment, and coercive purpose. The other records delayed voyages, reduced fixtures, higher compliance staffing, lost premiums, redirected services, and the daily effort of turning a public rule into private action. A coalition remains strong when those reading the second side still believe the first justifies it. Once that belief weakens, the ledger begins to look less like solidarity and more like subsidy.

This is why the issue cannot be dismissed as mere complaining from commercially exposed actors. Uneven exposure is part of the mechanism by which maritime sanctions either retain legitimacy or slowly lose it. A state positioned near the trade, or a firm structurally central to it, can support a sanctions regime while still asking whether the distribution of burden is drifting beyond what coalition discipline can reasonably demand. That question is not a distraction from enforcement. It is one of the conditions under which enforcement remains governable.

The unresolved question follows naturally. When a sanctions coalition depends on some states and firms bearing markedly more compliance cost because of where they sit on the map, what they insure, or what fleets they run, how long can political unity endure before the actors carrying the heaviest weight decide that shared purpose no longer feels quite so shared?

Neutral carriers and contested legitimacy

In June 2022, as sanctions pressure widened across Russian-linked maritime trade, one of the quietest and most consequential struggles unfolded around ships that belonged neither to the principal sanctioning states nor to the principal target. Neutral carriers found themselves in an awkward position. Their voyages might remain lawful on the face of the contracts. Their cargoes might be documentable. Their flags, owners, and managers might sit outside the direct political quarrel. Yet insurers, banks, ports, brokers, and service providers increasingly asked whether legality alone was still enough. The answer was often hesitant.

That hesitation reveals a hard truth about maritime neutrality. A carrier may remain outside the formal alignment of coercive policy and still be drawn into its operational consequences because private services do not treat neutrality as self-executing. Insurance, classification, payments, bunkers, port acceptance, and trade finance all run through institutions that make their own judgements about exposure. A neutral carrier can therefore be lawful and still become commercially awkward. The file goes grey.

This is the first point that matters. Neutral shipping does not resist geopolitical drafting only through public argument or diplomatic posture. It resists through practical insistence that lawful commerce should not be punished by private caution masquerading as inevitability. Show the ordinary scene. A neutral shipowner fixes a cargo that, on the owner's reading, complies with the relevant rules. The vessel is not designated. The charter is facially lawful. Yet the payment bank asks for more. The insurer slows confirmation. A port agent signals discomfort. A service provider seeks stronger ownership and cargo assurances than would normally be required. The concept is indirect conscription. The implication is severe: a carrier can be pulled into enforcement discipline not by legal command alone, but by the surrounding private network's refusal to treat legality as sufficient comfort.

This is why contested legitimacy becomes more important than formal law in the daily life of neutral shipping. Legitimacy here is not an abstract moral quality. It is visible in whether counterparties still regard the voyage as reputable enough to service without later regret. A neutral carrier may possess a clean legal position and still fail that quieter test if the route, cargo, buyer, insurer, or payment chain looks too close to a political fault line. The visible behaviours are familiar: longer due diligence, revised freight expectations, more intrusive document demands, narrower clauses, delayed berthing, or a simple decline explained in the language of internal policy rather than external prohibition. Open commerce meets coercive policy in precisely that grey zone.

A named example from the Black Sea grain disputes after 2022 helps clarify the structure. Several shipments and vessel movements linked to grain trade from the wider region became objects of dispute not because every neutral carrier involved had obviously broken a rule, but because documentation, origin claims, and political narratives had become difficult enough that private and public actors alike began treating some otherwise plausible voyages as reputationally charged. The lesson was not that neutrality had disappeared. It was that neutrality no longer guaranteed commercial ease once the broader ecosystem of ports, banks, insurers, and service providers had begun reading certain trades through a more anxious political lens.

That anxiety matters because neutral carriers often sit inside market roles that make abstention costly. They may specialise in routes, cargo classes, or service segments where demand remains strong precisely when political controversy grows. They may not wish to become instruments of one coalition's strategy, yet they also cannot easily abandon major lanes of lawful trade without harming their own business model. The concept is exposed neutrality. The implication is that the neutral carrier's problem is not simply whether a voyage is legal. It is whether enough of the private governance system will continue to recognise that legality in operational terms.

This is where private services pressure changes the meaning of neutrality. A state may declare itself outside a sanctions coalition. A carrier under that state's flag may still require insurance from institutions aligned with sanctioning markets, payment rails influenced by allied banks, or port access shaped by service providers unwilling to distinguish sharply between legal permissibility and reputational discomfort. The carrier remains neutral in formal status while losing autonomy in practical terms. The voyage becomes a test of whether private infrastructure can be used to extend policy beyond the states that officially adopt it. The implication is not merely commercial. It touches the legitimacy of the sanctions system itself, because the more enforcement leans on private pressure, the less clear the boundary becomes between lawful trade management and informal coercion.

A second named example can be drawn from the wider service environment after the European Union's 2022 sanctions expansions and the associated price-cap architecture. Even where neutral carriers tried to continue participating in trades they believed permissible, the practical question often turned on whether the surrounding service chain would still accommodate them. Could they obtain acceptable insurance? Would banks process the payments without repeated escalation? Would ports or terminals require more documentary comfort than before? The answer varied, but the structural point remained constant. Neutrality did not settle the file. It merely opened the argument.

A credible limitation must be faced directly. Neutral carriers are not innocent by definition, and neutrality can itself be used strategically.

Some carriers may seek to exploit the ambiguity around non-alignment, offering services precisely because they expect others to treat them as less politically exposed. Some may build business models around the tolerance gap between what law allows and what more cautious firms refuse. It would therefore be naive to imagine neutral shipping as a morally pure category injured only by overreaching coalitions. The grey zone exists partly because lawful neutrality and opportunistic proximity can look uncomfortably similar from the outside.

That limitation does not weaken the central argument. It sharpens the analytical task. The issue is not whether neutral carriers are beyond scrutiny. The issue is whether scrutiny remains tied to evidence and proportion rather than drifting into a broader reputational presumption that some lawful trades should simply be made too awkward to continue. Once that drift occurs, the distinction between open commerce and coercive policy begins to fray. A sanctions system that cannot preserve that distinction clearly may still pressure the target. It will also pressure confidence in its own fairness, especially among states and firms whose support remains contingent rather than enthusiastic.

This is why neutral carriers often resist not through defiance but through argument about process, scope, and commercial reasonableness. They ask why private institutions should impose burdens not clearly required by law. They challenge assumptions that reputational discomfort equals disqualifying risk. They seek clearer guidance, more specific documentary thresholds, or contractual structures that preserve room for lawful trade without pretending political pressure is absent. The resistance may look technical. It is actually constitutional in miniature. It asks who gets to decide when a lawful voyage becomes too uncomfortable to support and on what basis that judgement should travel through the market.

The quiet motif here is the stamp. A neutral carrier may have the proper documents, the lawful charter, the acceptable flag, the cleared cargo description. Yet the decisive issue is often whether the next institution still stamps the file as tolerable enough to proceed. The stamp does not merely certify legality. It signals willingness to stand beside the trade. When neutrality becomes contested, the stamp begins to wobble even before the law does.

This is why the tension between open commerce and coercive policy is so difficult to manage in maritime sanctions. Open commerce depends on carriers being able to rely on legal categories and documentary sufficiency with some confidence. Coercive policy, especially when operationalised through private services pressure, thrives on making that confidence conditional. The neutral carrier inhabits the point where those logics collide. Too much indulgence and sanctions lose force. Too much informal pressure and neutrality begins to look like a formal status stripped of practical content.

The unresolved question is therefore not whether a neutral carrier can point to a lawful voyage on paper. It is whether a sanctions system that increasingly relies on private caution can preserve any meaningful space in which lawful neutrality remains commercially viable - or whether that space shrinks each time reputational risk is allowed to do work that law has not quite claimed for itself.

Humanitarian and safety externalities

On 23 March 2021, when the *Ever Given* grounded in the Suez Canal, the world was reminded that delays in shipping are never purely administrative. A vessel held in the wrong place at the wrong time can turn contractual inconvenience into wider disruption with startling speed. That incident was not a sanctions case, and it should not be forced into one. Its relevance lies elsewhere. It shows how quickly maritime systems reveal their dependence on timing, routing, service availability, and safe operating margins once ordinary movement is interrupted.

That dependence becomes more serious in harsher environments, where distance, weather, ice, and limited alternatives narrow the room for error. A delay that might be commercially irritating in a dense southern corridor can become operationally consequential in cold waters with fewer ports, fewer repair options, and longer intervals between safe havens. A reroute that looks manageable on paper can lengthen exposure to fatigue, uncertain weather windows, thinner service support, or degraded scheduling for crew changes and resupply. Risk accumulates quietly.

The waiting matters physically.

This is the first point that must be stated plainly. Sanctions rarely produce only political pressure or commercial inconvenience. They can also generate humanitarian and safety externalities when enforcement tools alter the practical conditions under which ships, crews, and cargoes continue to move. Show the sequence in ordinary terms. A port delays entry while documents are checked. An insurer hesitates. A service provider declines support. The vessel reroutes, waits offshore, or continues under narrower margins than originally planned. Nothing in that chain requires dramatic misconduct. The concept is induced strain. The implication is that even lawful and prudently designed enforcement can create downstream consequences that exceed the immediate target and land on people and operations far from the original decision.

That is especially true where harsh geography amplifies every disturbance. Cold-water operations already depend on tighter planning, more specialised support, and greater sensitivity to timing than many other trades. Add longer verification cycles, contested service access, or narrower routing options, and the voyage begins to carry burdens that are not fully visible in the legal file. A crew faces longer periods aboard because relief plans slip. A ship remains exposed to deteriorating seasonal conditions because a cargo or payment issue has not cleared. A technical deficiency that would normally be addressed at the next suitable facility becomes harder to manage because the suitable facility is no longer available or no longer willing to engage. The implication is not melodrama. It is that externalities arise when enforcement friction meets operational thinness.

A named example from the pandemic crew-change crisis helps clarify the human dimension. In 2020 and 2021, as border controls and travel restrictions disrupted maritime labour movement, vessels around the world experienced prolonged service by crews unable to disembark as planned. The crisis was not a sanctions product, yet it exposed a durable truth: administrative barriers imposed ashore can become welfare and safety burdens aboard ship with surprising speed. The lesson for sanctions practice is not that all delay is equivalent. It is that decision-makers should never assume that holding a file still means only holding paper still. The human timetable continues.

This matters because safety and humanitarian risks rarely appear as cleanly as policymakers would like. They do not always arrive as dramatic emergencies. More often they accumulate through slower processes: fatigue, deferred maintenance, degraded confidence in rescue or repair options, longer voyages under uncertain conditions, delayed medical access, frayed crewing schedules, and the pressure to preserve commercial performance after a costly interruption. The concept is cumulative externality. The implication is that legitimacy in sanctions enforcement depends partly on whether institutions recognise these secondary effects early enough to avoid treating them as somebody else's downstream problem.

The same is true of rerouting. A ship diverted from a preferred or familiar corridor may not merely travel farther. It may travel under different operational assumptions, with different service ecosystems, new port dependencies, and altered exposure to weather or political uncertainty. A route chosen to reduce sanctions risk can increase other forms of risk without anyone in the decision chain explicitly intending that result. A carrier may accept the change because it sees no better lawful alternative. An insurer may tolerate it because the original route became too exposed. A port may insist on it because the paperwork is not acceptable in time. Each decision can look individually defensible. The combined effect may still be a vessel operating under a tighter safety and welfare margin than before.

A second named example comes from Arctic and sub-Arctic shipping more broadly, where operational resilience depends heavily on specialised support, predictable access, and careful seasonal judgement. In such contexts, service denial does not simply inconvenience the trade. It can force difficult choices about waiting, diverting, or continuing in environments that punish thin planning more severely than milder seas do. One need not offer operational advice to see the institutional problem. If enforcement pressure narrows the range of acceptable ports, insurers, repair options, or support providers, it may make lawful caution more difficult to practice. The intended coercive effect therefore shares space with an unintended safety cost.

A credible limitation must be acknowledged. Externalities are real, but they are often invoked too loosely by those seeking to soften sanctions pressure for commercial or political reasons. Not every delay creates a serious welfare risk. Not every reroute is materially unsafe. Not every service denial threatens humanitarian consequences. Shipping has always involved waiting, diversion, and imperfect support. Markets adapt. Crews and operators handle disruption as part of the trade. A serious analysis must therefore resist sentimental inflation. If every inconvenience is redescribed as a humanitarian emergency, the term loses credibility and the discussion becomes unusable.

That limitation does not weaken the central argument. It strengthens it by insisting on proportion. The real issue is not whether all enforcement friction produces unacceptable externalities. It is whether institutions have built any serious method for recognising when ordinary commercial delay begins to interact with geography, weather, crew welfare, technical dependency, or emergency planning in ways that change the moral and operational meaning of the decision. Good enforcement does not abandon pressure at the first mention of hardship. It does recognise that hardship can become part of the case rather than an afterthought to it.

This is where legitimacy becomes inseparable from administrative discipline. A sanctions regime that ignores humanitarian and safety externalities may still coerce effectively for a time. It will do so at a cost. Private actors will grow more defensive. Neutral carriers will become more resistant to participation. Allies bearing heavier operational exposure will ask harder questions. The market will begin to interpret sanctions not as disciplined pressure but as a system too willing to externalise risk onto crews, service providers, and difficult operating environments. That perception matters because legitimacy is not maintained by rhetoric. It is maintained when institutions show that they can pursue coercive ends without pretending secondary harms are invisible or irrelevant.

The quiet motif here is the weather window. It captures something larger than meteorology. A weather window is a period in which movement remains possible, safe enough, and commercially meaningful. Delays can close it. Rerouting can strain it. Service denial can narrow it. The phrase reminds us that maritime time is not infinitely elastic. Administrative hesitation ashore may consume operating margins at sea more quickly than office procedures tend to imagine. Once the window begins to close, the distinction between compliance friction and operational consequence becomes harder to maintain honestly.

This is why the chapter's broader concern with allies, neutrals, and economic costs cannot remain confined to finance and politics alone. Humanitarian and safety externalities test whether sanctions systems understand the medium through which they operate. Sea transport is not a spreadsheet. It is a human and technical enterprise conducted under physical limits that do not pause while institutions argue over documentation, permissions, or exposure. The strongest sanctions regimes are not those that deny this. They are the ones that account for it without surrendering seriousness.

The unresolved question is therefore not whether coercive policy can impose maritime strain. It clearly can. The harder question is when the strain it creates stops looking like legitimate pressure on a target and starts looking like a transfer of risk onto crews, lawful carriers, and harsh operating environments that never chose to become the place where the policy's hidden costs would be paid.

Dispute resolution and commercial fallback

In March 2022, as sanctions pressure widened across Russian-linked maritime trade, one of the most revealing changes occurred not at sea but in contracts. Clauses that had once lived quietly at the back of charterparties, sale agreements, insurance wordings, and service contracts moved abruptly to the front of commercial attention. Parties began reading for interruption rather than performance. The voyage still mattered, but so did the question of what each side could refuse, suspend, reroute, or demand if legality became uncertain after the deal was struck.

That shift tells us something important about maritime sanctions. They do not only prohibit. They reorganise the ordinary architecture of commercial prudence. A firm facing a politicised trade does not usually begin by searching for heroic solutions. It begins by asking how to preserve room to move if the file becomes harder to defend. Can the vessel call elsewhere? Can performance be delayed? Can a payment be paused? Can further documents be demanded? Can a service be withheld without collapsing the entire contractual structure? The contract becomes a hinge.

Paper prepares the detour.

This is the first point worth fixing clearly. Dispute resolution and commercial fallback are not peripheral legal niceties added after the real trade has been arranged. They are how maritime actors absorb the uncertainty created when sanctions risk enters ordinary commerce without warning or without stable interpretation. Show the sequence. A seller, buyer, owner, charterer, bank, or insurer senses that a once-routine transaction may become difficult. Rather than abandon the trade immediately, the parties revise the paperwork around it. Clauses are sharpened, alternative ports are named, documentary conditions multiply, and rights to pause or re-route are drafted more carefully. The concept is contractual buffering. The implication is that compliance changes maritime contracting from a framework of expected performance into a framework of managed interruption.

This matters because maritime commerce depends on promises made across time, distance, and incomplete information. A cargo may be sold before loading, financed before arrival, and contracted through several layers of service before anyone knows whether a future sanctions development, payment refusal, port query, or insurance hesitation will disturb the chain. Firms, therefore, use contract language not simply to allocate ordinary risk, but to decide which party must absorb the cost of uncertainty when compliance pressure appears mid-voyage. That allocation is never morally neutral. The side with greater leverage often writes the safer fallback. The side more dependent on the fixture often accepts a broader zone of suspension or refusal. The contract becomes a map of who can step back first.

A named example from the Russian shipping environment after February 2022 makes the point plainly. As sanctions rules, guidance, insurer appetite, and banking behaviour shifted, parties across maritime trade revised contractual expectations in real time. Some trades failed because the new burdens were too great. Others survived only because firms inserted or activated sanctions-related clauses, demanded stronger documentary support, or reworked performance terms to preserve an exit if a bank, port, insurer, or service provider later balked. The lesson was not that contract language solved the uncertainty. It was that contractual fallback became one of the few ways to keep commercial relationships functioning at all once ordinary assumptions no longer held.

Alternative ports are one visible expression of that fallback logic. Their significance lies less in geography than in institutional substitution. A party naming an alternative port is not simply choosing another point on the map. It is trying to preserve commercial optionality if the original port becomes politically, administratively, or reputationally difficult. This is not tactical evasion in the sense that concerns this book elsewhere. Often it is the behaviour of lawful actors trying to keep a legitimate trade alive within a more restrictive and nervous environment. Yet the alternative port also changes costs, timing, service dependencies, and dispute dynamics. A fallback location may be legally available while commercially inferior. The concept is substitute access. The implication is that sanctions pressure does not only close routes; it rewrites the hierarchy of acceptable ones inside the contract itself.

Additional verification works in a similarly double-edged way. A party may ask for more origin documentation, ownership clarification, insurer confirmation, payment assurances, or route explanations not because it has decided the trade is improper, but because it wants a defensible basis for continuing. Verification thus becomes a bridge between outright refusal and blind performance. It gives firms a way to say, in effect, that the deal may proceed only if the paper grows stronger. Trust, here, is visible in the number and specificity of the extra conditions attached to performance. A file that once needed one certificate now needs three. A vessel that once required routine screening now triggers escalated review and written internal approvals. The implication is that the transaction survives only by becoming more administratively self-conscious.

This is why dispute resolution under sanctions pressure often begins before any formal dispute exists. Contracts are not merely instruments for settling broken relationships after the fact. They increasingly function as anticipatory devices through which firms decide how disagreement, delay, or legal unease will be managed before the voyage reaches crisis. A bank delay, a port question, an insurer's hesitation, or a service provider's refusal can all be treated not as shocking interruptions but as contingencies already acknowledged in the commercial structure. The concept is pre-dispute governance. The implication is that maritime contracting adapts to sanctions not by abandoning performance, but by drafting uncertainty directly into ordinary business practice.

A second named example can be seen in the broader use of sanctions clauses and force-majeure-adjacent drafting across shipping and commodity contracts after 2018 and again after 2022. The precise language varies, and one should resist pretending that all clauses do the same work. Still, the structural trend is clear enough. Parties increasingly seek wording that gives them lawful and reputational room to stop, delay, or redirect performance if compliance conditions change after conclusion of the deal. The significance lies not in any single clause, but in the growing expectation that a prudent contract must contain a pathway out, or at least a pathway sideways, before the market will trust the transaction. Sanctions have become part of standard contractual weather.

A credible limitation must be faced directly. More fallback language does not necessarily produce more fairness or more clarity. Broadly drafted clauses can become instruments of opportunism. A party may invoke compliance concern selectively to escape a now-unfavourable commercial bargain, shift costs onto a weaker counterparty, or justify delay that is as much about market movement as legal discomfort. Alternative ports can become expensive half-solutions. Extra verification can harden into endless requests that function like soft refusal. The existence of fallback mechanisms therefore does not prove institutional maturity on its own. It can also reflect the legalisation of distrust.

That limitation, however, sharpens the core argument rather than weakening it. The issue is not whether fallback devices are pure. The issue is what their spread tells us about the changed texture of maritime trade. A sector confident in the stability of legality does not need every ordinary contract to prepare for refusal, redirection, and documentary escalation with such intensity. A sector living under sanctions pressure does. The contract becomes heavier because the surrounding environment has become more brittle. This is why commercial fallback should be read as institutional adaptation, not merely legal drafting. It shows where the market no longer expects smooth performance and where private actors have learned to govern uncertainty without waiting for states to resolve it neatly.

This matters for legitimacy as well as efficiency. If sanctions regularly force lawful firms to rely on broader clauses, more elaborate verification, and secondary ports merely to preserve the possibility of normal trade, then compliance is no longer an external check added to commerce. It has become part of commerce's internal grammar. That can be stabilising. It can also quietly redistribute costs towards parties with less bargaining power, less administrative capacity, or less access to alternative service networks. A large trader or shipowner may absorb thicker drafting and verification with tolerable discomfort. A smaller carrier or regional service firm may find the same burdens transformative. Ordinary contracting thus becomes one more site where uneven exposure is written into the market.

The quiet motif here is the side letter. One party asks for an assurance not quite covered by the main contract. Another seeks a clarification, an additional certificate, a fallback payment route, a written statement on ownership, destination, or insurer comfort. The side letter is modest, almost embarrassed by its own necessity. Yet it reveals what the formal contract can no longer carry by itself. When side letters proliferate, the market is admitting that ordinary language no longer provides enough shelter from compliance risk.

For maritime sanctions, the broader lesson is austere. Dispute resolution and commercial fallback show how deeply enforcement has entered the bones of ordinary trade. Firms are not simply reacting to blocked voyages or denied services after they happen. They are redesigning contracts, routes, verification practices, and dispute pathways in anticipation of the next interruption. This is not tactical evasion. It is the legal and commercial metabolism of a sector learning that performance now depends on preserving defensible ways not to perform.

That leaves the harder question where serious commercial judgement now begins. When a contract is drafted less to guarantee the voyage than to manage the moment the voyage becomes too difficult to defend, has maritime trade adapted prudently to sanctions pressure - or has it quietly accepted that ordinary commerce now proceeds only on the condition that everyone carries, in writing, a better-prepared route to disagreement than to trust?

Chapter 14

Future Arctic Governance and Enforcement

What does successful enforcement look like in a place where the hardest task may not be stopping a voyage, but building the conditions under which stopping, checking, rescuing, or even reliably observing a voyage becomes possible at all? That question unsettles many of the habits sanctions analysis has acquired in warmer, denser, and more institutionally mature theatres of trade. In the Arctic, law cannot be separated for long from distance, weather, infrastructure, and the blunt fact that authority without capability is often only a promise written too far from the scene.

That is why the future of Arctic enforcement turns less on dramatic moments of interdiction than on the slower construction of systems. A route becomes more accessible. A port becomes more capable. Monitoring improves in one corridor while remaining thin in another. Search and rescue capacity, communications reliability, ice support, commercial services, and institutional trust all accumulate unevenly. The result is not a single geopolitical map but a layered one, in which physical access and governance access do not always advance together. A harbour without services cannot enforce much. A rule without reach cannot persuade for long.

The checkpoint matters.

This is the chapter's central tension. Arctic governance is often discussed as though changing ice and changing law were the main story. They are not. The harder issue is whether the region's growing commercial and strategic relevance will be met by a comparable growth in the capacities that make enforcement meaningful, proportionate, and credible. The checkpoint stands here as a concrete test: not merely a place of inspection, but the whole chain of support that allows a state, a port, an insurer, a classifier, or a coalition of partners to decide that a rule can be applied and defended without creating more danger than discipline.

That tension matters because the Arctic punishes institutional fantasy. A state may declare standards. A coalition may announce restrictions. Private actors may update compliance systems overnight. Yet if monitoring remains intermittent, rescue thin, ports sparse, and service nodes unequally distributed, the practical consequences of those decisions will vary sharply. Some routes will become easier to govern because they are more visible and more serviced. Others will become more tempting precisely because they remain administratively shallow. Enforcement, then, is not a matter of legal ambition alone. It is a problem of synchronising physical capability with institutional intent before trade learns to exploit the gap between them.

The stakes are larger than control of any one voyage. Arctic sanctions and compliance systems will be judged not only by whether they impose friction on targeted trade, but by whether they preserve legitimacy among the actors asked to carry them. That includes allies, neutral carriers, insurers, classification societies, port authorities, and service providers whose willingness to cooperate depends on more than strategic alignment. They need clarity they can operationalise, evidence they can trust, and burdens that do not look disconnected from the capacities actually available in harsh conditions. Where those conditions are absent, even well-meant governance can begin to look performative, selective, or careless.

This is one reason private rulemaking will matter so much. Public treaties and formal intergovernmental arrangements tend to move at the speed of negotiation, caution, and compromise. Commercial standards bodies, insurers, classification societies, and major service markets often move faster because they are reacting to operational risk rather than waiting for perfect political settlement. Their rules may begin as prudential adjustments and end as de facto entry conditions for trade. This does not make them illegitimate. It does mean that the future enforcement environment may harden through commercial standards before public law fully catches up, and that indirect pressure may continue to outpace direct coercion in shaping who can trade where and under what conditions.

The path ahead follows that asymmetry from the ground up. It begins with infrastructure, climate, and route politics, because governance in the Arctic will always depend on what can actually be seen, reached, serviced, and recovered. It then turns to standards bodies and private rulemaking, where market access may tighten through technical and insurance logic more quickly than public agreement can mature. From there the argument moves towards a more durable way of thinking about sanctions design in harsh environments, before ending with the harder problem of measurement:

how to judge success when visible seizures may tell less than reduced risk, accumulated friction, and preserved legitimacy.

A deeper friction runs through all of this. The more serious enforcement becomes, the less useful spectacle looks as a metric of success. A dramatic interception satisfies the political imagination, but Arctic governance cannot be built on exceptional moments alone. It depends on quieter achievements: better information, more reliable service nodes, clearer standards, stronger cooperation, and fewer incentives for trade to seek out the thinnest parts of the map. Those achievements are slower, less cinematic, and often harder to attribute. They are also closer to what real systems require if they are to endure.

That leaves the harder question waiting at the edge of every future Arctic route. If accessibility continues to grow unevenly, and governance capacity grows unevenly with it, what should count as a credible enforcement system: the ability to stop the occasional ship, or the harder and less glamorous achievement of building enough infrastructure, standards, coordination, and restraint that targeted trade finds the region steadily less permissive without lawful commerce finding it steadily less governable?

Infrastructure, climate, and route politics

In August 2007, a Russian submersible planted a titanium flag on the seabed beneath the North Pole and briefly gave the world the sort of Arctic image it finds easy to remember: dramatic, territorial, symbolic. The harder Arctic story has always been less theatrical. Power in northern waters does not rest only on claims, maps, or legal positions. It rests on who can see, reach, support, repair, rescue, and sustain traffic when conditions turn hostile and distances begin to punish institutional vanity. The port matters more than the gesture.

That is why Arctic enforcement cannot be understood as a problem of law layered onto ice. It is a problem of systems layered onto remoteness. A route becomes more accessible and the immediate assumption is often that governance has advanced with it. That is seldom true in any simple sense. Accessibility may grow faster than monitoring. Traffic may increase before rescue capacity is credible. Port services may improve in one corridor while remaining thin in the next. Communications can remain uneven even where commercial ambition is high. A state may possess jurisdiction and still lack reach. The map can lie.

The dock tells the truth.

This is the first principle worth stating plainly. Changes in accessibility and infrastructure reshape enforcement options because enforcement depends on physical capability before it becomes persuasive as policy. Show the ordinary sequence. A route becomes seasonally easier or commercially more attractive. More vessels consider it. More cargo follows. A government or coalition imagines stronger oversight because the route has become more relevant. Yet what actually determines the quality of that oversight is less the route's abstract availability than the infrastructure around it: ports able to receive and inspect ships, reliable communications, monitoring systems that do not collapse into guesswork, ice and rescue support that can respond to distress, and service nodes through which legality can be translated into practice. The concept is governed accessibility. The implication is austere: without those material supports, Arctic enforcement remains episodic, selective, and often more declaratory than operational.

This is why climate change and infrastructure development do not pull in a single direction. Greater navigability can strengthen enforcement in some respects by concentrating trade into corridors that become more visible, more serviced, and more institutionally legible. A better port, clearer communications, and more regular traffic can make verification easier, emergency response more credible, and service-based pressure more effective. The same developments can also create new vulnerabilities. More movement means more opportunities for difficult cargoes to hide inside ordinary flow. A corridor with improving commercial utility may attract actors who calculate that governance still lags behind traffic. The concept is asymmetrical maturation. The implication is that improved access does not inherently liberalise or securitise the Arctic. It redistributes the points at which governance can succeed or fail.

Monitoring sits at the centre of this redistribution because visibility is the first condition of credible enforcement. One need not reduce monitoring to satellites and AIS feeds to see the larger point. A ship becomes governable when its movement can be observed with enough continuity to support later decisions by ports, insurers, banks, and authorities. Arctic conditions make that continuity costly and uneven. Weather, remoteness, communications limits, and sparse traffic can all make routine awareness harder to sustain than in denser maritime regions. A troubling voyage may therefore disappear not because anyone has skillfully concealed it, but because the surrounding system cannot maintain the same evidentiary confidence across space and time. The implication is that monitoring capacity is not an accessory to governance. It is one of its constitutive parts.

A named example helps ground the issue. The 2011 Arctic Search and Rescue Agreement under the Arctic Council did not create sanctions tools, but it clarified something more basic: Arctic governance is inseparable from practical response capacity. Search and rescue is often treated as a humanitarian or safety issue distinct from enforcement. In reality, the two are closely related. A state or coalition that cannot credibly support a distressed vessel, coordinate information, or move assets through remote conditions will struggle to present its regulatory and enforcement posture as either serious or legitimate. Rescue capability signals something deeper than benevolence. It signals usable presence. The lesson extends well beyond emergency response. Ports, communications, and support services tell commercial actors which rules are likely to be real because they reveal which institutions can actually act on them.

Port services matter for the same reason. A northern harbour is not just a place of shelter or transfer. It is a governance multiplier. A port with inspection capacity, fuel, repair access, communications, pilots, local administrative competence, and links to service providers can turn legal standards into repeated practice. A port without those things may still exist on a chart while offering little more than symbolic jurisdiction. The visible behaviours that matter are unglamorous: whether documents can be checked without paralysing the ship, whether a delay can be managed safely, whether an insurer regards the facility as credible, whether alternative arrangements exist if the voyage is disrupted. The concept here is nodal enforcement. The implication is that Arctic route politics are inseparable from the politics of where serious ports are built, who funds them, who uses them, and whose standards they normalise.

This is where route politics becomes sharper than simple competition over shortened passages. States do not care about Arctic corridors only because cargo may move there. They care because routes anchored by reliable infrastructure create durable leverage over the legal and commercial meaning of that movement. A corridor with trusted ports, support services, and monitoring systems can become easier to govern, easier to insure, easier to classify, and easier to discipline through service denial or documentary scrutiny. A corridor lacking those supports may appear commercially open while remaining politically and institutionally thin. The result is not one Arctic, but several overlapping Arctics: some increasingly thick with governance capacity, others still governed mainly by distance and improvisation. The implication is that route politics is really about whose systems become normal.

A second named example can be found in the Northern Sea Route's long evolution from strategic ambition to more sustained commercial use under Russian administration. One need not settle every dispute about its future to see the relevant institutional lesson. The route's significance has always depended less on ice charts alone than on the surrounding infrastructure of permits, pilots, icebreaker support, ports, communications, and state capacity to coordinate movement. Whatever one thinks of its politics, it demonstrates a crucial truth: a route becomes governable when physical and administrative systems begin to reinforce each other. The broader implication for sanctions analysis is clear. Enforcement in the Arctic will follow the corridors where such reinforcement is strongest, not merely the areas where maps suggest transit is possible.

A credible limitation must be admitted. Infrastructure is not destiny. Better ports, stronger monitoring, and more capable rescue or support systems do not automatically produce wise or proportionate enforcement. They can centralise control in ways that exclude weaker actors, privilege certain states or commercial networks, and deepen political competition around access rather than reduce it. They can also create false confidence. A corridor that looks well governed may still contain blind spots, and a state with substantial physical capability may still use it selectively or politically. To acknowledge Arctic enforcement as a systems-building problem is not to celebrate every system that emerges. It is to understand the terrain on which legitimacy will be tested.

That limitation sharpens the main argument rather than weakening it. The relevant question is not whether more infrastructure is simply good or bad. The relevant question is what kind of governance the infrastructure makes possible, for whom, and at what cost. Does improved capacity make monitoring more reliable and externalities easier to manage? Does it create credible rescue and service support that allow enforcement to remain proportionate in difficult conditions? Does it strengthen ordinary compliance through better ports and clearer administrative pathways rather than leaning too heavily on exceptional coercion? These are the questions that turn Arctic governance from symbolism into institutional analysis.

The quiet motif here is the dock, because docks reveal what grand strategy often conceals. A dock with fuel, pilots, communications, repair support, inspection capacity, and dependable links to insurers and service firms says that a rule can be lived with, tested, and enforced. A missing dock says something else: that governance may still be thin enough for risk, opportunism, or mere confusion to outrun authority. The Arctic's future will be shaped not only by who claims a route, but by who can build and sustain the practical edge at which a ship meets a system.

For sanctions and enforcement, the deeper lesson is austere. Arctic governance will rise or fail less by the brilliance of legal design than by whether physical capability keeps pace with political ambition. Monitoring without ports, ports without rescue, rescue without communications, and jurisdiction without service capacity all produce weak forms of control that may impress on paper while faltering in practice. A serious assessment of future Arctic enforcement, therefore, begins not with the question of what rules states would like to apply, but with the harder question of which routes and nodes can actually carry the burdens those rules create.

That leaves the unresolved issue where it belongs: if climate and commerce continue to open parts of the Arctic faster than governance systems can mature around them, will enforcement become more credible because more of the region is finally becoming reachable - or more uneven because the places easiest to reach will be governed more tightly while the rest remain the very spaces where determined trade learns to hide in the growing gap between access and capability?

Standards bodies and private rulemaking

In January 2017, when the Polar Code entered into force under the International Maritime Organization framework, it was easy to read the moment as a triumph of public rulemaking. States had negotiated, adopted, and formalised a common standard for ships operating in polar waters. Yet anyone who has watched maritime commerce closely knows that formal entry into force is only the beginning of a rule's real life. Long before a treaty's language settles into routine practice, insurers decide what they will cover, classification societies decide what they will certify, and commercial counterparties decide what they will treat as prudent enough to touch. The market edits the text.

That is why Arctic governance cannot be understood through public law alone. A vessel may satisfy the minimum legal requirements for operation and still find itself commercially disabled because insurers dislike the route, class is uneasy about the ship's condition or documentation, or counterparties want a higher standard than the treaty strictly demands. Standards bodies, insurers, and classification societies do not legislate in the constitutional sense. Yet they often decide which ships can enter the market as credible participants and which ships must trade, if at all, on thinner terms. The certificate becomes a gate.

Private rulemaking matters here because harsh environments intensify the value of trust. Show the ordinary sequence. A shipowner considers an Arctic or near-Arctic voyage. The law provides one framework. Then the ship meets the private architecture around it. An insurer asks whether the route, crew, and technical condition fit its appetite. A classification society asks whether the vessel still satisfies the standards it is prepared to stand behind. Charterers, cargo interests, and ports look to those decisions before making their own. The concept is de facto governance. The implication is that access to Arctic trade often depends less on what a state has forbidden than on what a cluster of private institutions will no longer endorse.

This helps explain why private governance may harden faster than public treaties. States negotiate slowly because they must manage sovereignty, diplomatic compromise, uneven capability, and legal finality. Private actors move more quickly because they are reacting to concentrated exposure. If claims risk rises, cover can narrow. If route conditions become harder to defend, exclusions can tighten. If a vessel category begins to look politically or technically awkward, class and service providers can alter their treatment sooner than governments can reopen international bargains. The visible behaviour is practical and immediate: revised underwriting standards, more intrusive vetting, narrower clauses, reduced tolerance for ambiguous ownership or service chains, and heightened requirements before a ship is considered commercially acceptable. The implication is not that private actors outrank states. It is that they often reach the ship first.

A named example makes this plain. The Polar Code's entry into force in 2017 provided a public baseline for polar operations, but the commercial meaning of that baseline has always depended heavily on how classification societies, insurers, and other market actors interpret and extend it in practice. A code can say what must be done. Private governance decides, very often, what will count as enough. In Arctic conditions, that difference matters enormously because a vessel that is legally capable but commercially under-supported may still find the voyage impossible to arrange on terms anyone serious wishes to defend. The lesson is broader than one code. Formal standards often stabilise the floor. Private governance frequently raises the ceiling at market speed.

This is especially important for sanctions and indirect enforcement because private rulemaking does not need to announce itself as coercive in order to have coercive effects. An insurer narrowing appetite for a class of routes, counterparties, or ownership structures may be responding to safety, claims exposure, or reputational discomfort. A classification society tightening scrutiny around vessels with unstable documentation or questionable service histories may be acting from professional caution rather than geopolitical intent. Yet the combined effect can still shape which Arctic trades remain possible, which become expensive, and which are quietly forced towards less reputable service ecosystems. The concept is indirect exclusion. The implication is that market access in the Arctic can be constrained by a pattern of private refusals long before any state resorts to dramatic enforcement.

That dynamic becomes stronger in harsh environments because the cost of getting it wrong is so visibly non-routine. A questionable voyage in an ordinary corridor may be inconvenient. A questionable voyage in Arctic or sub-Arctic conditions can implicate rescue capacity, environmental harm, crew safety, infrastructure limits, and political blame in more acute ways. Private institutions know this. Their standards therefore tend to reflect not only narrow legal compliance, but broader judgements about governability. Can the ship be assisted if something fails? Can its records be trusted? Can the operator be relied on to respond credibly under stress? Is the route supportable by the surrounding service network? Those judgements are not written like statutes, but they function powerfully in the same direction. They decide who remains inside the circle of ordinary confidence.

A second named example can be found in the wider withdrawal or restriction by parts of the classification and insurance world from Russian-linked shipping after 2022. One should be careful not to flatten many separate decisions into a single script, but the structural lesson is unmistakable. Public sanctions created the political and legal environment. Private institutions then converted uncertainty, reputational exposure, and service risk into much more immediate market consequences. Ships and trades that might still exist in formal legal space discovered that credibility in the eyes of insurers, class, banks, and commercial counterparties had hardened more quickly than the treaty language or official guidance alone would have suggested. That is exactly how private rulemaking works. It advances through selective endorsement and withdrawal rather than headline proclamation.

A credible limitation must be acknowledged. Private governance is not inherently wiser, fairer, or more legitimate than public treaty-making. It can overshoot. It can reproduce unequal access. It can reflect concentrated

Western market power or the risk appetites of dominant institutions rather than any broadly debated conception of public interest. A classification society or insurer may apply caution that is commercially rational and still politically distortive. A standards culture built around the preferences of strong markets can marginalise weaker states or lawful operators who lack the resources to satisfy ever-thickening expectations. To note the speed of private hardening is not to celebrate it uncritically.

That limitation, however, sharpens the main point rather than weakening it. The relevant question is not whether private rulemaking is pure. The relevant question is whether Arctic governance can be understood at all without it. The answer is plainly no. A shipowner, port, bank, or neutral carrier planning operations in harsh waters does not experience governance as a neat separation between treaty and market. It experiences a layered order in which public law sets broad legitimacy, while insurers, standards bodies, classification societies, and commercial service networks decide what will actually circulate as credible trade. Enforcement follows this layered order because exclusion often travels through the private layer first.

This is why the book's larger theme of indirect enforcement finds one of its clearest expressions here. A state need not prohibit every difficult voyage if enough private institutions have concluded that the voyage no longer fits the standards they are willing to support. Access can narrow through underwriting. It can narrow through class scrutiny. It can narrow through chartering practice, terminal caution, and service denial. None of these decisions alone looks like a sovereign act. Together they can structure the Arctic market more effectively than a dramatic but poorly supportable assertion of control. The quiet motif here is the certificate, because it is small, technical, and easily underestimated. Yet the certificate carries the authority of institutions whose refusal can turn a legal possibility into a commercial impossibility.

This matters for future Arctic governance because the region is unlikely to wait politely for perfect treaty coherence before commerce, risk, and political pressure keep evolving. Where infrastructure improves, traffic grows, and stakes rise, private rulemaking will continue to adapt at the pace of claims exposure, market confidence, and institutional memory. That adaptation may reinforce public governance, outpace it, or occasionally frustrate it. But it will not stand aside. Anyone assessing Arctic enforcement without attending to standards bodies, insurers, and classification is therefore studying only the visible half of the system.

The unresolved question follows from that reality. If private governance can harden market access faster than public law can be renegotiated, who truly sets the operative rules of Arctic trade when the next politically difficult voyage appears: the states that wrote the formal framework, or the institutions whose signatures, cover, and certificates quietly determine whether the framework ever reaches the ship in time to matter?

Sanctions design for harsh environments

In March 1989, when the *Exxon Valdez* ran aground in Prince William Sound, Alaska, the catastrophe fixed a truth that polar and near-polar governance has never escaped: in harsh maritime environments, consequence travels faster than correction. Once distance, weather, ice, and weak redundancy are part of the operating setting, a bad decision is rarely confined to the original file that produced it. It spills outward into safety, rescue burden, environmental exposure, commercial delay, and political blame. That is why sanctions design in such places cannot be judged only by what it forbids. It must be judged by whether it can be applied without outrunning the conditions that make enforcement credible.

What kind of sanctions rule remains usable when the ship is far from support, documentation may be incomplete in real time, and the institutions asked to comply are already balancing legal pressure against physical risk? That question cuts through much of the false confidence that surrounds sanctions drafting. A rule may look forceful at a ministry desk and still fail in a harsh environment because it asks ports, insurers, service providers, or carriers to make distinctions they cannot verify quickly enough, or to absorb operational burdens they cannot safely manage. The test is not rhetorical severity. The test is feasibility under strain.

The checkpoint comes first.

That simple image helps because sanctions design in harsh environments is best understood as a problem of checkpoints rather than declarations. A checkpoint is not only a border or a port gate. It is any service node at which a transaction must become legible enough for someone to decide whether it can proceed: an insurer reviewing cover, a classification society examining the vessel's status, a bank processing payment, a port authority deciding entry, a bunker supplier weighing the file, a manager arranging crew or repairs. The central design question is whether a rule gives those checkpoints something they can actually recognise, compare, and defend. The concept here is operational clarity. The implication is that a sanctions measure which cannot be translated into usable decisions at service nodes is not truly designed for the environment in which it must work.

Clarity matters first because ambiguity grows more expensive in harsh settings. Show the ordinary problem. A ship operating in cold or remote waters needs insurance confirmation, route acceptance, support availability, and port confidence under tighter time and safety margins than a vessel in a denser, more forgiving trade. If the sanctions rule governing that voyage is vague about what documentation suffices, which counterparties trigger concern, or how competing obligations should be weighed, then the institutions involved will not produce subtle wisdom. They will produce caution. More files will escalate, more transactions will stall, and more lawful actors will be pushed into defensive behaviour that may itself create operational strain. The implication is not that clarity eliminates hard judgement. It reduces the volume of avoidable doubt at the points where delay carries physical as well as commercial cost.

A named example helps anchor the issue. The Polar Code's entry into force in 2017 did not create sanctions rules, but it demonstrated something highly relevant to sanctions design: Arctic and near-Arctic governance works best when obligations are translated into criteria that operational actors can actually apply. Where the standard is legible, classification societies, insurers, ports, and ship operators can build routines around it. Where the standard is blurred or internally unstable, private caution begins filling the gap unevenly. The lesson extends beyond safety regulation. A sanctions design that depends on interpretive heroics from dispersed commercial actors will tend to harden unpredictably, especially where the environment leaves little margin for leisurely legal refinement after the ship is already committed.

Verifiability is the second criterion because clarity without evidence is only good drafting. A harsh-environment sanctions measure must rely, as far as possible, on facts that can be checked with reasonable confidence at the moment decisions are needed. That sounds obvious and is often neglected. Ownership may be legally relevant yet difficult to verify in real time across layered entities. Cargo origin may matter strategically, yet become blurred by blending, storage, or transhipment. Intended destination may be central to the policy and still remain partly inferential when the ship is only on one leg of a longer chain. The concept is evidentiary fit. The implication is that a feasible sanctions design aligns its demands with what service nodes can genuinely confirm, not merely with what central authorities wish were knowable.

This is why verifiability should be treated as a discipline of modesty rather than a retreat from seriousness. A design that rests on unstable inferences will push the burden of doubt downwards onto ports, banks, insurers, and neutral carriers, who will respond by widening refusals and protecting themselves first. A design that uses more checkable triggers - stable identifiers, recognisable service relationships, coherent documentation thresholds, clearer attestation expectations - does not become morally weaker. It becomes institutionally stronger because the people asked to apply it can tell more reliably what the rule is speaking to. Trust, in this setting, is visible in whether a checkpoint can explain its decision by pointing to evidence that another serious institution would recognise, rather than to discomfort alone.

A second named example lies in the wider service-based enforcement that followed sanctions expansions on Russian-linked trade after 2022. What proved most workable, in practice, were often not the broadest political ambitions but the measures that could be translated into recognisable tests at finance, insurance, and shipping service nodes. The larger lesson is structural. In harsh environments, feasibility depends less on maximal legal imagination than on whether the rule can survive contact with the institutions that must process it under pressure. A sanctions design that ignores this becomes performative: strong in statement, brittle in application.

Proportionality is the third criterion, and it deserves more than ritual mention. In difficult maritime settings, disproportionality does not simply offend abstract fairness. It degrades compliance quality. If the consequences attached to ambiguous files are too blunt, or if lawful and unlawful trades become operationally hard to distinguish, then commercial actors will rationally broaden their own zones of refusal. The result is the compliance ratchet familiar from earlier chapters, now sharpened by geography and safety exposure. More lawful trade is delayed or rerouted. More neutral actors resist participation. More pressure falls on the least politically influential carriers, crews, and service providers. The implication is that proportional design is not a concession to weakness. It is one of the conditions under which sanctions preserve enough legitimacy to remain sustainable among those asked to carry them out.

This is particularly true where humanitarian and safety externalities can emerge from delay and denial. One need not give operational advice to see the design consequence. A rule that is formally coherent yet indifferent to route conditions, rescue thinness, seasonal compression, and service scarcity may create burdens that undermine support for the policy among allies, insurers, ports, and neutral carriers. Proportionality therefore means more than calibrating pain to target. It means asking whether the structure of the measure keeps secondary costs within a range that partners can continue to defend as prudent rather than merely punitive. That is why legitimacy belongs inside feasibility, not after it.

Coordination across service nodes is the fourth criterion, because no single institution governs a maritime transaction by itself. A ship can survive a vague rule in one part of the chain if other parts compensate with stable practice. It struggles when each service node applies a different threshold with different timing and different evidentiary expectations. Show the ordinary chain. The bank wants one document, the insurer another, the port a third, the manager a fourth, the classification society a fifth. None is irrational. Together, they create a maze that lawful trade must navigate and evasive trade may exploit through fragmentation. The concept is node alignment. The implication is that a good sanctions design does not merely identify a target or prohibited pattern. It also travels coherently across the institutions through which the voyage must still pass.

A credible limitation must be acknowledged. No sanctions architecture, however carefully designed, can eliminate uncertainty in harsh environments. Weather shifts, information arrives late, ownership evolves, commercial relationships mutate, and private risk appetites differ across jurisdictions and firms. A feasibility framework is therefore not a promise of clean execution. It is a way of judging whether a measure is likely to fail gracefully or fail chaotically. That distinction matters. Some rules produce friction that disciplined institutions can absorb and explain. Others trigger a cascade of inconsistent refusal, reputational panic, or practical non-compliance because they were never built for the world in which they had to operate.

That limitation points back to the everyday motif of the checkpoint. A durable sanctions framework in harsh environments is one that leaves the checkpoint with something better than instinct. It leaves it with standards clear enough to interpret, facts verifiable enough to test, proportionality tight enough to sustain support, and coordination good enough that the next checkpoint down the chain will not need to reinvent the entire problem. The checkpoint does not need certainty. It needs a basis for defensible judgement.

This is why sanctions design for harsh environments should be treated less as a matter of legal maximalism and more as an exercise in systems realism. The strongest designs are not those that describe the largest ambition. They are those that recognise the relationship between law, evidence, services, and physical operating conditions closely enough that enforcement pressure can move through the system without breaking the very institutional cooperation it depends upon. If that cooperation collapses, the measure may still exist on paper. It will have lost the medium through which it was meant to work.

The unresolved question, then, is not whether harsh environments require weaker sanctions thinking. They require stricter thinking. When a proposed measure reaches the point at which a port, insurer, bank, classifier, or service provider must decide whether to carry the burden of implementation, does it give them a rule they can actually use - or only a principle whose ambiguity will be paid for later by the next delay, the next refusal, or the next voyage forced to test the edge of the map?

Measuring success beyond interdictions

In July 2019, when the tanker *Grace 1* was detained in Gibraltar, the image was irresistible: a ship stopped, a cargo contested, a state demonstrating that sanctions could be made visible. Such episodes linger in public memory because they satisfy a simple appetite. They look like proof. A vessel is seized, and enforcement appears to have materialised in a form that can be photographed, debated, and counted. Yet maritime sanctions are often strongest where nothing so dramatic occurs.

That is the first difficulty any serious evaluation must face. If visible interdictions become the main measure of success, the assessment will almost certainly misread the system it is trying to judge. A sanctions regime can force costly rerouting, narrow service options, degrade confidence, deter counterparties, and reduce the willingness of ports, banks, insurers, and carriers to support a trade without ever producing a cinematic seizure. The absence of spectacle may indicate weakness. It may also indicate that pressure has become normal enough that the trade now bends earlier, or does not attempt the voyage at all. The empty berth can matter.

This is why effectiveness should be treated as a question of system behaviour rather than episodic drama. Show the ordinary distinction. An interdiction proves that one vessel, one cargo, or one transaction encountered a point of enforcement strong enough to stop it visibly. That matters. It does not tell us whether the wider trade has become riskier, more expensive, less trusted, or institutionally thinner over time. The concept is systemic effect. The implication is that sanctions should be judged by how they alter the operating environment for targeted trade, not merely by whether they occasionally produce an arresting public scene.

Risk reduction belongs at the centre of that assessment because sanctions rarely eliminate trade altogether, especially in maritime systems with multiple routes, intermediaries, and service layers. A more realistic question is whether the regime has reduced the space in which risky or politically targeted trade can move with confidence. Has the trade become harder to insure credibly, finance routinely, service safely, or disguise cheaply? Have the institutions around it grown less willing to assume that paperwork deserves belief? Risk, here, is visible in behaviour: slower payments, narrower insurance appetite, tougher port scrutiny, more intrusive due diligence, or a migration towards thinner and more fragile support structures. The implication is austere. If targeted trade must increasingly rely on marginal channels, unstable ownership patterns, and high-friction service networks, the sanctions system may be effective even when the number of headline seizures remains low.

A named example helps clarify the point. After the wave of sanctions expansions and commercial tightening around Russian-linked maritime trade in 2022, much of the practical effect appeared not in dramatic state interceptions, but in the restructuring of the trade's support conditions. Mainstream insurers narrowed appetite. Payment and compliance scrutiny intensified. Service ecosystems shifted. The relevant lesson is not that every subsequent trade became impossible or illicit. It is that the operating environment changed. A system can be coercively effective when it makes continuation more cumbersome, more expensive to defend, and more dependent on less trusted channels than before. That is a strategic outcome, even if it arrives without a single memorable boarding operation.

Increased friction for targeted trade is the second measure, and it requires a certain intellectual honesty. Friction is not success merely because it exists. All maritime trade contains friction. The analytical question is whether the sanctions regime has imposed friction that is selective enough to burden the targeted trade more heavily than ordinary commerce, and durable enough to affect strategic choices rather than just produce temporary inconvenience. The concept is discriminatory drag. The implication is that one should look for changes in the texture of the trade: thicker paperwork, more circuitous routing, greater reliance on alternative service providers, repeated ownership or management changes, or pricing structures that suggest the cost of uncertainty is being redistributed through the transaction. None of these signs alone settles the case. Together they reveal whether the system is making the trade work harder simply to remain possible.

That emphasis on friction matters because maritime sanctions are, in practice, often wars of patience. A targeted trade that remains legally arguable but commercially exhausting may still represent a meaningful strategic constraint. A cargo that can move only through slower finance, more nervous insurers, more disposable corporate forms, and narrower ports is not moving under the same conditions as before. The effort required to sustain it becomes part of the measure. This is especially important in harsh or Arctic environments, where every additional uncertainty interacts with geography, seasonality, and sparse infrastructure. Friction at one node can echo more widely than in denser southern corridors. The implication is that evaluation must remain sensitive to operating context. A delay that is modest elsewhere may be strategically and operationally weightier in the north.

A second named example can be found in the long-running scrutiny of Iranian shipping practices during the later 2010s and early 2020s. What mattered over time was not simply whether a particular vessel was named, boarded, or detained. What mattered was whether the broader ecosystem around the trade became less forgiving: whether insurers, banks, ports, and counterparties grew more cautious; whether the trade increasingly depended on transhipment, layered ownership, and less transparent financing; whether ordinary market actors began treating involvement as institutionally unpleasant. That is the kind of shift an effectiveness measure must capture if it wants to describe real strategic pressure rather than merely visible confrontation.

Maintained legitimacy among partners is the third measure, and in some ways the hardest to handle because it resists simple display. A sanctions regime can be forceful and still fail strategically if allies, neutral carriers, insurers, service providers, and coastal states begin to experience it as arbitrary, disproportionate, or indifferent to uneven burdens and externalities. Legitimacy is visible in whether partners continue to cooperate without needing constant political rescue, whether neutral institutions still find lawful participation possible, and whether private actors treat the system as demanding but intelligible rather than as a field of reputational panic. The implication is severe. A regime that produces spectacular seizures while corroding allied patience and market trust may win the news cycle and lose the longer system.

A credible limitation should be admitted. Legitimacy is not a soft substitute for coercive seriousness, nor should it become a euphemism for comfort. Partners may complain even when a sanctions regime is effective and justified. Commercial actors routinely resist cost. States exposed to maritime disruption will not always speak warmly about burdens they nonetheless accept. It would therefore be naive to treat every sign of strain as evidence of failing legitimacy. The real question is whether strain remains politically and institutionally manageable, or whether it begins to erode the willingness of others to supply the compliance, services, and information on which the regime quietly depends.

That limitation does not weaken the broader framework. It makes it more durable. A serious evaluation asks several questions at once. Has the targeted trade become riskier to sustain? Has friction increased in ways that meaningfully complicate continuation? Have partners remained willing to support or at least tolerate the system without widening retreat into defensive non-cooperation? These are not separate checklists. They interact. A regime may increase friction but lose legitimacy if the burden spills too widely. It may preserve legitimacy but reduce little if the targeted trade adapts too easily. It may generate visible interdictions and still fail if those moments reveal strength only at the margins while the main current of trade learns to flow elsewhere. The most useful measure is therefore relational rather than spectacular.

The quiet motif here is the wake. A ship passes, and the wake tells us something about the force of its movement without being the movement itself. Visible interdictions are like the crest of that wake - unmistakable, attention-grabbing, easy to point at. The deeper current is harder to see. It lies in the behaviour of insurers, ports, banks, neutral carriers, coastal states, and service providers whose decisions gradually make a trade harder or easier to sustain. If one watches only the crest, one mistakes noise for direction.

This is why sanctions in Arctic and near-Arctic settings especially demand a more patient method of judgment. The region's distances, service scarcity, environmental sensitivity, and uneven infrastructure make the costs of mismeasurement particularly high. A single seizure may reveal capacity. It does not prove strategic success. A quiet reduction in risky traffic, a narrowing of credible service support, or a sustained willingness among partners to carry the system despite uneven burdens may tell us more. Measuring success beyond interdictions therefore means accepting that the strongest forms of enforcement often leave their clearest marks not in the headlines, but in the altered behaviour of a maritime system learning what it will and will not carry.

That leaves the final question where any living sanctions regime must eventually face itself. If the most visible acts of enforcement can mislead, and the most important effects may be dispersed through risk, friction, and legitimacy, are institutions willing to judge success by the slower evidence of a system changing its habits - or will they keep demanding the spectacle of seizures even when spectacle is the least reliable guide to what the strategy is truly achieving?

About the Author

Rayan Veldaskar is a nonfiction writer focused on how large institutions turn policy into practice, especially where law, commerce, and security overlap. His work is driven by a simple suspicion: that the decisive features of geopolitics are often mundane. Contracts, inspections, registries, insurance clauses, and compliance workflows may appear technical, yet they determine which rules actually bite and which dissolve under pressure.

He approaches sanctions and maritime governance as problems of systems design and information integrity. Rather than treating enforcement as a contest of rhetoric, he is interested in the quieter struggle over proof, responsibility, and coordination across actors who do not share incentives: ports that need throughput, insurers that need predictability, carriers that need routes, and governments that need credible restraint without uncontrolled escalation. His writing aims to be precise about mechanisms while remaining readable to non-specialists.

A recurring thread in his perspective is the way frontier environments expose the true strength of institutions. Archives of shipping practice, public registry fragments, and the lived reality of remote logistics all show the same lesson: where margins are thin, governance becomes visible. In that sense, cold waters are not a niche setting but a revealing one. Veldaskar writes to equip readers to ask better questions of official claims, and to see enforcement not as a switch that is flipped, but as a chain that must hold.

www.ingramcontent.com/pod-product-compliance
Lightning Source LLC
Chambersburg PA
CBHW031321230926
51848CB00001B/41
* 9 7 8 9 3 7 7 9 4 0 2 9 4 *